The Bible:

Family Album

The Bible:

Family Album

Jack Good

Chalice Press

St. Louis, Missouri

All scripture quotations, unless otherwise indicated, are from the New Revised Standard Version Bible, copyright 1989, Division of Christian Education of the National Council of the Churches of Christ in the USA. Used by permission.

Scripture quotations marked NKJV are taken from the New King James Version. Copyright © 1979, 1980, 1982 by Thomas Nelson, Inc. Used by permission. All rights reserved.

Scripture quotations marked NEB are from *The New English Bible*, © Oxford University Press and Cambridge University Press 1961, 1970. Reprinted by permission.

Excerpts from *J.B.* by Archibald MacLeish. Copyright © 1956, 1957, 1958 by Archibald MacLeish. Copyright © renewed by William H. MacLeish and Mary H. Grimm. Reprinted by permission of Houghton Mifflin Company.

Excerpt from: *The Poetry of Robert Frost*, edited by Edward Connery Lathem, Copyright 1945 by Robert Frost, © 1973 by Lesley Frost Ballantine, © 1969 by Henry Holt and Company, Inc. Reprinted by permission of Henry Holt and Company, Inc.

Cover design: Lynne Condellone

Interior design: Elizabeth Wright

This book is printed on acid-free, recycled paper.

Visit Chalice Press on the World Wide Web at
www.chalicepress.com

10 9 8 7 6 5 4 3 2 1   98 99 00 01 02 03

Library of Congress Cataloging–in–Publication Data

Good, A. Jack, 1935–
    The Bible : faith's family album / by A. Jack Good.
        p.   cm.
    Includes bibliographical references.
    ISBN 0-8272-0225-3
    1. Bible—Theology.   2. Bible—Evidences, authority, etc.   I. Title.
    BS543.G66   1998   97-45698
    220.6—dc21   CIP

Printed in the United States of America

Table of Contents

Therefore, since we are surrounded
by so great a cloud of witnesses…

Hebrews 12:1

Introduction

Seldom is the Bible encountered as a unit. It is sliced and shredded. Sentences and paragraphs are lifted out of context. Ideas that have no relationship to one another are matched to buttress some thought the reader brings to the text. No wonder there is so much confusion about its role and authority!

The unity of the Bible must be reclaimed. Unfortunately, the scriptures do not reveal their unity easily. The Bible speaks in many voices, like a variety of musical instruments, each in its own voice and range. Readers must train themselves to hear both the distinctive instrument and the harmony that results as they speak together. For the person willing to do the work of preparation, the Bible as a whole becomes the orchestra through which "the music of the spheres," including harmonies and discords, human and divine, is played.

Of course some passages of scripture, such as the liturgical cadence of the psalms, the high ethic of the Sermon on the Mount, or the social analysis of the eighth-century prophets, can be read for their own sake. The skeptic, however, can destroy the value of such spiritual food by pointing to the Bible's much less savory passages. Genocide is apparently commended in the book of Joshua. Leviticus tells us not to wear clothing in which two fibers are mixed and calls anyone who has touched the carcass of a pig an "abomination."

For those who try to read the Bible all the way through, who attempt to let it speak on its own terms, the highs and lows of biblical writing cease to be barriers to spiritual travel. There is no way to level the two, to create an average common denominator of spiritual insight. Instead, a new way of understanding the Bible is needed. The new understanding must allow the high mountains and the muddy pits to co-exist. The two must create a landscape that makes sense, lifts the spirit, and reveals beauty.

The obvious way of dealing with a Bible that has such extremes of insights and ethics is to embrace the good and ignore the not so good. Not only is this obvious, but it is done. Churches both liberal and conservative cut and paste. They edit and digest.

The violence done to the Bible has come from two seemingly opposite directions. The more obvious way the Bible is dissected arises among conservative Christians who insist on an "inerrant" view of the Bible. The idea that every word of scripture is a direct communication from God is appealing in its simplicity and pervasive in its presentation from pulpit, radio, or television. Yet ultimately it is disastrous for understanding the Bible as a unit. If every phrase of scripture indicates the precise divine will, then the reader has no reason to worry about the time or place of its composition. Contradictions in the text must either be pushed under the rug or explained away with mental gymnastics that would make any respectable student of logic blush. An inerrant Bible is a divine message without spiritual or human context.

Those who believe in the inerrant view of scripture usually deal with problem areas of scripture by ignoring them. Their energy goes into finding creative ways to explain away the contradictions that refuse to disappear or re-directing attention toward more friendly passages. One could conclude from reading billboards and listening to TV programs from conservative Christians that John 3:16 constitutes half the biblical text!

A devout, articulate member of a fundamentalist church visited me recently. He had learned that I did not accept the divine origin of every biblical phrase. His mission was to convert me from the error of my ways. In our discussion I asked him to comment on a passage in which God seems to take a very unfriendly attitude toward women and children. His face visibly fell as he read. He insisted he had never read that chapter and asked that we move on to other topics. He illustrated an important point. In order to sustain a belief in God's equal participation in every page of the Bible, one must be very selective in what is read and preached.

In recent years I have come to be equally frustrated with another approach to scripture that is used by the mainline denominations (also known as the progressive, or liberal, churches). The seminaries and denominational authorities of these churches encourage their pastors to base their preaching ministry on a pre-selected set of scripture readings (Old Testament, Psalm, Gospel, and Epistle) appropriate for each Sunday of the church year. In its three-year cycle the lectionary includes most, but not all, of the New Testament and approximately half of the Old Testament. A common lectionary has been devised for Catholics and many major Protestant denominations.

This cut-and-paste approach to scripture, undertaken for many noble purposes, presents the worshiping community with "the divine plan of salvation," a plan that centers on the life, death, and resurrection of Jesus. A problem emerges, however. Anyone who has ever read the entire Bible—either in the order in which it appears in modern versions or (as in this volume) the order in which it was likely to have been written—knows that a "divine plan of salvation" is not the theme of the Bible. "The plan of salvation" is implied in scripture. It is certainly implied for those who see the revelation of God in Jesus as central to faith. However, it does not arise naturally out of the printed page. Reading only lectionary selections does not allow the Bible to speak on its own terms. A lectionary approach gives scant attention to the original context of passages.[1]

Thus, from both right and left come truncating approaches to the Bible. In contrast to these opposite, yet amazingly similar views, this manuscript insists that *the Bible as a whole is the bearer of divine truth.*

What is needed is a new way of viewing the Bible, a way that allows the reader to roam at will in its landscape. The seeker must be free to absorb the scriptures' bright sunshine and to breathe the dank air of its deepest caves. The framework of understanding must illuminate the Bible's sacredness and celebrate the strength scripture has afforded persons of faith through more than two millennia. This new vision of the Bible must embrace the entire volume—its beauty spots and its warts.

Two basic truths lie as foundations for this important search. One is that the Bible is the history-bearing document of a community of faith. As such it belongs to the entire people of God and not just to the ordained ministry. Certainly it does not belong exclusively to an unseen committee to determine what the people of God can and should hear. The second truth is that the Bible is the *spirit-bearing* document of that same community. This second truth draws attention to the complicated issue of divine participation in the writing and interpreting of scripture—an issue put in focus by the New Testament claim that "all scripture is inspired" ("God-breathed") by the Almighty. This issue will be explored at length in the final chapter.

---

[1] None of this is intended as a blanket indictment of the use of the lectionary. The lectionary is a useful discipline that keeps pastors from preaching *ad infinitum* on their favorite themes. I use the lectionary readings approximately two-thirds of the Sundays I preach. The remaining Sundays I use to explore the rich scriptural resources that receive little or no exposure in the lectionary readings.

Fortunately, such a new way of envisioning the Bible is available. The concept is not original with this writer. I know of no other volume, however, in which this way of approaching the Bible has been applied in helpful detail to all of scripture. While the view is described as a metaphor, I am convinced it is more than metaphor. It is an accurate way of describing the intent of biblical writers.

A Helpful Metaphor

Some months ago a friend brought my wife and me a copy of the family album that he and his kin had assembled. His family had collected items that described and celebrated their common history—a task requiring considerable energy. They had gone to this trouble because they see themselves as unique (a claim that every family can make—some more convincingly than others). Their claim to uniqueness comes from two sources—the unusual individuals they have produced and the location of their family dwelling. The residence, in a now-declining part of what was once the capital of the Confederacy, has had a deep impact on their family development. I thumbed through that album with fascination. The story it tells began when ancestors moved to their special location. The persons who inhabited that home are described—sometimes, one suspects, with accuracy, and on other occasions with loving exaggeration. Mixed into the historical materials are artistic materials created by family members. Local conditions and history are described. Impressive framing has been placed around pages that contain especially important information.

The album was interesting to me, but, I suspect, precious to the members of the family it describes. Every word helps them know who they are. The album details the traditions that have sustained the clan through its changing fortunes. Each modern member of the family can examine these traditions, embracing some and rejecting others. The album is not a straitjacket that insists "This is the way you must act," but an invitation to continue the basic commitments of a unique people. I realized I had in front of me the answer to a question that had persisted through my years of pastoral work: "What is the organizing principle of the Bible?"

The Bible is the family album of my community of faith. Or, more succinctly, it is my *Faith's Family Album.* When I accept it in this light, I am much less bothered by its inconsistencies and moral incongruities. No longer need the burden of such inconsistencies be placed on God, for I accept that the Bible was not written by God. Its major actor is not the divine, but the faith community. The Bible, as a family album, introduces me to the other imperfect people who make up my community of faith and invites me to identify and embrace that community's highest traditions. In a strange way it also encourages me to take ownership of its seamier heritage—those passages that describe an embarrassingly low ethic. It invites me to know and identify with people whose lives I would never accept as role models. All these variegated, sometimes misshapen parts make up my long and complex spiritual history. When concepts clash I can say with a smile, "That's the way my family is. Sometimes it is right, sometimes wrong. It disagrees a lot. It is, nonetheless, a wonderful and remarkable family!"

What Do Non-Fundamentalists Believe About the Bible?

At times, I find myself almost envying my fundamentalist friends. As I have already explained, one of the tenets of such religious groups is the concept of biblical "inerrancy." Inerrancy means that the Bible was written, at least in its original documents, without error. God, inspiring the human writer, either dictated the actual words, or so guarded the writer that no errors were allowed to be placed on paper. The so-called problems of the Bible are only in the minds of modern readers—or so the argument goes.

Those who can accept the idea of an inerrant Bible have no trouble describing its authority. The words of the Bible are, to them, the actual Word of God. Thus the words are to be obeyed in their entirety. (The fact that its advice is often contradictory does not seem to bother those who assign the Bible a certain divine status. Ways are found to reconcile apparent conflicts, or ways are found to ignore that which is most difficult to explain.)

Appealing as this approach might be, I could never allow myself the luxury of accepting it. Any effort I might have made to convince myself of biblical inerrancy fails in the Bible's first verses. Chapters one and two of Genesis contain, as any objective reading will reveal, not one but two stories of creation. In the first, a distant God systematically makes the universe, crowning it with human life. In the second, a very near and involved God begins with human life, making male and female in two creative acts. No amount of mental gymnastics can reconcile the quite different facts or the opposing implications of these two stories. It is as if a wise editor had hung disclaimers on the outer door of scripture: "This is not a book of scientific information; this is not a book of history in the modern understanding of that term."

If I, as a non-fundamentalist person of faith, cannot accept the Bible as inerrant, what can I accept?

While fundamentalist churches have confronted the authority of the Bible and come up with an inadequate answer, mainline churches have ignored the question and thus come up with a pretense. By giving attention only to the spiritually-enriching portions of scripture, and by rearranging them to provide an artificial plot (the story of salvation), the liturgical denominations have been able to *appear* to accept the Bible as a product of divine thought. This pretense is certainly less honest, and may ultimately be more destructive, than the fundamentalist's concept of inerrancy.

An alternative answer can be found. I *can* and *do* accept that the Bible is a series of writings about a human community, written by members of that human community. The writings were preserved because the community experienced itself as called into a unique relationship with the Holy One, the Creator of all the universe (although some early biblical writers believed their God was only one deity among many). Knowing that it had this special role, the faith community preserved the writings that would define it and that would explain and celebrate its faith.

The authority of scripture, then, is that it describes my heritage as part of a unique community of faith and challenges me to embrace its privileges and responsibilities. Because the Bible is so varied, because it reveals human life in all its wonderful and terrifying manifestations, it invites me in. No amount of evil-doing on my part can exclude me, for I find my own evil and more described in its pages. It forces me to ask, in any ethically confusing situation I might face, "How should I, as a part of this continuing family of God's people, handle this question?"

The Bible, then, is not primarily a book about God. It was not written by God. *It is a book about a community of people who had experienced a call to serve God and who, after much struggle, came to recognize that they were also called to reveal God to the remainder of humanity.* The Bible traces this community through a stage of narrow self-centeredness, through the traumas that would cause it to re-examine its role and finally through radical changes that caused it to open itself to all regardless of ethnic backgrounds.

This book is an effort to trace that history as the scriptural writers offered it and to identify themes that knit the varied writings into a colorful whole.

Traditional Vs. Non-Traditional

The Bible's focus on community has far-reaching implications. What seems at first glance a struggle over the meaning of scripture is, at another level, a battle over the nature of our current communities. Societies can be distinguished by their attitude toward change. Traditional societies tend to take a negative view of change. Parents in traditional societies attempt to rear their children in ways that impart the values of the past and insure that the offspring will live essentially as did their ancestors. Non-traditional societies are more open to the new. Parents in non-traditional societies rear their children with the hope that they will build different and (it is assumed) better communities. People in traditional societies wrestle with a fear of the unknown when change occurs; people in non-traditional societies have an equal fear of what they perceive as a diseased stagnation.

Much of scripture is the story of a traditional society attempting to pass its values on to younger generations. In this sense the Bible is a weapon in the hands of those who fear change. It is clear why those who prefer radically non-traditional communities are likely to reject the entire idea of biblical authority—just as such people reject the concept of absolute, enduring values. The fundamentalists, who insist that every word and phrase of the Bible represents the definite will of the divine, have discovered an excellent way to encourage a society to remain in its traditional mode. Fundamentalists show their deeper agenda in this regard when they attack concepts of modern science, especially evolution, and use the term "modernity" in a thoroughly pejorative manner.

On the other hand, Catholics and mainline Protestants, who focus almost exclusively on a limited number of pre-selected texts, are also laying the foundation for an unchanging faith. They want us to accept a "faith once given," reiterated year after year, cycle after cycle. Worshipers who listen only to lectionary readings will never appreciate the degree to which the Bible is a dynamic document, filled with heated arguments and developing concepts.

Embracing the Bible as a faith family album opens a middle ground between the traditional and radically non-traditional approaches to community living. Accepting the Bible as a special and unique volume, a volume that calls modern people into a community with roots three thousand years long, means that the values of the past have not been rejected. Yet acknowledging these writings as fluid products of their time and culture allows an openness to the future. The writer of the 46th Psalm offers an excellent model in this regard. He looked at the changing landscape around him and rejoiced that in the midst of this flux God was his "refuge and strength." Yet he also knew that God was involved in the emerging new realities. Referring to the changes taking place, he remarked, "Come, see the works of the divine!"

Background

Christians of the last several generations could not take the Bible for granted as their ancestors did. "The battle over the Bible," a phenomenon of the last century and a half, has forced people of faith to examine the meaning of scripture. Previously, common worshipers were content accepting the Bible as "the word of God." Both Jesus and Paul referred appreciatively to sacred writings that had nourished them in their faith. For them, scripture was the Torah, essentially the first five books of our modern Bible. Other Hebraic writings were held in almost equal esteem. When Jesus read from the holy scrolls in his home synagogue, he read from the prophet Isaiah. When the author of 2 Timothy wrote that "all scripture is inspired" he referred to these same Hebraic works. He certainly had no idea that his own letters would someday be included among holy writ. The Gospels had not been written at that time. The reader is given no idea what "inspired" implied, other than the fact that such writings were to be taken with great seriousness.

As the church grew, the Catholic Church accepted the Bible as an authority alongside its own tradition. The Protestant reformers, feeling that the concept of church tradition was open to abuse, made the Bible the only written authority of faith. But even the Protestant reformers made no case for biblical inerrancy. On the contrary, Martin Luther referred to one book of the New Testament (James) as "an epistle of straw." Later John Wesley would teach his followers that the Bible is one among several sources for faith. Other authorities to be consulted, according to Wesley, included church tradition, human experience, and human reason. So it was with all Christian leaders up through the middle of the nineteenth century. The Bible was a prime influence in matters of faith; yet they had read the Bible with enough care to know one of its central teachings: nothing was to be worshiped other than God. They never made the Bible an object of adoration. They would have been shocked by the idea of inerrancy.

Two events of the nineteenth century set the stage for serious disagreement over biblical interpretation. One (actually the second in chronological order but the first to receive wide-spread publicity) was the publication of Charles Darwin's *Origin of Species* in 1859, followed in 1871 by his *Descent of Man*. In Darwin's view, biological life was not created in some single, divine act, but evolved over millions of years in a process he called "natural selection." Thus humanity was not a special species with dominion over the remainder, but simply one highly differentiated product among many products of this process. No divine Creator was needed in Darwin's view; no sacred goal was envisioned toward which all creation was moving.

The concepts of Darwin were not entirely new. Other scientists had written about a long and gradual development of the natural world. But Darwin stated his theory persuasively, documented it with a wealth of information, and then explained the process through the concept of natural selection (survival of the fittest). The scientific community, both in Europe and the United States, was divided over Darwin's ideas. A turning point for scientists in the United States came with the appointment of Charles William Eliot, a Darwin defender, as president of Harvard in 1869. Only after this did the churches begin to hear about and react to the concepts of natural selection.[2] The resulting division in the religious community has been deep and long-lasting.

Following the publication of Darwin's books, some individuals of faith in both Germany and America argued that the Bible's view of creation and the new scientific view of creation could comfortably coexist. The coexistence was seen as possible so long as the Bible was approached as a book of faith and not as a book of science. Other persons, concentrated in parts of the United States, felt that the accuracy of the Bible, and thus the entire authority of the Bible, was under unacceptable attack. The concept of biblical inerrancy was largely an effort to re-establish that authority.

The second challenge of the nineteenth century was also centered in Europe. Earlier, a group of German scholars had set in motion an attempt to solve some of the mysteries of biblical writings. They approached the sacred pages as they would any other literature, asking questions about such things as the vocabulary used, the age of the events referred to, and the peculiar style of each writer.

---

[2] Ahlstrom, Sydney E., *A Religious History of the American People* (New London: Yale University Press, 1972).

These scholars found not only two creation stories in Genesis, but also two interwoven stories of Noah and the flood. They insisted that the book of Isaiah was the product of at least three different writers. They said that Moses could not have written the first five books of the Bible (a person cannot write about his own death), nor could the psalms have been written by David or Solomon.

A very unfortunate term was used to describe the effort to better understand scripture: "biblical criticism." In common speech the word criticism has a negative ring. Critics are assumed to be those who point out faults. For those who had a high respect for scripture, the term biblical criticism put the project off to a very bad start!

Biblical critics, however, were not on a campaign of destruction. They were using the term in its other meaning—like a newspaper critic who reviews musical presentations. Such critics were simply reviewing and evaluating; they were as likely to say positive things as negative.

Indeed, biblical criticism, while seen as a threat by the emerging fundamentalists of the United States, has been, on the whole, a very positive endeavor. It has allowed the Bible reader to find deeper spiritual realities beneath the dry, factual surface. Because biblical criticism has been so important to the understanding of scripture in the past two centuries, some examples of its work should be noted.

Biblical criticism has led to a better understanding of the Bible by placing it in its cultural context. This helps us see additional meanings in certain passages. Psalm 121 is a good example.

"I lift up my eyes to the hills," the psalmist begins. Older translations of the second phrase ("from whence cometh my help") made it seem that the hills were symbols of the strength and endurance of the Divine. Other parts of the psalm, however, speak of protection against the sun and moon; the poem has references to a person coming in and going out. All this seems quite removed from the announced theme.

Further language study has convinced most scholars that the second phrase of the psalm is a question: "From where will my help come?" Why would the writer wonder about protection?

Historians know that caravans were a vital part of the culture of Israel, sitting as it did astride the major trading routes of that part of the world. Other information from non-biblical sources teaches us the following facts: the hills, rather than a source of strength, were often hiding places for gangs of thieves waiting for the caravans to rest in nearby valleys. The caravans' only human protection was by exhausted, sleepy guards. Other dangers beset the traveler. The hot desert sun could be fatal. Folklore insisted that the moon by night could be as dangerous to the mental health (a myth common to many cultures; thus the term "lunatic") as the sun was to physical health.

These facts allow the reader to capture a much more accurate and consistent interpretation of the psalm. When the poet lifted his eyes to the hills he saw not a symbol of divine strength, but a place of threat! Thugs likely were hiding there! From where would this frightened traveler receive help? His help "comes from the Lord, who made heaven and earth." In contrast to the tired guards, God "neither slumbers nor sleeps." God's power was greater than the ravages of sun by day and moon by night. God would preserve the traveler's coming in and his going out not only in this earthly life, but forevermore!

In many modern hymnbooks is "The Navy Hymn," entitled *Eternal Father, Strong to Save*. It is a request that the divine

> hear us when we cry to thee,
> for those in peril on the sea.

Psalm 121 was the Hebrew equivalent of "The Navy Hymn." It was a prayer for protection for those who traveled in dangerous situations. Biblical criticism has helped us correctly understand a lovely part of our devotional history.

Biblical criticism, carried to deeper levels, can help us understand other mysteries, such as the two creation stories that open the biblical drama. Modern students of the Bible have come to recognize that the creation stories were the product of two writers whose accounts were woven together by an editor. The editor had an important agenda: the preservation of the Jewish community.

The Jewish community was under threat from many divisive forces. The tribe of Judah was considerably larger than the other eleven tribes. They, the smaller tribe of Benjaminites, plus the tribe of priests named Levites, became a separate unit. Following the death of King Solomon, the ten tribes of the north (to be known as Israel) and the two tribes of the south (to be known as Judah) became two nations, each with its own government. At times these two groups cooperated against some common enemy. At other times they fought against one another. Never, however, did they lose sight of their common ancestry.

As might be expected, these two groups developed separate understandings of their shared history. The understandings were similar, but often differed in important details. (My wife and I, who grew up in the south, moved north of the Mason-Dixon Line soon after our marriage. When we first heard people in New England discuss the Civil War, we were amazed. Enough common facts and events existed to assure us that we were discussing the same war. Yet the differences in interpretation of that war and its aftermath were so severe as to give it an entirely different meaning. A similar dynamic was at work in the interpretations of national history given by Judah and Israel.)

To oversimplify a very complex story, an editor, whose concern was the preservation of the larger Jewish community, took the written history of Judah and the written history of Israel, plus some other documents, and wove them into a common history. The opening was the most difficult. The creation stories from the two estranged groups were so different that they could not be reconciled. Thus the two stories were included in their original forms. The two accounts of Noah and the flood, however, were similar enough that, with skill, they could be woven together. A casual reader would not notice the difficulties. The careful reader, however, will note that there are discrepancies in the number of beasts entering the ark and the way a bird, or birds, are sent out to confirm the receding of the flood. Later in the nation's history, violent stories of David and his offspring were told with gentleness, so that descendants of David's other children might live peacefully with the descendants of Absalom, who staged a fatal (for Absalom) rebellion against the mighty king.

Thus, in examining the early books of the Bible, biblical criticism has given us important clues to hidden goals. The purpose of biblical editors was to reconcile differing views of Jewish history *to better preserve the Jewish community!* Many problems and contractions are thus explained.

Some aspects of biblical criticism have dealt with the essence of the Christian faith. This is especially threatening to those who are anxious about the critical process. Knowing that the Gospel stories were written several decades after the life of Jesus, some scholars have attempted to determine which of the sayings of Jesus were authentic and which were altered to fit the needs of an emerging church. This is a complex and controversial undertaking. For the most part, these careful students of the New Testament have concluded that the first three Gospel stories give us a generally accurate picture of the man Jesus. The fourth Gospel, which differs in many ways from the first three, is a highly spiritualized product of the early church and is less reliable in its historic facts. Early in the twentieth century there was fear, even among relatively liberal church people, that criticism at this depth might destroy the very basis of faith. Additional information and additional time for reflection, however, have allowed these anxieties to subside. It is possible to continue to be faithful followers of Jesus even as we attempt to sort out which records of his life give the most accurate picture. Passages added by the early church are not to be rejected. While these words may not have come directly from the lips of Jesus, they can nonetheless reflect the purposes of Jesus. They can also be channels by which the divine speaks to the current scene.

From the point of view of the non-fundamentalist, therefore, biblical criticism has been a boon. It has helped us have a better understanding of certain passages. It has helped us cope with the "human noise" that threatens to distract us from the Bible's central themes. Ultimately, it has helped us see the purpose of the entire scriptures.

Unfortunately, the pulpits of non-fundamentalist churches have been largely silent about the understandings offered by biblical critics. Many clergy with whom I have had contact assume that their pews are filled with people whose beliefs match those of their more conservative neighbors. It is easier to preach from those same assumptions by making minimal references to such things as cultural context and human writers. Better to present the text as if the shallowest meaning of the phrase "the word of God," were operative than to risk shattering someone's fragile faith. Or so the theory goes.

Thus the twin challenges of Darwinism and biblical criticism have affected both fundamentalist and mainline churches, but in far different ways. The fundamentalists have been hardened in their interpretation of scriptural authority and forced to reject much of what is seen as modern or scientific. Non-fundamentalists—those who accept the truths put forth by Darwin and the Bible critics—find their challenges painted in a different hue. We cannot buy into the "all or nothing" implication of inerrancy. On what basis, then, can we look to the Bible for spiritual direction? Can we accept the ethical norms of certain passages as divinely inspired while dismissing others as simply the work of well-meaning, but misguided, individuals? We Christians who are non-fundamentalists were taught to revere the Bible. Its message has been a support and guide through our lives, "a very present help in time of trouble." Yet, dare we allow it to guide us on our spiritual journey? What authority, if any, do we assign it?

What the Bible Is Not

In order to answer questions put forth by modern knowledge, Christians of many positions have rushed into some dead-end streets.

In the first place, both fundamentalists and non-fundamentalists often act as though the Bible is the Christian equivalent of the Islamic Koran.

The people of Islam insist that their holy book is inerrant. The Muslims make a consistent case for their view. Their belief is that Mohammed, claimed to be illiterate, was put into a trance, received the precise word of God, then dictated it in its original form. Christians cannot make a simple case for the same view, for the Bible was written by many people over a long period of time. No one, so far as I know, believes, for example, that David was put into a trance to compose the psalms; neither does anyone suppose that Paul, in writing what came to be a major portion of the New Testament, was doing other than composing letters to his friends in far-away churches. Nonetheless, in actual practice, the Bible is treated by many Christians of varying persuasions as if it were another Koran, dropped down out of heaven in its present form.

A second way of approaching scripture is equally inadequate: the Bible is often treated as if it belongs to the genre of how-to, self-help, or recipe books.

Beside the computer on which these words are written is a large volume with the interesting title, *The Macintosh Bible*. As one might suspect, it contains several hundred pages of helpful hints about ways to make the computer more efficient and for repairing it when it might need adjustment. Whenever I have need for the computer book's information I find myself reacting to its title. How interesting that the word *Bible* has so thoroughly attached itself to the helpful hints/recipe concept that this how-to book about computers could be entitled *Bible* and immediately communicate to potential consumers exactly what its nature is.

A recipe book is constructed on similar assumptions. It is, of course, a volume that contains many foods for many tastes and occasions. One is seldom likely to sit down and read page after page of a recipe book. Instead, you identify your need (I want a dessert to impress my new friends) and turn to the pages that have elaborate sweets.

The Bible is often used by Christians today as a how-to or a recipe book. It is picked up only in case of particular need—when I need direction for dealing with a particular situation, or I am depressed or grieving.

Harry Emerson Fosdick, famed preacher of the early twentieth century, is said to have complained that people read only the beauty spots of scripture. Certain familiar passages have a nostalgic (and sometimes spiritually helpful) ring. To these passages people turn again and again. The remainder, which is the vast majority of the Bible, is left unread. Thus few texts are ever understood against their original background.

The Bible works as a book of "helps" as long as people are only looking for assistance in some narrowly-defined situation. People who determine to go deeper into faith will want to discover what is in the remainder of the scriptural pages. Then problems arise. Such people find themselves reading chapter after chapter of arid history; they discover a sexual ethic designed to produce as many babies as possible—an ethic that, if followed today, would quickly overpopulate the globe. They discover an ethic toward war which, today, would be called genocide and condemned as war crimes. The beauty spots of scripture all have their counterparts in warts and wrinkles.

A Better Metaphor

If the Bible is neither the Christian equivalent of the Koran nor a book of helpful hints, then what role does it play in the development of the spiritual life?

Another way of approaching the Bible is needed. A much more helpful approach is the one already described—to see the Bible as the family album of a community attempting to define itself and its special role in the plan of God.

Freeing Assumptions

The Bible as faith's family album means I can approach the reading of scripture with certain freeing assumptions:

1. The Bible is not about God so much as it is a collection of writings about a community. It is a community that found itself called by God to be the servant of the divine and custodian of the divine message. Therefore I do not need to feel embarrassed for the divine when unsavory passages are encountered.

2. The Bible is a human document written with gentle prodding from a divine Spirit—a Spirit that some writers responded to with sensitivity and accuracy, and other writers largely ignored. The ultimate inspiration is in the impact of the total Bible, not in any individual word or passage.

3. Reading the Bible as a my faith's family album means I do not have to imagine a different divine-human relationship than the one I know and experience in my own day. God, in God's own basic

being, has not changed. Neither have God's methods changed. The Holy Spirit continues to invite people through her gentle prodding. People today listen for that "still, small voice"[3] against the noise of many competing voices. Some today hear the sacred voice with accuracy; others hear the competing sounds and think they have responded to the divine. All that was true of biblical writers. God's methods have not changed.

4. The Bible is, then, seen as a continuous and continuing story. Christians need no longer look for major breaks between an old covenant (Old Testament) supposed by some to have been annulled, and a new covenant (New Testament) based on entirely different assumptions. Too many Christians have determined that our sacred writings establish a harsh divide between two religions: Judaism and Christianity. These two are, it was assumed, stacked one on top of the other. Their primary relationship is assumed to be that the first was there to warm up the crowd in preparation for the main act to follow. Instead, the Bible is a *single* story about a *single* community. The community tragically divided when one part determined that the Messiah had appeared. The other part disagreed. The two separated in anger and misunderstanding. Their estrangement could not, however, hide the fact of their shared history.

5. The Bible is the arena in which family arguments are openly and often heatedly debated. This notion absolutely reverses the idea of scripture as a magic answer book, a "how-to" response to every spiritual need. It becomes clear why people on both sides of so many important arguments have been able to quote the Bible. This is possible because somewhere in our faith family's development, some writer can be found taking almost every conceivable side in a variety of crucial matters.

6. The concept of faith's family album frees the reader from the necessity of defending the factual information in the Bible. Family albums are constructed to answer a broad question: What are the unique characteristics of this particular clan? Those who want precise information about a family's history consult a genealogist whose work is a science. Family albums are put together by poets—persons who use language, photographs, and works of family art to create an impression. The accuracy of particular facts is not nearly so important as the accuracy of the overall picture—of the gestalt. Effectiveness, not accuracy, is the important consideration. For the Bible,

---

[3] As heard by Elijah, 1 Kings 19:12, RSV.

effectiveness is measured by the degree to which it can help persons know what it is to be part of this sacred community.

All Christians, then, can claim the Bible as *their* book. It was written by and about *their* faith family. It was inspired by the God who reaches out to *them* in a way similar to the way that same God touched those who wrote, compiled, and translated its pages. The entire Bible can be embraced. Even those parts with an unsavory ethic can be accepted as insight into the development of one's spiritual ancestry.

The material that follows consist of an overview of the biblical message seen through the metaphor of a faith family album. A book of this length cannot claim to embrace nearly all the ideas that scripture contains. This volume is an effort to identify and follow the threads that hold the fabric together. Certain ideas and questions form a consistent background against which all other themes must be viewed. I am convinced that for many readers the integrity of the Bible and the meaning of its overall message will become clearer as it is traced along these continuing lines and seen through the lens of the family album metaphor.

Two Unusual Approaches

To accent the concept of scripture as a family album, I have taken two unusual approaches to the biblical overview.

First, the books of the Bible are addressed, inasmuch as possible, in the order in which they were written, not the order in which they appear in our modern Bible.[4] It is important to note that while the Bible itself may be holy, the order of the books is not. The Hebraic parts of the Bible, for example, come in one order for Jewish editions and in quite a different order in Christian Bibles. Many editions of the Bible contain some books called the Pseudepigrapha and the Apocrypha, books not considered a part of the canon (official list) in other editions. By taking the books essentially in the order in which they are most widely understood to have been written, the reader is better able to see the community working its way through issues such as the doctrine of God, or the meaning of joy and suffering. In the New Testament, taking the books in the order

---

[4]This goal of chronological order must be fudged somewhat by writings such as the book of Psalms, written over a very long period and thus overlapping many other writings. Reaching the goal is further complicated by material such as Genesis, edited after the eighth-century prophets spoke, but pieced together out of quite ancient fragments. I have tried, imperfectly, to trace ideas along a reasonable time line.

in which they were written allows family arguments over grace and law, for example, to be seen much more clearly.

A second unusual approach is to include a parable about an island community that felt called to record the history and meaning of its unique existence. I hope this will encourage readers, most of whom enter Bible study with deeply ingrained assumptions about the way the Bible was written, to refocus on a religious community assembling an album that will pass on its ideals, commitments, and history to later generations. Some who read advance manuscripts found this helpful; others found it distracting. Those of the second persuasion are encouraged to skip the parable.

Method

My preparation for this writing took many forms. Recent formal study at two theological schools was important to the preparation of the manuscript. Most of my time, however, has been spent in intensive reading of the text. But why mention this? Surely there is nothing unusual about reading the Bible in preparation for writing about it!

The danger for me was that I previously had read the entire Bible several times, and parts of it innumerable times. It was entirely too easy to approach a passage with an "I've read that before" attitude that would profit me nothing.

Modern technology has helped me read more intensely. I designed a data base for my computer that allowed me to type a brief summary of each chapter, indicate by a code the major topics addressed, and add the name of the writer (if known), the probable date of composition, and, finally, comments about the way the information affected the faith community. I then read and recorded this information in the approximate order in which it was written. This allowed me to experience the progress of the community. It showed me how each writer responded to those just previous. It was a laborious, but exciting, adventure.

One of the obvious advantages of reading at this level was that it forced me to come to grips with what the biblical writers actually said—not what a Sunday school teacher or religion professor told me it said. For example, as one who grew up near the Bible Belt, I was informed, in education and worship, Sunday after Sunday, that the primary theme of scripture was my personal salvation. I have known for considerable time that this was not so. The recent reading confirmed this in unmistakable form. While the Bible does address the issue of personal salvation, especially as Paul struggled for ways to bring Gentiles into the faith community, it deals much more extensively with other issues. Radio and television evangelists, who seem to have co-opted the Bible for their message of personal success and eternal salvation, need to consult a good concordance. The word "heaven," for example, occurs often, but the vast majority of these passages refer to the place where stars, moon, and sun reside. "Hell" is mentioned only thirteen times in all the Bible, and not all of those relate to personal punishment. By contrast, the word "justice," a social concept, is referred to more than one hundred times. Volume alone may not be an accurate measure of biblical concern, but where the differences are this great, the frequency of occurrence cannot be ignored.

Of course I did not depend solely on my own reading. All local pastors, aware of the limitations of time and knowledge, learn to lean on the insights of major commentaries and acknowledged scholars. The major sources are designated in the footnotes.

Appreciation

Community United Church of Christ in Champaign, Illinois, where I share in the life of the faith community, gave me a sabbatical study leave that made concentration on this task possible.

My preparation took me to the Presbyterian School of Education in Richmond, Virginia, were I consulted with Dr. Carol Reynolds. Dr. Reynolds was extremely helpful in reacting to some preliminary ideas about this writing. She stimulated my thinking. She will recognize the way many of my earlier ideas have been modified in light of our discussions; she should not, however, be held responsible for anything here in its final form.

Three weeks at Princeton Theological Seminary, studying with Dr. James Moorhead in the history of Protestant thought, completed my formal preparation for this writing. Dr. Moorhead will also recognize the influence of his excellent teaching; the ideas here, nonetheless, are my own.

Finally, special thanks go to more than thirty members of Community United Church of Christ who participated in a Bible study based on an earlier edition of this manuscript and whose insights and criticisms have been invaluable. Deep appreciation goes, also, to Dr. Jo Ann Fley for her editorial suggestions and perceptive comments. Deepest gratitude goes to my wife, Diana, who has shared in and stimulated my spiritual growth for more than three decades, and who also shared in my sabbatical study. Without her wisdom and support this writing would not have been possible.

1

The Community
Defines Itself: Justice

The community was on an island, not far off the coast. Its people had occupied that spot for more generations than could be accurately counted. Evidence for their long occupation came from written records, some damaged but later restored. Ancestors of the record-keepers had been on the island even earlier, before the skills of writing were developed.

The community had a unique relationship to the sea. This relationship to the water was much more intimate than that enjoyed by people on the mainland; it had continued longer than that of any other island people.

Those on the island had come to understand four important realities about the water that surrounded them:

1. The sea was the source of their life. Fish from it filled their tables. They had observed how the sun seemed to lift moisture into the sky so it could fall in the form of rain for their crops and water for drinking and cleaning.

2. The sea was a source of inspiration. The salt air was invigorating. Sometimes visitors from the mainland came and told them that their island stimulated their mental and spiritual health. The islanders recognized that, compared with other communities of similar size, they had produced an unusual number of poets, painters, dramatists, and essayists.

3. The sea was their protector. Not only did it provide a formidable moat around them, but their knowledge of the forces of the ocean gave them an advantage over invaders who tried to take away their precious island.

4. The sea also was a source of danger. What gave them life could also cause their death. If encountered without caution—without respect for the disciplines of the sea that had evolved across the generations—people could be swept away.

As the generations passed, the islanders became increasingly aware of the importance of preserving their records and insights. For some, this was a simple matter of helping the community survive by passing on traditions to a younger generation. Others, however, were aware that they had a truth that might be shared with people beyond their community, people who also were influenced by direct contact with the sea. So some leaders of the community began to collect a community album.

Easiest to collect, of course, were current documents. Certain persons were recognized by most islanders as particularly skilled in understanding the sea and how the community should adjust to its omnipresence. While these individuals were seldom universally recognized, they had enough respect among the general populace that their words were taken with great seriousness. These individuals had given recent and forceful presentations on the defining aspects of their island homeland. These speeches, written as people remembered them, became the first complete entries in the island's special book.

The Community Is Defined: The Work of Four Prophets
The Eighth Century B.C.E.

The eighth century before the Common Era was a time of tragic transition for the Jewish people. Despite their division into two often hostile nations, they had managed to prosper. The prosperity, however, was not well distributed. The rich grew richer, often by taking advantage of the powerlessness of the poor. Perceptive people know that such prosperity is always doomed to a short life.

Additional storm clouds could be seen by any who had the courage to look. Assyria, a strong nation to the north, was increasing its military strength and expanding its influence. Cities were growing at the expense of the countryside—a development that was abhorred by those who saw the nation's land as a primary source of its strength. A coalition of smaller states had organized itself to oppose Assyria.

Some people of influence insisted that Israel and Judah should change their foreign policy and ally themselves with that group.

For many, the most distressing aspect of their lives was the loss of ethical mooring. Strength and prosperity could be preserved, according to religious precepts, only by faithfulness to the nation's covenant with Yahweh, their God. Yahweh was worshiped, but in a superficial manner. The wealthy brought their fine animals to the sacred altars in the most ostentatious way possible. In between Sabbaths, however, these same prosperous merchants could be seen using one set of scales for selling and a quite different set for purchasing.

Because of these problems, several sensitive, far-sighted individuals predicted dire consequences for both Israel and Judah. These persons shared a common assumption: the assumption that God controlled earthly events and gave evidence of that control by rewarding those who were morally good and punishing those who were morally evil. Since those who spoke out saw evil all around them, they were confident Yahweh would soon correct matters through an awesome upheaval. This idea of automatic rewards for faithful behavior and punishment for evil behavior has been given a name: *the theory of retribution.*

As might be expected, these spokespersons, who were later to be called prophets, were not received kindly by the wealthy and powerful. Complacent in their prosperity, those atop the social pyramid wanted to hear only the optimists speak.

By the end of the eighth century, however, the optimists had been thoroughly discredited. Assyria attacked and completely destroyed the northern kingdom of Israel. Judah, the southern kingdom, survived by becoming a vassal state. Assyria demanded huge tributes. Then the people remembered the voices of four articulate prophets and realized that their words should have been given greater respect.

Amos

A country boy moved to the city. The event has been repeated millions of times in the history of human migrations. Yet this particular episode was unique. The impact of Amos' unadorned background upon the complexities of urban life gave birth to the first complete book of the Bible. In developing his ideas—ideas later written into the book that carries his name—the prophet Amos gave several important defining characteristics of the faith community into which he had been born.

Amos, as the author of the first completed book of the Bible, deserves a personal introduction. Scripture refers to him only as Amos, herdsman of Tekoa. The absence of a father's name signifies that he belonged to a low class. Of material wealth he had little. He described himself as a "dresser of sycamore trees," a profession followed only by the very poor. It was a vocation easily combined with shepherding. Amos apparently did both.

His materially poor life was rich in experiences of God. In the scattered oases in which his flocks had fed, Amos discovered that the Creator had provided adequate resources. No doubt he associated his watchful care of his animals with the divine desire to protect God's human flock. Amos also knew of Yahweh's judgment. Wild beasts and rough terrain waited to destroy any animal that willfully wandered from its companions. Staying within the caretaker's oversight meant life, Amos discovered; straying from it meant death. A similar justice must attach itself to the Designer of this world. The warm sun spoke to Amos of the goodness of his Maker, the cold wind at night disclosed the Creator's severity. The lightning suggested divine wrath. This concept of a God thorough in love, mighty in power, and fixed in righteousness, accompanied Amos as he moved from a rural area to the city.

His relocation caused painful culture shock. Instead of the still waters and quiet fields, the city confronted him with crowded, dusty streets where people pushed and shoved along their harried way. The chariots of the wealthy rushed by, oblivious to those who chanced to be in the way. Amos learned by distasteful experience that one must deal carefully with merchants. Their dual set of scales meant a hidden charge to each unsuspecting customer. In every direction his careful eyes observed realities that were in direct contrast to the divine justice he had known in his former life.

His personal pain was severe. Yet he saw others suffering much more than he. The poor, the widows, the ill, and the children were defenseless against the powerful urban forces. No one defended them if they were cheated by ruthless merchants. If employed at all they were hired by unscrupulous landowners who paid only a pittance for their labor. He saw a vicious cycle in motion, one in which the strong became stronger, the weak weaker.

One other reality jarred Amos. He watched as wealthy persons used part of what they had wrung from the poor to purchase elaborate sacrifices for the sacred altar. The powerful, who had found that money would purchase whatever was desired at the human level, thought they could use money to purchase the favor of the Divine.

Amos had been a shepherd in Judah. He chose to make his religious statement, however, in Israel, the other part of the divided nation. Already, by making himself an early carpetbagger, he had planted the seeds of his unpopularity!

Nonetheless, Amos managed to capture the attention of his audience. He used an effective device. He spoke first of the sins of people far away. After describing the anger of God at the people of Damascus (a clear statement that the deity who was worshiped by the Jews was also the God of other nations), he moved slightly closer by railing against the transgressions of the city of Tyre. Closer and closer he came, still talking about foreigners, but tightening the noose around the people to whom he spoke. After nearly a quarter of his address had been given, he spoke directly to those before him. "Hear this word that the Lord has spoken against you, O people of Israel..."

And what were the sins that had generated the anger of the Creator? Amos was quite specific. The powerful "store up violence and robbery in their strongholds." God was furious at those who "oppress the poor, who crush the needy." Dishonest economic practices were singled out:

> We will make the ephah small
>   and the shekel great,
>   and practice deceit with false balances,
> buying the poor for silver
>   and the needy for a pair of sandals,
>   and selling the sweepings of the wheat.
>   (Amos 8:5b–6)

Remembering that the money he had seen flowing into the temple in the effort to purchase the favor of God, Amos vented his anger into one of his most famous passages:

> I hate, I despise your festivals (says the Lord)
>   and I take no delight in your solemn assemblies.
> Even though you offer me your
>   burnt offerings and grain offerings
>   I will not accept them....
> Take away from me the noise of your songs;
>   I will not listen to the melody
>   of your harps.
> But let justice roll down like waters,
>   and righteousness like an
>   everflowing stream. (Amos 5:21–24)

Amos spoke at a time of apparent prosperity. Yet he, with the prophet's eye that sees beneath the surface, recognized that a lack of social ethics[1] had eaten away the nation's core. Their wealth was only a fragile shell. Because Israel had been guilty of these evils, Amos predicted a dreadful demise for their entire society.

It should be no surprise that Amos was quickly and forcefully ushered out of Israel. The relatively brief message that became a part of scripture is the only recorded message he left. He had accomplished, nonetheless, an amazing amount. He had given posterity the earliest, complete book of the Bible. He had also done much to define the nature of his faith community.

Micah

Micah, the second of the eighth-century prophets, was in many ways similar to Amos. He, too, had grown up in a small community, the kind of town that nostalgia often fills with "dear hearts and gentle people." Yet Moresheth, the place of his birth, was hardly idyllic. It lay near the border of the nation. The people there felt especially vulnerable to foreign powers. It was natural, therefore, that Micah would want his nation to remain strong.

National strength, as Micah envisioned it, could not be found in armaments. On the contrary, he was sure the divine was calling the nation to "beat their swords into plowshares, and their spears into pruning hooks" (4:3). Their strength would be found in an entirely different area: in their religion. The people's covenant with God should cause them to relate justly to one another. Justice would mean that the weak would be lifted, that every member of the nation would feel a part of the whole and thus contribute to a powerful nation woven together by the bonds of trust and compassion.

Micah was especially incensed by his knowledge that the leaders of the nation were involved in widespread corruption. His words vividly convey his feeling:

> Listen, you...rulers of the house of Israel!
> Should you not know justice?—
> > you who hate the good and love the evil,
> who tear the skin off my people,
> > and the flesh off their bones;

---

[1] Amos also felt that Israel should change its international alliance and ally itself with a group of states in opposition to Assyria. It was, however, his concern for social justice that gave lasting meaning to his words and helped define the religious community.

who eat the flesh of my people,
  flay their skin off them,
break their bones in pieces,
  and chop them up like meat in a kettle,
like flesh in a caldron. (Micah 3:1–3)

Surely, Micah reasoned, the religious leaders would call down the wrath of God upon such practices. Instead, he found the temple authorities to be primarily interested in their own welfare. Those who brought food to the priests received a pleasant message of "shalom," but those who were unwilling or unable to make large contributions heard themselves condemned (3:5).

Micah was a more perceptive economist than Amos. Concerning the wide gap between rich and poor, he was able to describe in detail both the problem and the solution. The problem was greed—a greed that caused those already materially comfortable to want even more and to devise unscrupulous schemes to take away what should not be theirs. "They covet fields, and seize them; houses, and take them away; they oppress householder and house, people and their inheritance" (2:2).

The solution Micah offered was an economy in which every family had "a piece of the action." The nation would be strongest, and best able to defend its borders, when all people owned enough land to secure their economic well-being. After declaring that armaments should be converted into tools of agriculture, Micah offered this formula for national strength:

but they shall all sit under their
  own vines and under their own fig trees,
and no one shall make them afraid;
for the mouth of the LORD of
  hosts has spoken. (Micah 4:4)

While Amos had used the literary device of speaking first of distant peoples and then working his way back to his target audience, Micah employed another approach. He described a courtroom scene in which God brings a controversy with the people. The Creator had been good to the nation, had brought it out of slavery and offered it effective guidance. Yet the people had gone their own way and ignored their covenant with the Divine. God would not let them forget, however. God told them that they could not win divine favor with impressive gifts at the altar. Then comes this summary statement of Micah's message:

> He has told you, O mortal, what is good;
>   and what does the LORD require of you
> but to do justice, and to love kindness,
>   and to walk humbly with your God? (Micah 6:8)

Hosea

Hosea's message was similar in content to that of the other eighth-century prophets, yet quite different in form. He shared intimate details of his marriage, allowing that relationship to become a window through which the reader could glimpse the depth of God's patient love for the people of faith.

Hosea mentioned his father's name, indicating that he was a person of social standing. From such heights, however, he found he could descend to remarkable lows.

For reasons that are not spelled out in the book that carries his name, Hosea found himself in a disastrous marriage. His wife, Gomer, was a whore. Three children were born into the marriage, but questions about their paternity led the parents to give them very negative names: Jezreel, (meaning "God sows") became a reminder of a tragic chapter in the history of the land; Lo-ruhamah, which translates "no pity," was a reference to the punitive side of the Divine; finally and most tragically, Lo-ammi, which means "not my people" (obviously, Hosea was especially suspicious that he had not fathered this child!). One must hope the book of Hosea is a parable and not a reality. Otherwise three children lived out their lives with some of the most prejudicial names in history!

Gomer finally tired of the charade of their marriage and left Hosea for full-time prostitution. She was less than successful at this oldest of vocations, however. Soon she was sold into slavery.

At that point a man of Hosea's social standing could have declared himself divorced from the evil Gomer and rebuilt his life from other materials. Instead, he performed a remarkable and humble act. He went to the slave market and *purchased back his wife!* In simple words awash in both pathos and hope, the prophet announced, "So I bought her for fifteen shekels of silver and a homer of barley and a measure of wine" (3:2). Hosea did this because he saw a reflection of the nation's covenant with God in the tragic rending, then the compassionate mending of his own marriage covenant.

Hosea's analysis of the problems of his people was significantly different than that of Amos or Micah. Hosea was confident the source of the estrangement between God and the Jewish community was to be found in the history of the relationship itself. God had, in the wilderness, taken the people as a husband takes a bride. God had been faithful to this covenant, but the people had gone "a-whoring" after other sources of protection and pleasure. Hosea knew there had been a previous debate between those who wanted a king to rule over the nation and those who resisted the monarchy on the grounds that only God could ultimately rule. Just as the anti-monarchists had once feared, the king had become a competing object of worship and adoration. Hosea spoke also of the many altars established to false gods. Developing the metaphor of marriage, Hosea saw this idol worship as an act of adultery.

Even the worship of Yahweh, when it took place, was less than satisfactory. As both Amos and Micah had pointed out, the people brought their sacrifices and sang their songs of praise simply to give themselves a false sense of security—an experience of having won the protection of the Divine. It would not work, Hosea warned. "For I desire steadfast love and not sacrifice, the knowledge of God rather than burnt offerings" (6:6).

Like the other prophets of the same era, Hosea predicted tragic results from the people's unfaithfulness. God would utterly dissolve the relationship between God's self and the adulterous generation, "for she is not my wife, and I am not her husband" (2:2).

Hosea's ultimate message, nonetheless, was one of hope. He believed that God would totally abandon the people who had once been chosen; yet the purpose of the break was to establish the basis for a more permanent relationship. "For it is he who has torn, and he will heal us; he has struck down, and he will bind us up" (6:1). Hosea's children, once a symbol of estrangement, would become symbols of the restoration. "And I will have pity on Lo-ruhamah, and I will say to Lo-ammi, 'You are my people'" (2:23).

Hosea made clear that forgiveness and restoration are not inexpensive gifts. The sorrow of the marriage, the painful names carried by the children, and the utter humiliation of Hosea's visit to the slave market are indications of the cost of grace—especially divine grace. Nonetheless, God, according to Hosea, is willing to bear the cost. The people, after much suffering, will be restored. Such is the qualified optimism of this remarkable prophet.

Isaiah (First)

The name Isaiah is associated with a very long book of the Hebraic Scripture. Scholars are confident that the man who carried that name was responsible only for most of the first thirty-nine chapters of the book. He was the fourth of the prophets of the eighth century.

Isaiah continued the concepts of the other three prophets. Like Hosea, he portrayed the relationship between God and the nation as a romance. "Let me sing for my beloved" (Isaiah 5:1). Also like Hosea, Isaiah knew that the course of this romance was anything but smooth. The suitor built a vineyard for his beloved. "He expected it to yield grapes, but it yielded wild grapes" (v. 2). Like Amos and Micah, Isaiah condemned a society and an economy that encouraged greed by allowing some persons to grow wealthy while the majority sank into deeper poverty.

> [God] expected justice, but saw bloodshed;
> righteousness, but heard a cry!
>> Ah, you who join house to house,
>> who add field to field,
>> until there is room for no one but you,
>> and you are left to live alone
>> in the midst of the land! (Isaiah 5:7–8)

The book of Isaiah has several unique features. One is the fact that its writer, though basically a person of religion, was also deeply involved in foreign affairs. He was apparently both a friend of and advisor to the king. Many of the middle chapters of his book are oracles[2] describing the sins of neighboring countries and the punishment that their actions will bring upon them.

Surprisingly, Isaiah's concern for political happenings became the soil from which grew a passage important to the worship life of succeeding generations of the faith family. At news of the death of his friend, King Uzziah, Isaiah went into the temple to cope with his grief. In that moment of spiritual vulnerability he experienced the divine presence. His description of that encounter, and the emotions that overtook him, is an often-used model for worship (Isaiah 6:1–8).

Isaiah is helpful, also, in demonstrating that the prophetic task is to speak with depth and concern *to the situation of the present day.* Unfortunately, the word "prophet" has come to mean, to some ears, one who peers into a crystal ball in order to foresee the distant future. Indeed, some future gazing is integral to the prophetic task, for the person who dares speak for God must often say, "If this trend continues, then certain results will inevitably occur." But the prophet

---

[2] An oracle is a religious address, usually made in the setting of a temple or synagogue.

is not a professional seer. He or she is called by God to speak the divine message to the current situation and to the present place.

The seventh chapter of Isaiah illustrates the point. The Jewish capital was under attack. Siege had been laid around the city. The situation was remarkably bleak. Isaiah, because of his wisdom and understanding of the ways of God, was invited to go with the king to view the foreign army. Isaiah recognized the gravity of the scene. Yet he was sure that God was not ready to allow the destruction of the holy city. So he made an informed prediction that some horror would befall the visiting army and they would be unsuccessful in their siege. When the king expressed his dismay at this welcome news, Isaiah tried to put the matter more forcefully. God would give a sign, Isaiah promised. A pregnant young woman would bear a son, and before that son was old enough to be responsible for his own actions, the armies that had attacked Jerusalem would be entirely vanquished.

The time span to which Isaiah referred could not have exceeded a dozen years. Efforts by over-eager Christians to make this a promise of the birth of Jesus, an event that would not take place for more than seven hundred years, have no foundation. If this were a prediction of Jesus, then poor King Ahaz would have had to postpone deliverance from the foreign armies for much longer than he or his people were prepared to wait! Like all good prophets, Isaiah was speaking to an immediate situation.

Isaiah introduced another important element. Looking at their current situation he saw the need for a radically new situation. He predicted the future arrival of a saving individual—a Messiah!

Isaiah spoke at a low point in Jewish life. One half of their divided nation had already been taken captive. The other half was under severe threat. Nostalgic memory carried the people back to another time, when King David was feared by Jewish neighbors and when conquering armies brought back rich spoils from their foreign victories. Those glory days of the nation would, according to Isaiah, someday be restored. Their saving figure would come, naturally, from the family of David. "A shoot shall come out from the stump of Jesse" (the father of David) (Isaiah 11:1). This saving figure would be king. He would rule with authority, wisdom, and power. His strength would be beyond challenge, both for the citizens who lived under him and the nations that surrounded him.

The military power of this offspring of David would be such that genuine peace would be enforced in the land. Using compelling, poetic language, the prophet described his reign as one in which

> the wolf shall live with the lamb,
>> the leopard shall lie down with the kid,
> the calf and the lion and the fatling together,
>> and a little child shall lead them. (Isaiah 11:6)

The vision of tranquillity, however, should not hide the fact that Isaiah assumed this peace would be the product of wisely-used, overwhelming power. In the day of this new David the Jewish people would be raised to a position of respect in the council of nations. "The nations shall inquire of him, and his dwelling shall be glorious" (Isaiah 11:10). Much of the respect that this saving figure would demand would be the result of military power. "Therefore strong peoples will glorify you; cities of ruthless nations will fear you" (Isaiah 25:3). Isaiah had defined the vision of the Messianic Age that would dominate the Hebraic Scripture.

The first thirty-nine chapters of the book of Isaiah (the part for which a person named Isaiah is responsible) end with an ominous story concerning King Hezekiah. In a moment of foolish pride, the Jewish king received a delegation from an increasingly strong northern nation named Babylon and *showed them through the royal treasuries!* The act was exceedingly foolish. The delegation would carry a description of those treasures back to their merciless king. The Babylonian king would surmise that it would be quite worthwhile to attack the small nation of Judah. Isaiah rebuked his king and predicted (it certainly required no special spiritual powers to foresee the result of this absurd action) that the entire land would be destroyed.

In several different ways, then, Isaiah illustrated an important truth: *the role of the prophet was to speak the wisdom of God to the present situation.*

Thus the first books of the Bible to be written in essentially their present form (other scrolls were later added to the work of Isaiah) were the work of four remarkable men who lived between seven and eight hundred years before the birth of Jesus. They had no identified works of scripture to guide them, only the remembered history and faith of their people.

Their words, which were probably recalled and written down later by their followers, establish some of the continuing, identifying realities of the community of faith.

Identifying Marks of the Faith Community

The four eighth-century prophets differed in their imagery and their emphases. Yet they presented several common themes that, in turn, help define their faith community. The most important of these characteristics were monotheism, a unifying sense of community, a high ethical commitment, and a definition of the unique role of the prophet.

Monotheism is the first mark of this religious community. The prophets spoke for Yahweh, the God who brought the Jewish people out of slavery, established a covenant with them in the desert, and guided them into their own land. As these spiritual geniuses saw it, the nation's well-being was dependent on its focused commitment to their saving God. As long as the people remained committed in both word and action to the God of compassion, power, and justice, all would go well with the land. The fact that the nation had moved away from this central focus was responsible for their present troubles. Their idolatry would lead to other, even more ominous difficulties. In the imagery of Hosea, sin was the act of "going a-whoring" after other gods. Other gods represented a division in the Jew's unified worldview.

The Jews had observed neighboring cultures worshiping one god of the sun, another of harvest, and yet another god of sexual fertility. To their minds this divided realm of the divine meant a divided creation. *It was this divided creation, this tearing of the fabric of a unified worldview, that the Jews defined as idolatry.* Certain forms of idolatry created a separation of sexual activity from its intended role of pro-creation, that is, a sharing in God's creative activity. Idolatry meant focusing on the pleasure and well-being of the individual apart from the well-being of the larger community.

A second identifying mark was *the communal nature of their faith.* The prophets' messages had implications for the individual, of course. Yet it was the *nation* to whom the message was addressed. No divisive individualism was to be found in the words of God's spokespersons. All within the religious community were challenged to seek justice by caring for the widow and orphan because *commitment to the welfare of other people was inseparable from commitment to God.* Thus the reward of righteous living was not an individualized eternity in the presence of God, but a here and now nation of peace and justice—one that the current generation could happily turn over to posterity. Ultimately it was the nation that either served God faithfully and thus would find *shalom*[3], or else it was the nation that fell short and would be severely punished.

---

[3] *Shalom,* the popular word for peace, means much more than the absence of war. It is a rich word referring to a state of well-being for both the individual and the nation.

A third identifying mark of the religious community was its *ethical character*. Ethical behavior was the keeping of the moral law. In this we anticipate a later argument within the faith family: Is keeping the moral law alone adequate to satisfy the demands of the Divine? The limits of the law would be spelled out later by many persons, both before and after the birth of Jesus. Yet these prophets made clear that *behavior matters*, that keeping the demands of justice and righteousness are the bedrock on which all else must be constructed. No one could claim to be a full member of this faith community who was not committed to the demands of law, especially as the law specified ways of relating to the sojourner and the dispossessed.

The eighth-century prophets were well acquainted with their nation's history. They knew the stories of decades of desert wandering. Their nomadic ancestors had been under constant threat from other, often more powerful, peoples. Two realities became serious dangers. One was the individual who, because of age (too old, too young) or illness, was unable to move quickly. An equal threat came from the one who had accumulated too many unnecessary resources and thus was, for different reasons, unable to be flexible in moving quickly away from danger or toward a needed oasis.

In their wanderings the people developed a concept of *mispah*, translated by one wise teacher as "desert justice." In the desert the people had been forced to move quickly away from enemies and toward distant sources of water. They learned to share strength with the weak, lest the entire community suffer. The elderly and the lame needed special care. The community had also learned to be on guard against the temptation of greed. Owning too many possessions was as dangerous as the lack of mobility among the weak. Poverty and excessive wealth were twin dangers to their economy, their nation, and their relationship to God.

In their settled communities it was easy for the nation to forget the lessons of the desert. The prophets called them back to this reality, clearly measuring the faithfulness of the nation by the yardstick of concern for the widow, the orphan, the ill, and the elderly. Materialism, they reminded their contemporaries, could create dead weight as damaging to an agricultural community as to a nomadic one.

Finally, the fourth identifying mark of the community offered by these four men was the *extraordinary role of the prophet*. Politically, the nation had been ruled by kings. These kings had little or no concept of democratic rule; on the contrary, they were totalitarians of the first order, dealing ruthlessly with those who opposed them. Religiously, on the other hand, the nation was ruled by the Creator of the universe, the God who had entered into special relationship with their ancestors.

The prophets were living proof that, in actual practice, the religious realm stood decidedly above the political. The words of these eighth-century prophets had often been harsh. Because the nation was seen as a unit, their criticism of the nation was a criticism of the king who set the tone for the nation's life. In the closing chapter of Isaiah is found an example of the prophet scolding the king to his royal face! (Isaiah 39:5–8). (Many other similar examples of prophetic controntations with the king can be found in the historic books to be examined later.) In any other autocratic society a monarch would have quickly separated such an upstart faultfinder from his head. Yet, in Jewish society the prophets gave their stern opinions to the royal throne and walked away safely. They knew themselves to be safe because the ultimate ruler of the land was the God for whom the prophets spoke. Any power hungry king (or queen) who attempted to usurp that ultimate authority would have met a quick and ugly fate. Jezebel would later unwittingly prove that point! (See 1 Kings 21.)

As much as any other single reality, the unique role of the prophet shaped the nature of the faith community.

Family Arguments

Already, in the words of these four relatively similar writers, it becomes clear that the Bible is not a document that can be used as a giant how-to book. It is not a volume that can be consulted for consistent answers to controversial questions. The Bible is, instead, the stage on which the most important issues of the faith family are debated.

The careful reader of these four prophets will note evidence of a disagreement concerning the nature of God. The deviations here are not nearly so great as will occur when other biblical voices join the chorus of concepts. Yet even among these four essentially similar spokespersons, some differences are obvious.

Amos, the person of poverty whose concepts were molded in the often harsh world of nature, called the people to worship a God of precise ethical demands. Their failure to seek justice within their community would bring down the wrath of the Divine, just as sheep wandering from the flock put themselves in severe danger. Hosea, on the other hand, while seeing the suffering the people were bringing on themselves, felt that God's ultimate purpose was healing. The debate over the nature of God would later become more pronounced. It is introduced in a relatively serene form in these earliest books of scripture.

The words of these earliest prophets point, however, to another argument in which the two sides are more clearly defined. How is God to be served? The eighth-century prophets were united in their view that God is pleased by ethical living—by constructing a community in which the special needs of the weakest members are acknowledged and the basic needs of all are met. The strength by which they make their point, however, is a clear indication that an opposing view was widely held. The opposing view had a name. Over against the *prophetic* view of religion was the *priestly* view. In the understanding of the priestly party, God could best be served by proper services of worship and by sacrifices given in accordance to liturgical demands. Had the people sinned? Then, according to the priestly party, sin offerings were to be brought to the altar, and God would be placated. Against this understanding Amos shouted defiantly what he was sure was the opinion of the Divine: "I hate, I despise your festivals...But let justice run down like waters, and righteousness like an everflowing stream" (Amos 5:21, 24).

This debate, also, will be revived in many forms as other writers contribute their opinions.

Afterword

The four earliest writers of scripture had appeared. They spoke in the extraordinary role of prophet. As the first to compose biblical books these four prophets had a unique opportunity to define the faith community's core characteristics. They also foreshadowed at least two of the basic debates that would occupy the minds and spirits of those who would follow them: What is the nature of God? and how is God to be served?

Amos, Micah, Hosea, and Isaiah defined the community's commitment to justice. Justice, however, is a concept in need of further definition. How is it achieved? What actions are necessary to preserve it? Written rules were needed, rules that reflected not only the concern for a just society, but also the divine source of their severe demands. Law, therefore, would become another defining element of the community. To that topic we turn next.

2

The Community Defines Itself: Law

After collecting current writings that defined the purpose of their community, the islanders turned their attention to writings that defined their unique behavior.

"Do we behave in ways that make us unique?" The answer to this question was given in a code of rules and behaviors. Some of these rules pertained to their purpose, defining the way the purpose was to be achieved. The major means used to transmit the rules was to pass them on from person to person and from generation to generation within structured families. In addition, some written codes of behavior were circulated informally. One code was especially revered, for it seemed to summarize all that the community had learned about relationships among its people and their relationship to the sea. Most of the people on the island had memorized this brief but crucial list of rules.

This informal regulation of behavior worked reasonably well while the community was young and small. As the group grew in number and age, however, people began to sense a need for a more formal arrangement. Pressure in this direction increased when severe storms brought considerable damage to the island. Between storms a nearby group of islanders nearly succeeded in invading their precious space. These reversals caused some community leaders to question whether they were being faithful to their way of life. If they had been more clear about the proper rules of the sea, they were sure they could have moderated the damage of the storms. Following clear rules would also help them fight off hostile invaders, or so they reasoned.

Working secretly, some members of the community compiled a long document that brought together the major rules of behavior that had guided the community in the past. Laws that had been passed along only by verbal means were now committed to paper. Various written fragments of rules were edited and added to the document. The summary list of laws, the commands that almost all islanders had memorized, was given a prominent place in the writing.

What emerged from this work was more than simple rules of behavior. The finished document was a description of an entire way of life. It contained social rules and moral laws. The writing included proper ways to relate to the nourishing but awesome power of the sea. It included traditions, new rules, regulating the relationship between male and female.

After much work the document was completed. The few leaders of the community who knew that this had been written devised a clever scheme for sharing it with all the islanders. They hid the document where they knew someone would discover it. Its origins they kept secret, hoping the islanders would assume some transcendent power had left it for their guidance.

The plan worked perfectly. When the document was discovered, the king pretended to be amazed. He ordered that all the islanders gather for a formal reading of this "mysterious" code of laws. The people heard it and were delighted. They knew the way of life that made them unique was more secure now that it had been defined in a written, legal code.

Deuteronomy

The psalmist's description of righteous persons includes this remarkable statement: "Their delight is in the law of the LORD" (Psalm 1:2).

In most circumstances people see law as, at best, a necessary evil. Law restricts one's options. Laws usually come attached to threatened punishments—those who fail to obey will pay a price. Law takes power from the individual and places it in the hands of those with authority. Laws, by their very existence, tempt one to break them. A later religious writer from this faith family would expand on the interconnection between law and sin.

Nonetheless, the writer of the first Psalm insisted that the Law is a delightful part of righteous living! The Jewish people seemed to have approached the concept of law in a way different from most others.

Understanding the developing faith community is impossible without understanding the meaning and role of law among this people. The book of Deuteronomy introduces us to the concepts necessary for this understanding.

Deuteronomy is a book "discovered" in a time of religious renewal. The circumstances of the discovery are these: The nation had endured through several centuries with a set of rules that were poorly organized and vaguely understood. The Ten Commandments had formed the basis of all religious regulations. These commandments (the Decalogue) were securely protected in the nation's most sacred place of worship. Other laws, expansions of the Decalogue, existed also and were found in shorter documents. Additional regulations were preserved orally, although none of the other rules held the authority of the commandments, claimed to have been handed down through Moses.

The nation had existed for centuries with its peculiar mixture of formal and informal regulations. Many of those years were times of peril. Threats to the kingdom came from weaknesses within and from the strength of neighbors beyond its borders. The religious leaders became convinced that the low times occurred because God was sending punishment for the people's lax response to their religious duties. Yet those duties were not spelled out in any systematic way.

About a hundred years after the eighth-century prophets, a reform-minded king came to the throne. His name was Josiah. His goal was to restore the nation to its former strength. A major component of this effort was the reform of religious practices. Religious reform, however, would be difficult without a clearer definition of religious requirements. In other words, a full listing of the religious law was needed.

The circumstances of the "discovery" of the book of Deuteronomy are not clear. We are told, in 2 Kings 22:8, that the Book of the Law was found in the temple. Many students of scripture surmise that King Josiah ordered that a proper summary of the Law be written. Then he commanded that it be hidden (not too well, for it was important that it be found without much delay) in the temple. Its discovery there would give it an aura of authority that a normal, public unveiling would have lacked. The manuscript was duly found. The king seemed surprised. Josiah ordered the people to assemble before the temple. The entire book of Deuteronomy was read.

The people rejoiced to have so clear a statement of their religious requirement.

The above is probably a good description of how most of the book of Deuteronomy came into being. Parts of the text, however, seem to have been added later. A group of editors, many biblical scholars assume, all with a similar point of view, began with a basic set of Jewish laws and expanded these into the original book of Deuteronomy. This was done during the time of Josiah, before the breakdown of the state of Judah.[1] After the exile, so the argument has gone, other editors added brief passages to complete the manuscript as it is today.

Lately Richard Friedman[2] has made a persuasive argument for another possibility. He believes that Josiah commissioned Jeremiah to write Deuteronomy. This is quite conceivable, since Jeremiah was a prophet whose career began before the exile and lasted until after the exile. If so, then Jeremiah, building on a document that contained the body of Jewish laws, composed the majority of the text in the later part of the sixth century B.C.E. After the exile the same Jeremiah added passages to explain why God had abandoned the people to the Babylonian armies. The reason, of course, was their lack of faithfulness to the Law.

The Law: More Than Religion

The book of Deuteronomy, while written as a part of Josiah's religious reform, touches on more than religion, narrowly defined. Deuteronomy offers helpful insight into the intimate relationship between ethnic Judaism and religious Judaism. Deuteronomy is a summary of the laws that make a Jew a Jew.

When members of a religious community, using Psalm 1, declare that they "rejoice in the law," they are saying, in essence, that they rejoice in being Jewish! (Christians, as they use this psalm, can rejoice that they are part of a faith community that has its roots in Judaism.)

Thus the phrase "the Law" covers a multitude of rules and regulations that are amazingly broad, amazingly malleable, and often distressingly ambiguous. One especially perceptive writer put its meaning this way: "In brief, a charter of civilized life constitutes the bulk of the Mosaic Laws."[3]

---

[1] More will be said of this history in chapters 3 and 4.

[2] Richard Elliott Friedman, *Who Wrote the Bible?* (New York: Harper and Row, 1987).

[3] Geza Vermes, *The Religion of Jesus the Jew* (Minneapolis: Fortress Press, 1993).

The meaning of the term *law* is important in understanding the history of the faith community. A clear definition of this term became even more important later in the faith family's development, when followers of a Jewish leader named Jesus attempted to bring non-Jews into that faith community. How many of the laws of Judaism would these new members be required to embrace?

Because law was central to the self-understanding of this people, it is not surprising that the book of Deuteronomy—the book devoted to stating and interpreting the Law—was the next book after the eighth-century prophets' to be written in its present form.

When the book of Deuteronomy is set beside the works of Amos, Hosea, Micah, and 1 Isaiah, a clear definition of the faith community emerges. The prophets had established that the descendants of Abraham were a people in covenant relationship with the one, true God. They had determined, also, that the community was a community of justice—a justice shaped on the anvil of their experience in the wilderness. The prophets had also shown that the experience of liberation from slavery had defined the Jewish people, both in their fierce determination to preserve their freedom and in their understanding that God was and is a God of freedom.

To the prophets' works the book of Deuteronomy adds another crucial dimension. The faith community is a community based not on the whim of the moment, and not on charismatic personalities, but on law. The firmness of the Law pointed to a God who is not a fluid adjuster to each changing circumstance, but who is faithful across the fluctuating landscape of time. In its non-religious aspects, it insured a lasting community whose nature would not be altered by oppression or conflict. In short, *the written Law gave the Jewish people an established body of rules and commandments that made it easy to define themselves as a unique community and to pass their tradition on to future generations.*

The book of Deuteronomy begins with a brief summary of the nation's forty years of existence in the wilderness.[4] Just as the eighth-century prophets had based their idea of justice on their history in the desert, so the concept of law was also rooted in the nation's unusual background. Release from bondage and legal requirements were two realities that could not be separated.

The editor(s) of this new book had a second purpose in mind. Not only did they seek to codify the Law; they also sought to insure the place of the law-giver in Jewish history. Throughout the book of

---

[4] The circumstances of this history will be given in the chapter to follow.

Deuteronomy, Moses is a towering figure. His role is consistently more prominent than that of Aaron, his one competitor for the allegiance of the people. He is even shown as their great advocate in the divine courts who convinces God not to exact punishment on a sinful people (Deuteronomy 10:11). In Deuteronomy, chapters 4 and 5, the purpose of the editor toward Moses is especially clear. Never is this great leader more appealing and authoritative than in his defense of and interpretation of the Ten Commandments (Deuteronomy, chaps. 4 and 5).

The Varieties of Law

The reader of Deuteronomy quickly discovers that the concept of "the Law" is not monolithic. The term refers to many realities. The English language uses the term *law* in a similar, ambiguous way. For example, if a college graduate today announces her intention to study law, it is assumed that she will study the entire body of rules that govern society. On the other hand, a person working through his income tax forms calls out to his spouse, "I wonder what the law is about the special income we had last year?" In this second instance the word *law* refers only to a specific regulation that applies to a particular situation.

The Hebrew Scriptures operate with even more ambiguity about the meaning of the word law. "The Law" can mean the entire body of rules found in the book of Deuteronomy (613 by one count) plus the many additional regulations in other biblical books of history. This broad meaning is the one that defines Judaism. It is apparently this meaning that the psalmist had in mind when he said that the righteous person takes delight in the Law.

The phrase "the Law" can also refer to summaries of the rules. Two such summaries are given in Deuteronomy. The first is the Ten Commandments. The editors of Deuteronomy went to considerable lengths to insure that any reader would recognize the importance of the Decalogue. The paragraphs leading up to its listing expound on their meaning. The people are reminded of the remarkable circumstances in which the basic code of conduct was delivered by God. The ultimate source of the Law was clearly identified: "I am the Lord your God who brought you out of Egypt..." The editors thus designed a frame around this passage, alerting any reader that this was information of the highest importance.

The Decalogue includes three basic forms of Law. The first four commandments deal with matters between people and God. Monotheism is prescribed as the first requirement of the religious life. The second reinforces the first: You shall not represent the divine in any earthly medium. The third commandment insists that the name of Yahweh be held in respect. The fourth commandment insists that a Sabbath be observed.

The fifth through the ninth commandments deal with matters between persons. These deal with basic rules for the preservation of a just society. The elderly are to be honored. Murder, adultery, stealing, and false witness are proscribed.

The tenth commandment deals with dynamics within an individual. To prevent destructive activity, the person faithful to the Law will attempt to head off even the desire to do evil. "You shall not covet..." moves the concept of Law from outward behavior to inward attitude.

An even shorter summary of the Law is contained in the chapter of Deuteronomy following the Ten Commandments. The Shema (the Hebrew word for "hear") boils down the intent of all religious rules to these words:

> Hear, O Israel: The LORD your God is one LORD; and
> you shall love the LORD your God with all your heart,
> and with all your soul, and with all your might.
> (Deuteronomy 6:4–5 [RSV])

The brilliance of this summary of all legal requirements cannot be overstated. Religious persons should put the Divine at the center of their existence. All else will follow in good order. A member of the faith community who lived at a much later time would say, "Love God and do what you want to do." Luther was simply restating the Shema.

The early chapters of Deuteronomy give us another interesting insight into the meaning of "Law." The legal requirements of the faith community are not solidly fixed. There is a certain pliant element even in those laws—even those written in stone! For example, the Ten Commandments as given in Deuteronomy were altered slightly in the process of copying them from the temple's sacred scrolls. (The version recorded later in the book of Exodus is assumed to be the based on older records.) The rationale for the fourth commandment is altered. In the list of the Ten Commandments given in Exodus it says that the Sabbath was designed in response to the fact that God rested after six days of labor. In Deuteronomy a seventh day of rest was ordered because the people had been slaves in Egypt with never a day off, never a moment of rest. Keeping the Sabbath, in the Deuteronomy version, became a symbol of their liberation.

Also, the tenth commandment reference to coveting a neighbor's wife, present in the Exodus version, disappears from the Deuteronomy version.

The pliant nature of the Law gives it its strength. Through the tortured course of Jewish history the Law has adjusted to new circumstances, bending frequently without breaking. By the early centuries of the Christian era the Jewish community had learned to ignore most of the laws relating to animal sacrifice. In the modern time Judaism has quietly dropped those legal requirements that fall most heavily on women. Pliability has its limits, however. The Law has always been firm enough to prevent assimilation into non-Jewish cultures, but flexible enough to allow adaptation when needed.

The laws that make up the book of Deuteronomy can be divided into many other categories.

Some laws resemble operating instructions on how to live most effectively in God's world. The Ten Commandments are prime examples. Note that no specific punishment is given for breaking any of these rules for living. The punishment is built in. Break one of these laws, and the community begins to crumble. Without its commitment to Yahweh and its respect for the divine name the nature of the community would be seriously altered. Without respect for their elderly, the chain of authority would disappear. If murder, adultery, stealing, or false witness were allowed, the community would collapse from lack of trust. Coveting is the acid that could eat away the sinew that holds the community together. By seeing the Decalogue in this light and recognizing that all other laws are, in a sense, commentary on these basic rules, one can understand the enthusiasm of the First Psalmist. He could rejoice in God's Law because these laws helped him understand how the game of life is played with greatest effectiveness.

Much later, in the uniquely Christian scriptures, Paul (and his followers) would seem to dismiss the role of Law in religious development. A closer reading of Paul, as will be shown, reveals that he never intended to release his converts from the security and guidance of the larger legal code. Paul was to stand in the more flexible school of Jewish interpreters. Indeed, sensitive Jewish thinkers have long been aware of the complications that occur when people make a straitjacket of the multitude of laws contained in the Hebraic Scriptures. The most respected of Jewish thinkers have always counseled what Paul would later insist: that the Law be applied with maturity and love.

The brilliance of the Law is recognized, also, in the summaries. The Decalogue, for example, is clear. It is realistic. It takes account of our relationship to the Divine and our relationship to one another. It also addresses those internal dynamics that become the breeding ground for destructive behavior. The basic meaning is this: Those who share in the faith community are expected to live at a high, though not utopian, ethical level. This expectation would never be set aside, certainly not by Jesus, and not even by Paul.

The family arguments noted at the end of the previous chapter are reflected in the nature of the laws. Some rules relate particularly to prophetic religion. That is, they regulate the way justice is to be dispensed. In particular, one law decrees that all debts should be forgiven every seven years (Deuteronomy 15:1–6). Cities of refuge are established for anyone who had accidentally killed another member of the community (Deuteronomy 4:41–43). The laws regulating slavery are an effort to lessen the crushing weight of this institution (Deuteronomy 15:12–18). Payment of wages to the poor is not to be delayed (Deuteronomy 24:14). Not even the king is allowed to accumulate disproportionate amounts of wealth (Deuteronomy 17:17).

Priestly religion is acknowledged in many laws. Rules are given to regulate cultic practices, proper sacrifice, and consumption of meat offered on the altar (Deuteronomy 12:13–19; also 16:1–17). The editors of Deuteronomy placed more importance on this style of religion than had the prophets. For breaking these cultic laws the punishment was, in many cases, death. Central to priestly religion was the concept of being spiritually clean or spiritually unclean. Some persons, because of their practices (or, in the case of women, because of their menstrual cycles or pregnancy) were considered unclean and thus unable to appear before the Divine. In extreme cases the unclean were banished from the community or put to death. The matter of the clean and unclean is introduced in the book of Deuteronomy (Deuteronomy 14:1–21). It becomes a larger issue in the book of Leviticus. Elaboration on this theme will wait for the discussion of that book in a later chapter.

Different views of the nature of God are also reflected in the laws. Some laws stress the forgiving, loving face of theDivine. Examples include the establishment of cities of refuge, deferments from battle for newly married soldiers (Deuteronomy 20:5–6), and laws that include blessings (Deuteronomy 28:1–8).

Other laws point to a harsher Deity. The rules of military combat call for extermination of enemies (though people at a distance, who posed less of a threat to the community, are to be treated with slightly more leniency); sons who cannot be disciplined by a father are to be stoned to death (Deuteronomy 21:18–20); death is also the fate of a woman who cannot prove her virginity on the night of her marriage (Deuteronomy 22:13–21).

Laws also vary in their breadth. Some embrace all of life in a few words (e.g., "[love] the LORD your God, and [serve] him with all your heart and with all your soul. [Deuteronomy 11:13]) Others are amazingly specific (e.g., "you shall not wear clothes made of wool and linen woven together [Deuteronomy 22:11]).

Almost every aspect of life is regulated by the laws of this book. Rules are given for punishing crimes, handling dead bodies, punishing idolatry, the giving of the tithe, sex and marriage, and ways to support the priests.

So much detail in law raises the specter of legalism. Legalism is the rigid application of rules with no consideration of the unique circumstances or the particular needs of the individuals to whom the rules apply. In Deuteronomy legalism is a genuine danger. Religious persons who bring rigid attitudes to the book of Deuteronomy will find abundant fuel for their compulsiveness. Nonetheless, a fair reading of the text shows that legalism was not the intent of the writers. The covenant demanded not just outward obedience, but also a commitment of the total person to the God who had given the nation its freedom and its permanent place of residence. The Law was to be internalized rather than be applied mechanically. Words of the prophet Micah are echoed: "What does the LORD your God require of you? Only to fear the LORD your God, to walk in all his ways, to love him, to serve the LORD your God with all your heart and with all your soul, and to keep the commandments of the LORD your God" (Deuteronomy 10:12–13).

Legalism, in the form of the old theory of retribution, reappears in the later chapters of Deuteronomy. Before the book ends, however, the reader encounters a concept of God that allows the Divine to act autonomously and not simply in response to human behavior. "See now that I, even I, am he; there is no god beside me. I kill and I make alive; I wound and I heal" (Deuteronomy 32:39).

The overwhelming majority of the book of Deuteronomy is taken up with rules to regulate almost every aspect of life. Yet the pages of this book also show that law and grace, (i.e., externalized response and internalized commitment) can coexist, and can be intertwined in ways that strengthen both. The living out of the Law is shown to be a response to the covenant of God, a covenant that was offered not because the nation was large, strong, or deserving; but in spite of its small numbers and its moral weakness (Deuteronomy 7:7–10). The rationale for obeying the Ten Commandments is not some threatened punishment. The people are to be obedient in response to God's initiative in lifting the community from slavery (Deuteronomy 5:6).

In addition, the book of Deuteronomy also shows that priestly religion (attention to proper ritual and other outward acts of piety) and prophetic faith (the attempt to build communities of justice) can also coexist. In the middle portions of the book the priestly influence is strong and the moral level recedes. The fifteenth chapter of the book assumes the reality of human slavery. Genocide of those already occupying the promised land is approved (Deuteronomy 7). Overall, however, the book of Deuteronomy shows a high respect for prophetic faith, with its emphasis on the life of the total community and its demand that people express their faith in acts of kindness toward their neighbor and the stranger in their midst.

Additional laws would be added when the books of Exodus, Leviticus, and Numbers were edited. Again, these would be closely associated with the history of a people who obeyed the Law because they had been delivered from slavery and sustained through their wilderness years. The book of Deuteronomy, however, remained the central depository of legal requirements for a people who had shown almost unbelievable skills of survival, and whose survival was due in large part to a body of written rules defining them as a community of faith.

Summary

By the end of the seventh century B.C.E. the faith community had developed five books in essentially the form we have them in our Bibles today. These five books defined the basis of belonging to the Jewish nation.

Membership in the community of faith (that is, being Hebrew in the seventh and eighth centuries B.C.E.) involved two factors. The first came by birth. One who was born into the ethnic community had received a free gift, a remarkable heritage bestowed on every Jewish child. No amount of good behavior could earn this priceless commodity. Poor behavior could, in later life, forfeit it. Entry into the community came, nonetheless, as a gift of grace.

The second defining element of Jewishness was behavior. The five books examined thus far spelled out the basic elements of the style of living that made a Jew by birth into a Jew through action.

Four prophets had defined basic elements of the religion that held this people together. Theirs was a community religion—not a faith of isolated individuals. Their community was bound in covenant to a God who called them to establish justice and righteousness. The role of the prophet was established. The fifth book to be written further defined the behavior required of those who claimed the community and its faith. Obedience to the Law was essential to the nation's existence. "Law" was a broad and adaptable term. By its breadth it gave stability to the community and defined the values it wanted both to embrace and to pass on to future generations. The poet could identify righteousness by the fact that a person might "rejoice in the Law." "Rejoicing in the Law" meant taking pleasure in membership in the Jewish nation.

As the community was being defined, so also were defined the issues over which the community disagreed. The primary family arguments at this stage of development centered on the nature of God. Some prophets, especially Amos, revealed a harsh and demanding Deity; some of the laws reinforced this view. Other prophets, especially Hosea, spoke of a kinder and more forgiving Deity; other laws reinforced this second view.

A second, related question asked how best to serve God. The eighth-century prophets had been unanimous in insisting that proper ritual counted for little, that distributing the essential goods of a society in a just way was what would please Yahweh. Many of the laws found in Deuteronomy buttressed this position. Other laws, however, insisted that God should be approached through proper rituals, else the essence of religion would be lost. At least an equal number of laws in Deuteronomy supported this second, priestly position.

These and other debates would soon capture the attention of the writers who took up the task of editing the history of this unique people.

3

The Community Traces Its History

The island community began its family album with current materials. During a time of trouble, however, and after a trauma in which the community was almost lost, leaders recognized the importance of adding an account of their history. So people searched through their attics and basements, remembered favorite stories their grandparents once told, and shared these with the album's editors. These fragments and stories were collected, rewritten, and included. The history stories were placed, logically enough, at the beginning of the album. This made for interesting clashes in sequence. A story about the early days of the community might have been recorded rather late in the community's development. Writings placed at the beginning of the album were, at times, a combination of the newest and the oldest materials.

Those collecting the earliest history of the island were privileged to choose from among many exciting stories describing how the community had begun. Some of the stories brought to them had been borrowed, in part, from other islands. They had been told and retold by the islanders as they were passed down through the generations. With each retelling the stories took on more of the characteristics of that unusual place. Some stories were rejected, for they had little relevance to those who were currently living. What was finally preserved were two stories that had been found on two widely separated parts of the island. These two stories had remarkable power to describe the islanders' understanding of their unique beginning and thus of their unique status. In somewhat different ways, the two stories affirmed the special relationship that they had to the life-giving power of the sea. Since one of the stories had been told in its earliest form on another island, it implied a continuing relationship to other people—even people who occasionally became their enemies.

Other stories, contributed from people's memory or from their attics, described later periods of the people's history. The facts given, however, were sometimes less than trustworthy. The events had occurred before anyone on the islands had learned to write, so these stories had existed for generations in oral form. In that process the facts themselves faded to the background, and the stories were told in ways that emphasized the meaning of the events. One concerned a leader who was born under conditions of great danger, was rescued by people of another community, then came to the island to lead them to freedom from an oppressor. This leader had come to have amazing insights into the ways of the sea and had taught the people many of the rules they should follow as a people of the sea.

Other stories concerned other aspects of the development of the island people. Some of these, also, originated before the beginning of writing. Again, each retelling was like a filter through which the story passed. Facts and interpretations that had little meaning were dropped. What remained after many generations were stories that delved deep into human consciousness and described in sometimes cryptic but moving ways what it meant to be a part of that island and in special relationship to the sea.

Other stories and other information came after writing skills were developed. Accuracy improved, although most writers of the time saw their task not so much as writing facts as recording the meaning of those facts. Like the history of any other people, this history concerned wars, rulers and their foibles, droughts and floods, and other unusual happenings. Many of the leaders described were people of low morals. Some did not heed the community's special understandings of the sea; they caused damage to themselves and to other islanders.

All this was recorded as a gift to the next generation. It was passed on partly for guidance, partly to simply help the youth know who they were by understanding their ancestry. As in any family or community, the elders knew there were some ancestors on the family tree whom they hoped would not be seen by the youth as role models. On the other hand, the more important and positive parts of the history were identified by framing put around certain pages and passages. At other places, the community elders *hoped the youth would recognize the special influence (inspiration) of the sea by the fact that the behavior of this island community differed in significant ways from the behavior of other communities. The reader could also identify traditions that evolved in particular directions. For example, additional data was accumulated concerning tides, gradually improving the way fishermen planned for their catch. By continuing this learning, youth could build additional skills in dealing with the sea.*

Tracing a History

The descendants of Abraham were confident that God had promised them an eternal kingdom. The promise included the assurance that someone from David's family would sit on the throne of their nation forever (1 Kings 2:4). By the end of the eighth century, however, doubts about the permanence of their kingdom grew. Already the nation had been tragically divided. Ten tribes of the original twelve had been taken captive, thereafter to disappear from human history. The people of the remaining nation of Judah knew that many of their kings had been disloyal to the divine covenant and that they, too, might be subject to destruction. Naturally there developed an interest in preserving their history and their unique concepts. These could be passed on to a younger generation who, after their present troubles were behind them, might rebuild on the old foundations.

Thus, to the works of the prophets and the book of Deuteronomy, additional sacred books were added. The first thirteen books of the Bible were brought together to trace the history of the land. (This omits the book of Ruth; it will be discussed in a later chapter.) Like peoples everywhere, the Jews knew they could identify most effectively who they were by first tracing what they had been. They especially needed to remind themselves of the traumas that had shaped their consciousness.

At a particularly difficult time in the life of the nation, when it was clear that a recorded history was needed to keep the community together, a group of editors set about the task of writing its history. Some of the stories and other writings that were collected to make this history had been in circulation for hundreds of years. Others were of much more recent origin.

The biblical history begins in Genesis (meaning, "beginnings"). The writers and editors who put this material together made no secret of the fact that they were not offering factual history, and certainly not accurate science. *They wrote and edited to convince their readers that their community held a special place in God's creation.* They presented stories that told the *meaning* of their community's beginning, and thus the *meaning of its continuing existence*. Those familiar with the deeper meaning of the rich word "myths" could use that term as an apt description of these tales.

The writers and editors of the historical material had a second purpose. Their words were designed *to justify the ways of God toward humankind*. History was interpreted (and sometimes adjusted!) to prove that God gives appropriate rewards for good behavior and appropriate punishment for evil behavior. As was indicated in chapter 1, "the theory of retribution" is the name given to this defense of God's ways. This theory is assumed in all the biblical books of history, but is especially apparent in Joshua, Judges, and the two books of Kings. Much more will be said on this subject later.

In most characterizations of Bible books, the first thirteen (omitting Ruth) are usually labeled as "history." Of these thirteen, the book of Deuteronomy was written early. As discussed in chapter 2, it is primarily a summary of the Law and helped define the nature of the community. In addition, 1 and 2 Chronicles were written later, and gave a very different perspective on historical events. These two books will be discussed in chapter 5 with the materials that were written following the exile.

A very brief synopsis of the remaining ten books of history might help the reader traverse some difficult ground. The first three books received scant attention in the early part of this chapter. This is not because these books are unimportant. Quite the contrary. The major part of their contents will be discussed later in this chapter, under the heading "Defining Moments."

Genesis

In the book of Genesis are the stories of beginnings: beginnings of humanity, of the physical world, of sex and art and evil and jealousy and families. With the introduction of Abraham (at the end of chapter 11) the focus moves to the development of the Jewish nation—the faith community. The adventures of Abraham's offspring are traced until, after a series of dramatic events, the growing nation is living in Egypt. They move, within a few generations, from positions of power and respect to servitude and then into slavery.

Exodus

Exodus contains the stories of Moses and of the nation's deliverance from slavery. Immediately after securing their freedom, the people struggled with life in the wilderness. Moses went to the mountain to receive the Ten Commandments while the people in the valley below furthered their romance with gods they could build and control. The struggle between the God who released them from Egypt and the alluring gods of neighboring tribes continued as they made their way across the desert. An ark of the covenant was constructed and carried as a symbol of the presence of the Divine.

Leviticus

The book of Leviticus is mostly concerned with cultic practices— proper procedures for worship. (*Levi* equals "priest.") This book adds to the already rich variety of laws governing the Jewish people—a variety already noted in the chapter on the book of Deuteronomy. While its material is very important in the life of the faith community, it is a difficult book for modern people to read with interest and understanding. The first ten chapters are concerned with proper procedures for animal sacrifice. The next chapters deal with a variety of topics, including what animals can be eaten and purification ceremonies for women following birth (a longer time of purification after the birth of a daughter than after the birth of a son!) and each menstrual period. The seventeenth through the twenty-seventh chapters are a special section sometimes known as the Code of Holiness. This section is concerned with ways that people can enter worship in a condition of spiritual cleanliness. More will be said later about this special code.

In contrast to the prophets' concern with prophetic religion, most of Leviticus deals with priestly religion. Priestly religion was concerned with cultic practices: how to worship correctly and how to prevent various forms of spiritual contamination from invading the sacred places of worship. Most of the laws given in the book of Leviticus are priestly laws (not to be confused with the Priestly Code, a technical term given to certain of these laws). Such rules have to do with the transcendent (God as distant and mysterious) realm of faith.

The subjects addressed in Leviticus seem of little relevance to the modern church. Nonetheless, the material in Leviticus has relevance to the way the Jewish faith developed. Later it will be clear that these priestly laws were important to the way the Christian community dealt with its Jewish roots.

Numbers

The book of Numbers is an interesting mixture of literary forms. It includes numerical lists of tribes and their assigned lands. It also has additional laws similar to those of Leviticus as well as songs and oracles (religious proclamations).

The Christian name for this book comes from two careful censuses of the people and the division of land between tribes. The book, however, is much more than impersonal numbers. The Jewish community knows this book by the more descriptive title of "In the Wilderness." It summarizes the forty years of wandering, the rebellions against Moses' leadership, and the development of a priesthood from the tribe of Levi. In addition, it adds to the store of priestly/individualistic laws.

The book seems disjointed to modern eyes. The editors seem to have spliced various literary forms together with a logic that is no longer discernible. First Moses, then Aaron, has the leading role.

One helpful way to approach the book of Numbers is to see it as organized around two general censuses. The original count was of the first generation of nomads; the first twenty-five chapters trace this group of people and their moral deterioration. The second census, in chapter 26, is of a younger and much more faithful generation—a generation that will be rewarded by entry into the promised land.

The book of Numbers goes from the depths to the heights of ethical understanding. One "teaching" in the fifth chapter is an embarrassment to modern members of the faith community. It instructs the priest on how to "catch" a wife whose husband suspects her of infidelity. The degradation of women in this passage is, by current standards of ethics, abominable (Numbers 5:11–31). On a more positive note, women are allowed, in a later passage, to inherit land—albeit in very specific circumstances (Numbers 27:1–11).

The book of Numbers also includes one of the funniest stories in all scripture—the account of a donkey with considerably more spiritual insight than its owner! (Numbers 22:22–25)

The book of Numbers is not lacking in social conscience. In its final chapter we find a call to observe the year of Jubilee[1] and thus to establish a permanent foundation for justice.

The first five books of scripture (the four discussed here, plus the book of Deuteronomy, discussed earlier) are difficult reading for many Bible readers. One must often read many pages before finding a mention of God or a word of encouragement to lift the spirit. Yet these books constitute what might be called the religious infra-

---

[1]The year of Jubilee was a call to the nation to redistribute ancestral lands once every fifty years. This will be discussed later in the chapter.

structure of the young nation. For many centuries Jews knew these five books as their total Bible. Under the titles of "Torah" or "Pentateuch" they continue to constitute a core element of Jewish religious life.

Joshua and Judges

The books of Joshua and Judges cover identical subjects. Each traces the story of the Jewish entry into the promised land. Yet they recount this history in quite different ways. These books deal with a period (approximately 1150 B.C.E. to 1030 B.C.E.) when the twelve tribes had no central government. As the loosely organized nation expanded in its new land, or when it was attacked by foreign powers, it occasionally experienced a need for centralized government. In those times a temporary ruler (a judge) was called to give the needed leadership. When the crisis passed, the tribes would go back to their status as a loose confederation.

The book of Joshua describes the entry into the land as a quick action, directed by God. Former residents of the area were annihilated, supposedly with the encouragement of God. The book of Judges repeats the same events but describes a slow process that included an ebb and flow of victory and defeat against foreigners who remained very much in place. Archeological evidence indicates that the book of Judges gives the more accurate account of those important years.

1 and 2 Samuel, and 1 and 2 Kings

The books of Samuel and Kings tell the story of the nation from its decision to call a king to the final downfall of the Davidic dynasty.

From a loose confederation the nation, gradually and somewhat reluctantly, moved to a monarchy. Over the objection of some of its religious leaders, Saul was appointed king. When Saul proved autocratic, competition appeared in the person of a young warrior/shepherd/musician named David. David prevailed in his rebellion and led the nation to its greatest military, economic, and religious successes. (All this was accomplished despite David's well-publicized moral flaws.) David died. His son Solomon ruled and built a majestic temple. But Solomon lacked David's keen political instincts, and the nation began to suffer from internal strains. After Solomon's death the already-existing hostility between the northern kingdom of Israel and the southern kingdom of Judah was deepened, and the two permanently separated (approximately 922 B.C.E.). Both kingdoms deteriorated under corrupt leadership, but the downfall of Israel was more rapid. By the later part of the eighth century before Christ, Israel was so weak it could not resist the invasion of an army from Assyria. The nation was destroyed and its people disappeared into exile. Judah fared only slightly better, enduring until the beginning of the sixth century B.C.E. when it was invaded by Babylon, and most of its people were taken into exile.

Thus was completed the first recounting of the history of the Jewish people. More would be added later, after a calamity in the nation's history caused some writers to want to posit another interpretation of that history.[2]

The extensive history of the faith community takes up a third of the Hebrew section of scripture and a fourth of the entire Christian Bible. Little of this historic material is easy reading. Many of the events described are soaked in the blood of violence; many of the people operated from what seems to be abysmally low moral standards. Since this is, for those who try to read the Bible "from cover to cover," the material that must be encountered first, it is no wonder that many people quickly become discouraged in that effort!

It is important to remember, however, that scripture is a family album. This historic material, dry though it may seem, and, at points, devoid of spiritual content, is essential to the biblical drama.

Defining Moments

In the extensive account of the nation given in the early books of history, certain defining moments can be identified.

Creation and Fall

As suggested earlier, the two creation stories in the opening chapters of Genesis are from two divergent sections of the Jewish nation. An editor drew the two together in an effort to reconcile the larger community.[3] Several foundational ideas were placed in the early chapters of this highly important book.

First, echoing a major concept of the prophets, these writers recognized that the entire universe was the product of a single God. Unlike their neighbors, who assigned the sea to one deity, the heavens to another, and the harvest to yet another, the Jewish people saw

---

[2]1 and 2 Chronicles were compiled after the exile, and will be discussed with the exile literature in chapter 5.

[3]For an interesting and exciting explanation of the process by which the early books of the Bible were edited, see Richard Friedman, *Who Wrote the Bible?* (New York: Harper and Row, 1987).

unity in all creation. Humankind had a special place in that universe, but was, nonetheless, a part of the whole. Even pain and death, even human rebellion, must be seen as a part of the unified creation.

Another insight was that God's creative process is one that brings order from chaos: "the earth was a formless void" (Genesis 1:2). Building on this insight, Isaiah would later give his vision of the reign of God, in which even hostile animals lie contentedly next to one another. Such order, such shalom, was viewed as the fulfillment of the promise of creation. Sin, by contrast, was considered to be that which causes separation and reestablishes the chaos. The stories recorded in Genesis, chapters 3 and 4, concern a tragic tearing of what God had drawn together: People were estranged from God, male and female became aware of their separateness, people were separated from nature, and brotherly love was replaced with sibling jealousy. Later, when the prophets would pour out their indignation over sin, they had a very clear definition of what sin meant. Evil was whatever tore creation asunder. The nation was, at that later time, being ripped apart, the poor were being denied their place on ancestral lands, and the gap between rich and poor was widening. This was clearly a violation of the divine will. It was sin because it caused separation.

The creation stories firmly committed the Jewish nation to some form of relationship to their neighboring communities. Amazingly, even in the time of trouble in which the Pentateuch was brought together, a time when ethnic exclusivity might be expected to be the order of the day, the editors recorded stories that concerned the creation *of all the world by the one God who rules over all peoples.* Once the book of Genesis was before them, the Jews, who would later insist that they had been chosen for a special role in the divine economy, could never dismiss their neighbors as subhuman or entirely outside the realm of divine concern. All people were a product of God's creation. All persons were descendants of the original human being, the *Adam.*

Despite their formation in a highly patriarchal society, the creation stories assumed a remarkable equality between male and female. The Hebrew people understood this better than we who must read these stories in translation. Translators (almost entirely men) have put sexual bias where there was none in the original texts. For example, the Hebrew *Adam* is often translated "man." This is incorrect, unless *man* is used in its generic (and confusing) sense. *Adam* refers to undifferentiated humanity. Thus, in the first chapter of Genesis "God said, 'Let us make humankind in our own image...'" A verse later the gender separation takes place, "male and female God created them…" This story is completely devoid of sexual bias.

The second creation story is somewhat more complex in relation to gender. *Adam* was made from dust (establishing clearly that humankind is part of the world of nature), but was lonely. God then put *Adam* to sleep (history's first use of anesthesia!) and caused a division to occur. *Adam* was divided into two sides (the word usually translated "rib" can also mean "side"), one male, the other female. The two then turned to encounter one another. Sexual love became, then, the reuniting of what had been separated. The two became, once again, one flesh.

The Jewish commitment to monotheism is reemphasized in the story designed to explain the entry of evil into God's good world. This account is usually known as "the story of the fall" (Genesis 3:1–7). Humankind was living in the idyllic arrangements of the garden of Eden. Some stirrings of dissatisfaction, however, seem to have been a part of humanity from the beginning. The original people wanted to be like gods, possessing the ability to unravel whatever mysteries were found around them. When the possibility of knowing all about good and evil was offered, they seized it. But God would not countenance competition. Too much was at stake. The people were punished. They were put out of their garden. Pain and death would accompany them.

A remarkable aspect of the story of the fall is that it creates no division at the center of being. The God who brought a good world into existence continues to reign over that world as evil enters. The struggle between right and wrong, good and evil, is not at the Center of Being, but within the soul of humankind.

Note that there is no hint in this story of anything like "original sin." Indeed, this story seems much less important in the ongoing biblical drama than it was to become later in Christian theology. No mention of humankind's fall from its original, idyllic state occurs anywhere else in scripture, unless one considers Paul's cryptic comment that "by a man came death" (1 Corinthians 15:21, RSV) to be a reference to this ancient tale. "Original sin" is not a biblical concept.

Nonetheless, humanity had been created in a way that insured a struggle between good and evil. People were made from dust, attaching them to the world of nature, to a strong drive for self-preservation, and to all animal desires. Into this dust came the divine breath, allowing these "dirt-people" to transcend their animal needs and to seek to serve their Creator. The inevitable conflict between these two sides of humanity is seen in the tragic account of Cain and

Abel and in the story of Noah. After sibling jealousy caused the first human murder, and after humankind demonstrated other ways it was capable of mischief, God repented (a remarkable statement about the divine mind—even God can change in response to human change). God regretted making such a troubled world and destroyed by flood all but the remnants that could be crowded into an ark. The story of the Tower of Babel was an effort to explain the sad divisions that had arisen between nations and language groups. These Genesis stories all show the human race reaching for heights that their earthy origin would never allow, and in that reaching, creating divisions that produce more sin and death.

The Beginning of the Nation

From the deeply spiritual, poetic stories of the origin of all humankind, the book of Genesis moves on to describe the beginnings of the Jewish nation. The reader meets Abraham (first known as Abram) and Sarah (first known as Sarai). God enters into a sacred agreement, a covenant, with Abraham. Through Abraham and the then-barren Sarah, God promised to establish a great nation. The remainder of the book of Genesis tells of the first members of the Jewish community and their struggle to establish a lasting foothold among human communities.

The early stories of the Jewish nation existed first in oral tradition. These tales were told from person to person, from generation to generation hundreds of times before being committed to scroll. Each retelling was in the atmosphere created by the community of faith. In each retelling the spiritual meanings of the stories were more clearly drawn. Concern for historic fact, while never lost, became secondary. Thus the stories evolved into more than simple descriptions of the beginnings of a nation. They were probes exploring the depth of human life.

One particularly piercing story relates the life of Joseph, the favorite son of Jacob.[4] It recounts how the other eleven brothers, jealous of Joseph's favored position, left him one day in a pit expecting him to die. They told their father that Joseph had been killed by a wild beast. Joseph, instead, unbeknownst to his brothers, was rescued by travelers and taken as a slave to Egypt. In Egypt a series of dramatic events put him first in jail, then into the service of Pharaoh, and finally in charge of the nation's grain reserves. A drought had sent its destructive tentacles across a wide area. One day Joseph's

---

[4]This remarkable and beautiful story is told in Genesis 37:1—46:7.

brothers appeared seeking assistance for their hungry family. Their younger sibling recognized them; they did not recognize him. For a time he manipulated them, tricked them, then identified himself and forgave them. Jacob and all his kin were brought to Egypt where they lived in prosperity, thanks to the exalted status of the ingenious Joseph.

Wrapped within this story are a remarkable number of insights into the depth of human life: parental favoritism, human pride, sibling jealously, sexual intrigue, estrangement, and forgiveness. Even the themes of death and resurrection were introduced as Joseph was left to die, then was rescued. Later he was buried in jail only to emerge in glory.

As the book of Genesis closes, Jacob's family, the seeds of a great nation to be, have settled in Egypt. Generations pass. Joseph is forgotten. The offspring of Jacob drift from positions of respect to a sad state of servanthood. God's chosen people had become slaves.

Slavery and Release: The Book of Exodus

The word *exodus* need never be translated for any oppressed people. The word contains a theology in itself. *The will of God stands over against any human arrangement in which one person or group of persons seeks to own or control another person or group.* This assertion is central to the biblical drama. It is a pillar supporting the faith family's understanding of its relationship to the divine Creator.

The book of Exodus is essentially the story of the leadership of Moses. Despite his central role, however, Moses is never shown as larger than life. Especially, he is never depicted as a man of exemplary character. He once was forced to flee the land after his anger exploded into a murderous attack on an Egyptian. He refused God's first call into leadership, using his poor speaking ability as an excuse. Finally he was persuaded. By leading his people out of slavery, by shepherding them through forty nomadic years, he became the leading individual of Jewish history. The details of Moses' struggle with Pharaoh, his dramatic parting of the Red Sea creating a path for the people's escape, and his leadership in the desert are among the more familiar of the biblical events.

The implications of the exodus have resonated through the centuries that followed. *God's power had lifted the oppressed.* This central fact has been deeply implanted in the collective memory of all members of this faith community. *Your ancestors were once slaves; God has called you forth into freedom!* Reminders of this part of their background were given on many occasions when some later spokesperson for God tried to challenge the people to faithfulness. Never was a member of the Jewish nation allowed to be patronizing to the widow, the orphan, the poor, or the stranger. One was to practice compassion toward such folk because: *You once were slaves, but God has blessed you with the gift of freedom.* Fifteen hundred years later an itinerant preacher named Jesus of Nazareth would open his public ministry by quoting a former prophet: "He has anointed me…to proclaim release to the captives" (Luke 4:18). Seventeen hundred years later still, slaves in the United States would gather in secret and sing softly, "Go down Moses, and set your people free." No other event of the Western world has echoed with such clarity across such expanse of time and distance.

The Name of God

Another defining moment for the Jewish people came in the process of the call of Moses. In the conversation surrounding that call God revealed a significant aspect of the divine nature. Moses, the reluctant future leader who was keeping sheep for his father-in-law, went to Mount Horeb, an especially sacred spot in Jewish history.[5] Moses' attention was captured by a nearby bush. It had caught fire, but, strangely, was not consumed. The shepherd realized he was in the presence of the Holy One. He also knew he was being pressed into a service he would prefer to avoid. Somehow he would have to lead his people out of slavery. Thinking quickly, Moses devised what he was sure was the perfect excuse. He could not explain to his people that he had been called by God, for he did not even know the name of God! God, however, would not be sidestepped so easily. To the question, "What is your name?" there came this astounding response:

> I AM WHO I AM. He [God] said further, "Thus you shall say to the Israelites, 'I AM has sent me to you.'" (Exodus 3:14)

Thus God received a name that is, in every sense, a name above every name. It can be argued that it is not a name at all, but a description of the divine nature. God was to be known simply by the verb "to be." The terms that have grown out of this encounter, *Jehovah* or *Yahweh,* are transliterations built on the Hebrew verb "to be."

Moses learned from this experience on the holy mountain that Yahweh could not be compared to the gods of other cultures. Each

---

[5]Placing this event at this spot is somewhat as if the editor had encased this page of history in an impressive frame. Whatever happens on the Mount of God is to be taken very seriously by all members of the faith community.

of those deities had a name, and thus became objects in a world of objects. The God whom Moses had encountered was not a being among other beings, but the *Ground of Being.*[6] As the ground of our being, God gives existence to all that is.

We know, therefore, that any effort to capture God in human language and human imagery can be, at best, only partial. The terms we use in this regard are similes and nothing more. Addressing God as Father, for example, has been quite meaningful for many people, including Jesus; yet this description must never be taken as normative. Other similes have included God as shepherd, God as rock, God as wounded marriage partner (Hosea). Jesus was not afraid to use feminine images for God, finding effective illustrations of the divine nature in women who place leaven in dough, or who lose and then find a precious coin. One favorite description of divinity is: "God is truth." That the Holy One is the essence of truth seems beyond dispute. Yet an interesting account in the Book of 1 Kings (22) says that God distributed, through divine messengers, disinformation in order to lure an evil King Ahab to his death. In this story, God is the author of untruth. The upshot of all the biblical metaphors and other efforts at identity is this: *God is who God chooses to be.* Efforts to describe the divine nature in human language are necessary and inevitable; they can never, however, be seen as full and complete. God is beyond both human understanding and human description. "I AM has sent me to you."

The Giving of the Law: The Decalogue

After its release from slavery, the faith community ventured with reluctance into the desert area beyond the Red Sea. Quickly came another defining moment. Moses received from God the summary of the Law that we now know as the Ten Commandments.

Again, the editor surrounded this page in history with an impressive frame. As in the naming of God, the event took place on the holy mountain. A period of spiritual preparation preceded the event. Thunder and lightning, thick clouds, and the blast of a trumpet preceded Moses' encounter with God. The reader cannot escape the fact that this material is to be taken with the greatest of seriousness.[7]

Not only are the Ten Commandments, the Decalogue, given under majestic circumstances, they also are written on stone. A short

---

[6]Paul Tillich, theologian of the twentieth century, popularized this incisive and helpful phrase.

[7]The preparation for the gift of the Ten Commandments is recorded in Exodus 19:7–25

life-span is not what either God or Moses had in mind for this summary of the religious Law!

The Decalogue is introduced with a reminder: The people are to be faithful to the Law because they were once slaves (Exodus 20:2). God, the source of their freedom, is also the author of the rules that would give order and decency to their daily living.

As described in the previous chapter, the first four laws center on God. Monotheism is reaffirmed. To preserve their central values and their unified view of the universe, no other gods must be worshiped. Because God is beyond human knowing, no visual representation of divinity is to be allowed. Even the name of God is to be received as sacred, for it participates in the nature of God. Following the example that God established in creation, work is to be completed in six days, and the seventh day of each week is a time of rest and holy contemplation.

The next five laws describe, in usually negative terms, what the person can do (or not do) to establish a community of peace and justice. Communities find stability when honor is given to the elderly. Communities cannot exist in peace unless persons respect the life, the marriage relationships, and the property of others. Truthfulness, especially under oath, is another necessary ingredient.

The tenth commandment goes beneath the surface of behavior to touch the level of motivation. The faithful person is to be on guard against the greed that breeds evil action.

The Giving of the Law: Subdivisions of the Legal Code

The previous chapter described how, in the early books of scripture, the concept of *the Law* became quite complex. This complexity increases in the book of Leviticus. In this book the editor made important distinctions between particular types of laws.

Beginning in the seventeenth chapter of Leviticus is found a set of regulations often called the Code of Holiness. The majority of these deal with the individual's relation to the Ultimate. This part of the Code of Holiness might be called "priestly/individualistic laws." These commands have some common characteristics:

—Priestly/individualistic laws have to do with making individuals spiritually acceptable to God. The guilty are purified by proper animal sacrifices, and purification ceremonies are described for those who are made impure by certain sexual occurrences (menstruation, giving birth, semen emissions).

—Priestly/individualistic laws include punishments that are given to those who are impure. In more severe cases the impure are labeled as "an abomination"; abominations are to be either "cut off from the people" or killed.

—Priestly/individualistic laws deal in absolutes. Persons under these codes are either pure or impure, clean or unclean, acceptable before God or unacceptable. Priestly/individualistic laws do not allow for any ambiguity in human life. An example of the absolute approach of these laws comes in the twenty-first chapter of Leviticus:

> The LORD spoke to Moses, saying: Speak to Aaron and say: No one of your offspring throughout their generations who has a blemish may approach to offer the food of his God. For no one who has a blemish shall draw near, one who is blind or lame, or one who has a mutilated face or a limb too long, or one who has a broken foot or a broken hand, or a hunchback, or a dwarf, or a man with a blemish in his eyes or an itching disease or scabs or crushed testicles. (Leviticus 21:16–20)

Interestingly, a few laws of a different sort make their way into the section known as the Code of Holiness. Because these laws deal with ways of building compassionate and just communities, they can be referred to as "prophetic laws." Yet the word "prophet" suffers from the association with crystal-ball gazers. One is then tempted to substitute the word "social," and simply speak of "social laws." However, these are more than prescriptions for ways to relate to the neighbors. Hebrew society developed these rules for a very special reason. Their prophets called for a just society because God is just. Thus the best (though admittedly awkward) term that can identify such rules is "prophetic/social laws." Examples are the commands concerning respect for the elderly, hospitality for the stranger, and honesty in commerce, all located in the nineteenth chapter (Leviticus 19:32–35). These laws, which occur infrequently in Leviticus, have a different set of characteristics;

—Prophetic/social laws relate to interpersonal matters, not to individual cleanliness or piety.

—Prophetic/social laws are not concerned with punishment, but with response to the love of God. Instead of ending with words such as "they shall be cut off," prophetic/social laws end with "I am the LORD your God."

—Prophetic/social laws deal with concerns in which ambiguity is possible. Matters such as respect for the elderly, hospitality for the stranger, and honesty in commerce allow for degrees of faithfulness.

The mixture of priestly/individualistic and prophetic/social laws in the book of Leviticus is further evidence of the work of an editor who attempted to blend two interpretations of the nation's history into one document that all members of the community could embrace.

Thus the historic material of the nation further complicated the term *law*. This complexity, and especially the distinction between priestly/individualistic and prophetic/social law, is of more than academic interest. It will be shown later why distinctions within the concept of *law* offer valuable clues to the continuity of the faith community before and after the life of Jesus.

The Establishment of the Covenant

Central to the self-understanding of the Jewish people is their special covenant with God.

The status of "chosen people" might, it could be assumed, make a people arrogant. In point of fact, a certain degree of overconfidence and arrogance is occasionally encountered in the history of this people. However, on the whole, the people seem to have lived comfortably with the knowledge of this special relationship. They knew that their covenant involved obligations as well as privileges; they lived constantly with the reality that suffering is often the price they must pay for their unique place among the world's ethnic groups.

The special role of the Jewish community was sealed by a covenant between themselves and Yahweh. A covenant defines a special form of relationship. A covenant is an agreement, yet more than an agreement. It concerns the essence of life. Because human beings are involved, the biblical covenant is subject to breakage; because Yahweh is also involved, the covenant is eternally renewable.

The word *covenant* first occurs in the sixth chapter of Genesis. It comes as part of the story of Noah. Noah is assured that, though a terrible flood is coming, no further effort will be made to destroy humanity. This promise is called a covenant (Genesis 6:18). In this first usage, the Bible reader can capture something of the profound meaning of this concept. A covenant had been made between parties who were far from equal. In the case of Noah and God, it was simply a promise, a one-way commitment, unbreakable in this case because God had asked nothing in return.

A different style of covenant is made later with Abraham (Genesis 17:2). Again, the promises come from God. Abram, later to be renamed Abraham, is promised that his offspring (and the offspring of his wife, Sarai, renamed Sarah) will become a great nation. (Interestingly, Ishmael, half brother to Isaac and the eldest of Abraham's sons, who is traditionally considered to be father of the Arab nations, also was given a divine promise of a great, though secondary, nation.) Circumcision was to be the physical sign of the covenant.

The covenant is renewed in the time of Moses. By then both sides of this relationship take on responsibilities. Yahweh will be guide and protector of the Jewish community; they, in turn, will keep the moral law.

Another covenant is established with King David. David is promised that one of his offspring will always occupy the throne of the Jewish nation. This promise was broken much later, not by God, but by an army from the northern kingdom of Babylon.

The people lived out their existence in the knowledge of their special relationship to the Creator. Both the privilege and the responsibility of the covenant were constant companions.

Some Christian interpreters have imposed on scripture the concept of two distinct covenants: the Old Testament covenant of Law and the New Testament covenant of grace. In the actual biblical record, events are not so neat. The Jewish nation was given several versions of a covenant. The prophet Jeremiah spoke of a new covenant, in which God would write the Law "on their hearts" (Jeremiah 31:33), a concept remarkably like the Christian ideal of a law of love. The concept of covenant is an evolving one, and is not neatly broken into one, old and obsolete and a second, new and grace-filled.

Entry into the Promised Land

If a list of key words from each chapter of the Bible were to be collected, the word "land" would occur as often as, if not more often than, any other word. A land promised to the Jews and to their children, a land that would offer them sustenance and protection from external enemies, is bedrock in the Jews' understanding of themselves and their relationship to God.

So connected was their faith to their land that when one group of Jewish people was carried into exile, the non-Jewish people who took over that land were expected, by the Jews, to keep the sacred Law! A priest was actually sent to these people to teach them about the Jewish faith, since they occupied the sacred places! (See 2 Kings 17.)

Much of the difficulty that non-Jewish people have reading scripture comes from this attention to land. It seems less than spiritually uplifting to have to read, in the book of Numbers for example, long passages describing the way the area had been divided between the twelve tribes. Nor is it spiritually enriching to read in the books of Joshua and Judges their two descriptions (often differing significantly in detail) of how the land was conquered. To the Jewish person, however, no material is more sacred. This land, given to them, as they strongly believe, by divine promise, has sustained them by its reality and its memory through generations of separation from that place. "Next year in Jerusalem," is the passover prayer given by every scattered Jew at the end of the seder.

The modern reader, sensitized by such phrases and words as "ethnic cleansing" and "genocide" is apt to be deeply embarrassed by the military actions of the armies of the faith community. Time after time leaders of the nation were confident they had been told by God to go into neighboring areas and annihilate every man, woman, and child. On rare occasions only virgin females were spared the sword, to provide women for some tribe that was short of wives.[8] In light of other biblical understandings of the divine nature, the reader must conclude that those who felt that God had encouraged armies in such unrestrained slaughter had simply gotten their instructions wrong. Nonetheless, two explanations (not excuses) for their extreme action can be given.

The first explanation is the depth of the people's emotional commitment to the concept of the promised land. To a group of people who had lived their entire existence under threat from more powerful neighbors, whose collective memory took them back into slavery and two generations of nomadic wandering, the idea of permanent land was immensely precious. The Jews were neither the first nor the last to set aside, in time of war, all ethical considerations and do whatever they felt was necessary to protect themselves and their homeland. The jarring reality for the modern reader is to find such naked violence done under the supposed auspices of God and described within a sacred book.

A second explanation for their violence is the Jewish commitment to a sometimes harsh monotheism. The religious leaders must have feared that their rigid, demanding faith in a transcendent God would have difficulty competing against the allure of the gods of nearby cultures. Jewish people were enticed to other altars by temple prostitution and by the promise of generous crops if the fertility gods of other cultures were appeased. It was not enough, the Jewish leaders possibly reasoned, to defeat such foreign cultures. It would not be enough to simply take away most of their land and leave pockets

---

[8] See especially Judges 21.

of such people within the captured area. The other cultures and their gods had to be completely eradicated, otherwise the acids of their idols would soon weaken the foundation of the entire nation. In fact, the early history of the nation, especially as recorded by the editor of the book of Judges, was an ongoing struggle to prevent this very corruption from occurring.

More compassionate teachings by later biblical writers, such as the authors of the books of Ruth and Jonah, and the more inclusive concepts of Jesus would throw an unfavorable light on the wholesale slaughters by which the Jewish nation was established. Condemnation must be tempered, however, by a recognition of the time and place. What cannot be approved can, at least, be understood.

One additional observation should be made about the relationship of land to faith. The territory the Jews were sure had been given to them by God was the source of more than protection and financial security. Land was also a means of achieving justice. An eighth-century prophet had already described the just community as one in which all families could dwell "under their own vines and under their own fig trees, and no one shall make them afraid" (Micah 4:4). In Numbers the reader discovers the careful distribution of land, so each family had enough to insure survival. To these facts the writer of Leviticus added another, remarkable, concept: *the year of Jubilee* (Leviticus 25:1–12). Every fifty years (the seventh Sabbath year), each family was to return to its ancestral land, even though that land might have been lost to the family in the intervening decades. The year of Jubilee, an ideal probably never carried out in its full meaning, was intended to ensure that once each generation every family would start the economic process on an equal footing with every other family. The land thus became the primary instrument for insuring a community of justice.

Family Arguments

The attentive reader will recognize, throughout the historic material of the Bible's early books, the continuation of some internal debates already introduced. New issues of disagreement become visible. These issues were debated vigorously. They concerned the ideas and commitments that would help this faith community define itself.

The Nature of God

The debate over the nature of God was (and is) unceasing. The prophets had introduced their varied concepts of God before the editors of the historic materials did their work. The first chapters of Genesis define another important division of opinion. The first creation story exposes the reader to a distant, transcendent deity who worked without direct involvement. Beginning with the fourth verse of chapter 2, by contrast, the reader encounters a very present, involved God who literally dirtied the divine hands in the creation of humankind. This second, immanent being walked through the garden of Eden, looking for the people he (the male pronoun is appropriate here; this anthropomorphic deity is a man) had just made but could not find because they were hiding in the bushes.

The stories of the nation's earliest history, as has been noted, concern God's relationship to all humanity. From this broad beginning, the view of God's rule narrows until the young nation is worshiping a deity that is assumed to belong only to them. As the people enter their promised land, God is often depicted as a tribal deity doing battle with the deities of other nations. (The strong monotheism of Judaism is, in these early stories, a monotheism belonging to them alone. Biblical writers of that period often assumed that other cultures had genuine gods; those gods were simply weaker than the Jewish Yahweh.) The belief that Yahweh was unconcerned about people of other nations made it easy for the Jews to depersonalize their enemies and to slaughter them without compunction.

Other issues about God were in dispute. For example, is God a demanding deity whose punishment falls automatically on those who do not keep the divine standards? Much of the historic material in scripture portrays a deity who is rigid in demands and forceful in punishment. A certain formula is followed, especially in the books describing life under the monarchs. When the nation (i.e., the king) did what God required, the nation prospered; when the nation pursued other gods, it was punished. God was, in this view, like a cosmic machine into which a certain amount of faithfulness could be inserted, producing an automatic amount of blessing. An input of rebellion produced an appropriate amount of punishment. As indicated earlier, this formula came to have a name: *the theory of retribution.* The theory of retribution was never absent from the community's effort to understand the ways of God and the responsibility of the nation. The theory offered a ready explanation for the presence of suffering: Suffering was the direct result of failure to fulfill the demands of the Law.

It is no wonder, given some of the views of the time, that fear characterized much of the relationship between the people and

Yahweh. Moses was confident, in his mountain contact with God, that looking on the face of Divinity would mean death. Much later, as the ark of the covenant was moved into the new capital city of Jerusalem, Uzzah touched the Ark and immediately died (2 Samuel 6).

A low point in the people's understanding of God (measured against the standard of the ethics of the prophets and of Jesus) came in the eleventh chapter of Judges. Jephthah, in order to ensure God's assistance in a military campaign, promised to sacrifice the first person he encountered following the victory. The victory was won, and the first person he saw was his own daughter. She was given time to mourn her lost life, then was killed. The story suggests that human sacrifice had not been completely eradicated at that time in the community's development. Of greater seriousness, the story implies that God would be pleased by such parental brutality.

Yet, woven into the fabric of these mechanical and often heartless views of God are threads of love and grace. In the wilderness the hungry people were provided with heavenly manna (quite undeserved, given the level of complaint!). Also in the book of 2 Kings, God's grace reached across national boundaries to grant a Shunammite woman a jar of oil that did not go dry; later, healing was provided for an Aramean military commander who was both an enemy of Israel and a victim of leprosy (2 Kings 4 and 5). At another place in the same book the theory of retribution was set aside temporarily during the rule of Jeroboam. The king had done evil in the sight of God, yet God concluded that Israel had suffered enough and allowed the nation to prosper under Jeroboam through his 41-year reign (2 Kings 14).

How Is God to Be Served

Another continuing debate that the eighth-century prophets had brought into clear focus was the question, "How is God to be served?" In the books of history this debate continued. Many writers took the side of the prophets. They insisted that God was best served through ethical behavior. On rare occasions a passage sounds very much like the words of an Amos or a Micah: "[God]...who executes justice for the orphan and the widow, and who loves the strangers...You shall also love the stranger, for you were strangers in the land of Egypt" (Deuteronomy 10:18–19).

In most cases, however, obedience took a form different from that described by the eighth century prophets. According to the editors of the historic material, proper response to God involved rejecting false gods and worshiping in the proper sanctuary in Jerusalem. Much of the material in the books of the Law concerns such worship practice. It was through proper worship practices, according to the priestly view, that the nation found its strength, and it was through proper worship that they pleased God. (This is precisely the view that Amos and Micah so vehemently rejected!)

The debate between the priestly and the prophetic views (i.e., whether the primary focus of the religious life lies in appropriate worship or in obedient behavior) reverberates across almost all biblical landscape. Those who listen sensitively to discussions in synagogues and churches today will discover that the debate has been neither settled nor set aside. The debate will not be easily won; both sides can find support for their arguments in the Bible.

Fortunately, the two sides of this debate are not mutually exclusive. All continuing groups, including families and religious communities, need both rituals and codes of behavior. The question is one of emphasis. The pendulum of this debate has swung, like a machine of perpetual motion, back and forth across the centuries of both Christian and Jewish existence.

Gender Roles

Is there a proper role for men vis-à-vis women, and for women vis-à-vis men? If so, what is that role? Many opinions on this crucial question can be found in the early books of the Bible.

One passage shows emphatically the importance of reading scripture in context. In one of the early chapters of Genesis, God said to Eve that she was to be ruled by her husband and would endure the pain of childbirth for her disobedience in the garden of Eden. Over the centuries many readers (mostly men!) have taken these words as prescriptive for all women. A more careful reading, however, shows that this is not a prescription at all, but a punishment, a sign of fallen humanity. Lifting the curse of women's subjugation can then be seen as a sign that the will of God is reasserting itself in human affairs (just as modern medicine's attempts to decrease the pain of childbirth is universally accepted as a loving and positive step forward).

The overwhelming majority of the material in these early biblical books depicts women in secondary positions. A paternalistic society, along with widespread polygamy, gave women little opportunity to develop their full humanity. The need for rapid population growth meant that women were valued primarily for their ability to produce babies.

Typical, in this regard, is the story of Jacob and Rachel. Jacob had seen Rachel and fallen in love with her (no indication is given that Rachel had fallen in love with him; love was a male prerogative). He promised Laban, Rachel's father, that he would work on his land for seven years to earn Rachel's hand in marriage. But Laban tricked Jacob, and at the end of seven years gave him Leah, the older daughter. Jacob then determined to work another seven years in order to wed his beloved Rachel. Thus far the tale has elements of an appealing romance. What is often ignored, in modern retellings, is the fact that while Jacob worked the second seven years he was fully married to Leah, and when he finally wed Rachel he simply added her as a second bride. Later, when both Leah and Rachel proved less fertile than Jacob had hoped, each woman offered a maid-in-waiting as a concubine. Thus the twelve sons of Jacob, who became the fathers of the twelve tribes of Israel, were the offspring of four women, two of whom were married to Jacob, two of whom were not. The story may be romantic, but is hardly a model for modern family values![9]

A careful examination of the sexual ethics of the young nation indicates that the driving force was the production of children. Israel (later, Israel and Judah) was a small nation surrounded by hostile forces. They needed sons for their armies and mothers to produce more sons. Thus the waste of any male sperm was a threat to their existence—an abomination, as the lawgivers were likely to say. Forms of this abomination included masturbation, homosexuality (especially between males—female homosexuality was less an issue), male contact with animals, and even sexual contact between married couples during the wife's infertile period. The emphasis on fertility put women in a decidedly subordinate position. Their role as producers of babies took precedence over all other roles.

In Jewish society (as in many cultures) names have value beyond simple identification. Names represented status. In many stories of the nation's history women play an important role, yet their names are not recorded. An example is the story of the healing of Naaman, a warrior from Aram. He was told by a Jewish slave girl about the prophet Elisha. Naaman contacted Elisha, and was healed. The slave girl was an important part of the drama, yet the storyteller failed to offer her name to history.[10]

Violence against women was frequently mentioned. One particularly offensive story concerned a man (this time both male and

---

[9]This story is told in Genesis 29:1—35:26.
[10]This story is told in 2 Kings 5.

female are left without names) who, along with his concubine, had accepted hospitality for the night. Men of the city surrounded the house and demanded that the traveler be released to them for their sexual pleasure. The host refused, and offered his daughter instead. When this did not satisfy the rogue gang, the visitor's concubine was sent out to be raped and abused until dead. Later her body was dismembered and sent to the twelve tribes of Israel as a way of calling for action against such barbaric activity.

This story has been cited in modern times to prove divine displeasure with homosexual activity. However, no homosexual activity took place, only heterosexual rape occurred. A simple reading of this account leads one to conclude that the rape of a female is a lesser evil than the rape of a male. Rather than giving any ethical guidance, this story indicates the low esteem in which women in general were held.[11]

Further documentation of the point, if it is needed, comes from a startling passage in the book of Leviticus (chapter 27). If inadvertent damage was done to a male between the ages of twenty and sixty, the fine should be fifty shekels of silver; for a female, the fine was only thirty shekels. For children, the price was twenty shekels for male, ten for female.

Amazingly, however, despite an atmosphere that gave women little status other than that of producers of sons, individual women managed to make remarkable contributions to the life of the community. Two especially prominent examples are Rahab and Deborah. Rahab won her fame by overcoming a variety of drawbacks (Joshua 2). In addition to being a woman, she was a foreigner and a prostitute. Yet she was instrumental in helping the Israelites overcome their enemies at the city of Jericho. Deborah was a prophet (some translations use the diminutive "prophetess"), the most respected role in Jewish culture at that time (Judges 4). How a woman attained this status is not explained. She also became a skilled military leader. Indeed, it can be argued that isolated women take, at some point, every role in Jewish society—including that of the sovereign.

In a seldom-mentioned story, Athaliah, daughter of Ahab (and possibly daughter of the notorious Jezebel) seized the throne after the death of her father and managed to hold it for seven years. She had tried to murder all the king's other legitimate successors, but

---

[11]This story is told in Judges 19—20. It is probably a retelling of the story of Sodom (Genesis 19) in which there was a threat of both homosexual and heterosexual rape. The sin that angered God in both cases was the failure to provide safe and pleasant lodging for the stranger in one's midst.

one of his sons (her brother or half-brother Johoash) had been spirited away and kept in hiding. At the end of seven years Johoash was produced, and the queen's own guards killed Athaliah. This entire event is treated as an unfortunate secret by both the editors of 2 Kings and 2 Chronicles. Both tell the story; neither can bring himself to refer to her as queen. She reigned, nonetheless, breaking the exclusive male hold on the thrones of Judah and Israel.

Thus the gender roles were defined in ways that gave an inferior position to women. Yet those roles were not so rigid as a first reading might suggest. There is much in these books of scripture to strengthen the case of one who would argue for sexual equality. This faith family debate is another that will be continued.

Relationships to Those Outside the Family of Faith

Another ongoing debate concerned proper behaviors and attitudes toward those outside the religious community.

The early chapters of Genesis, as has already been noted, set a foundation for concern and compassion that reaches across all human barriers. The *Adam* into whom God breathed the divine breath represents humankind and was not an ethnically identified individual.

Quickly, however, the story focuses on a particular people. The community that descended from Abraham began to understand themselves as in a special relationship with God. "Special relationship" easily shifted to "exclusive relationship." The God of the Jews was seen to be at war with the gods of other cultures, as in the story of Elijah's triumph over the priests of Baal (1 Kings 18).

The ambivalence of the Jewish nation toward its neighbors is shown in an incident from the book of Joshua. The Gibeonites were about to be thoroughly defeated by Jewish armies, but staged a trick on their invaders. A deputation pleaded for their lives on the basis of the lie that they were from a nation far away. The Jewish leaders agreed, seeing no reason to destroy people who were no threat. When it was learned that the Gibeonites were actually near neighbors who could indeed become a danger, the pledge was nonetheless kept. Immediately, the Jewish armies continued the task of slaughtering all in other nearby towns, yet leaving the Gibeonites intact. The message seems to be this: People in other communities are human to the extent that pledges to them should be kept, but their humanity is not enough to prevent, when it seems in the best interest of the Israelites, their being exterminated!

Some passages that were intended to show the power of Yahweh over other gods actually reveal that the reign of God extends over all the earth. A clear example is in the travel of the ark of the covenant. The path of destruction that it created as it moved across the land of the Philistines showed that divine power does not cease at the Jewish national boundaries.[12]

Somehow, amid the history of violence between the faith community and its neighbors, some religious spokespersons saw the full implication of Jewish monotheism. If there is but one God, then that God must have some relationship to and some concern for people outside this one nation. A particularly striking example of this came when the temple was completed, and Solomon gave a temple prayer of praise and thanksgiving. He evidenced a very open attitude toward all people. This remarkable passage is included in the prayer:

> Likewise when a foreigner, who is not of your people Israel, comes from a distant land because of your name—for they shall hear of your great name, your mighty hand, and your outstretched arm—when a foreigner comes and prays toward this house, then hear in heaven your dwelling place, and do according to all that the foreigner calls to you, so that all the peoples of the earth may know your name and fear you, as do your people Israel. (1 Kings 8:41–43)

In another passage, notable for its balance, Moses heard these words of God that show that God could be concerned about all creation, yet is in special relationship to the Jewish people: "Indeed, the whole earth is mine, but you shall be for me a priestly kingdom and a holy nation" (Exodus 19:5–6a).

How were the members of the faith community to relate to their neighbors? To what degree are people who do not acknowledge the God of Abraham and Sarah also carriers of the divine image? The debate over this issue began as the faith community traced its history. It would later form the backdrop for the drama of the life of Jesus of Nazareth. It would not cease even after a redefined faith community began to welcome anyone who, in trust, embraced the concepts of a gracious and universal God.

---

[12]This story is told in 1 Samuel 5:1—6:12.

Summary

Thus the community laid out its history. It was a history told not to convey facts so much as to make a statement: *we are a people chosen for a special relationship to God and are called to serve God.* In telling this history and making this statement the writers and editors carried forward the work of the eighth-century prophets. In addition, they further defined their community. With the inclusion of these prophets and the historical materials, the faith family's album had delineated all the major issues that would later be developed and debated in the Hebraic writings. Nothing, however, had been settled. Later traumas would provide new vistas for examining these issues. Artists, including poets, short story writers, and dramatists would add their unique perspectives.

The material describing the history of the Jewish nation is the most difficult reading in scripture. This is especially so for those of non-Jewish background. Hard reading though it is, it is highly important. The history is essential in defining the community and identifying its major subjects of dispute. What would be built on those foundations is more exciting. To that material the scriptural readers can now turn their attention.

4

The Community Survives Crisis

The island community had become complacent in their apparently unassailable location. The presence of water around them and their knowledge of the ways of the sea had, in the past, protected them from major threats. Some invasions had taken place, but the intruders had been expelled within relatively short periods of time.

So complacent had they become that they forgot their special relationship to the sea. They failed to teach their young all they needed to know about tides and storms. Thus they were vulnerable when people from the mainland came in force. The invaders were looking for workers to tend their crops and run their mills. As a result, many of the people of the island were taken captive. Their new home was an environment quite different from any they had known before. The island was left to a few stragglers who failed to appreciate its significance.

For six decades the people of this community lived in a loose form of slavery among their landlocked captors. It was a terrible time. During some years the captors allowed the islanders limited freedom to practice some of their old rituals and tell their young the stories of life near the sea. Then, without warning, new governors appeared and punished the people for any such efforts. During these times of oppression some of the islanders rebelled, refusing to obey unjust orders. The list of martyrs grew long.

During the long years of captivity the people had many important questions to ponder. The more pressing were:

1. Why had the sea not protected them, as it always had in the past?

2. What had they done wrong to cause this suffering?

> *Other questions followed:*

3. Was it possible that something constructive could come from their suffering? If so, should they reevaluate their previous view of suffering? They had always assumed that all pain was an unadulterated evil.

4. If their island community was ever reestablished, could they relate to foreigners again without seeing them as a threat to all their values?

5. Had they been too narrow in their understanding of their special relationship? Could their unique concern for the sea be shared beyond their island community?

During their time of captivity, skilled writers recorded their best thoughts on these questions. Many of these writings were in poetry. Others pondered in memorable prose. In these writings they recorded surprising conclusions. Even though they had been forced to live in landlocked conditions, they recognized that they were still under the influence of the sea. Storms came, providing needed moisture. During the more peaceful periods they came to like some of their captors, recognizing in them many similarities to themselves. They also recognized the degree to which they had been deepened and toughened by their suffering.

After sixty years of homesickness and other forms of despair, conditions changed. The mainlanders were defeated by another nation. The islanders were free to return. Boats were built and they sailed to the home most of them had never seen.

The next years were spent rebuilding. They had to protect themselves from other islanders—people willing to take advantage of their weakness to attack and plunder. Some energy went into internal conflicts. Certain angry individuals among them wanted nothing to do with foreigners. Wives from the mainland who had married islanders were driven away, causing great dislocation to their families. Other zealots drew up rigid laws about ways to relate to the sea, hoping that obedience to such laws would better protect them in the future. Others argued with equal vigor that people on the mainland were often good people—else the sea would not provide nourishment for them. These people argued against rigid rules, for they were sure that what they needed was the flexibility to discover new ways to improve their sailing and fishing capacities.

A Time of Severe Trouble

The last years of the reign of David's offspring were not good years. Judah had become so weak that it found itself paying tribute to foreigners and devising schemes to play one foreign power off against another. It seemed obvious, to any who had the courage and foresight to consider the future, that the end was near.

The actual end of the kingdom came when Babylon became the leading power among Judah's neighbors, and Judah's king refused to pay the tribute demanded. (We remember Josiah's foolish tour of the royal treasury, given to a delegation from Babylon.) A Babylonian army invaded Jerusalem and took the king and several thousand residents to Babylon as slaves. A puppet king was put on the throne. When that puppet king rebelled, the Babylonians showed no mercy. This time (597 B.C.E.) Jerusalem was leveled, and all remaining healthy people were carried into exile. The rebellious king was taken to a field where the last thing he saw was the execution of his sons. His eyes then were pushed out (2 Kings 25:7).

In exile, a loose form of slavery was established. The degree of oppression varied. Changing Babylonian rulers meant changing circumstances. During the relatively good times the Jewish people were able to establish their own homes, even to start businesses, and occasionally to marry into Babylonian families. The bad times were horrible. When oppression descended the people were forbidden to discuss their faith or do anything else to preserve their culture. For sixty years this alternating pattern continued.

The years of captivity gave the people opportunity to reflect on their faith. What had gone wrong? Their former religious leaders had been confident that God had promised them an eternal dynasty of David's offspring (2 Samuel 7:13). Either God had broken a promise, or some of their religious leaders had misunderstood the divine will. Granted, they had been unfaithful to their covenant, but the severity of their punishment seemed far out of keeping with their crimes. One writer spoke of being punished double for his sin (Isaiah 40:2). Previously they had been confident that God issued rewards and punishments automatically and appropriately. Suffering, under this assumption, was always a sign of sin and the resulting divine displeasure. Was there something about suffering they had failed to understand? And how were they to continue their worship life, now that they were hundreds of miles from the place that had symbolized the presence of God? Was it possible, one psalm-writer mused, to sing God's songs in a foreign land? (Psalm 137:4)

The crisis brought forth a variety of writers and thinkers. It might be argued, in fact, that the period from just before to just after the exile produced the best and the poorest of the material that would be included in the faith family's album.

Writings of the Exile Period

Zephaniah and Nahum

Two writers made concise contributions as the kingdom careened toward its demise.

Zephaniah was a prophet during the time of King Josiah. Josiah was a reform king, responsible for discovering the book of Deuteronomy and calling the people back to their historic faith. Perhaps Josiah's success was due to his willingness to listen to the counsel of Zephaniah. This prophet predicted dire consequences if the people did not repent and reform. Unlike most prophets of the time, however, he included other nations in his judgments. Judah's neighbors would also meet a bad end, he insisted, if they did not accept the faith of Judah. (Note the assumption that these non-Jewish people would be welcome within the faith community should they choose to convert.)

Zephaniah's message was not confined to predictions of destruction. He also painted a hopeful picture of a nation at peace with itself and its neighbors. Such peace simply awaited the reforms he sought. Like the other prophets of this time, Zephaniah accepted the formula of retribution: If the people worshiped at the altars of false gods, they would be responsible for their own destruction; if they served only Yahweh, then peace—*shalom*—would come to their land.

Among the least inspiring of the writings that were to become scripture is a book attributed to a poet named Nahum. Nahum dreamed of the destruction of the city of Nineveh, capital of the powerful land of Assyria. Assyria had long harassed Judah. Earlier it had utterly destroyed the Jewish nation of Israel. As Assyria weakened, Nahum wrote a poem celebrating ("gloating over" would be more accurate) the downfall of Nineveh. The pleasure that the poet found in the death of his enemies is understandable, though not spiritually enriching. Nahum had lived his entire existence under the threat of loss of his homeland. He dreamed of the time when a messenger would bring word that Nineveh was no more. His most memorable lines are often quoted quite out of context: "Look! On the mountains the feet of one who brings good tidings, who proclaims peace!" Unfortunately, the "peace" this messenger was to bring was due to the utter decimation of one of the world's great cities!

Nahum's major contribution is to help the modern reader experience, in poetic form, the anxieties of the faith community as the seventh century B.C.E. came to a close.

Jeremiah

The prophet Jeremiah gave us some of the most interesting, though often some of the most perplexing, material in scripture. He is of special interest, since his tenure as a prophet began just before the Babylonian invasion and continued until some hope for release from captivity could be seen.

Jeremiah was known primarily for his pessimism. So bleak was his outlook that he put a new word into the English language. A "jeremiad" is a long lamentation, or a tale of woe. Many passages from this lengthy book are precisely that. He could foresee the disaster that was ahead, and he missed no opportunity to tell his contemporaries about the woe they were about to bring on themselves.

As might be expected, the pessimistic view of the future made this prophet's voice unwelcome. Jeremiah's words were dictated to his secretary, Baruch. Baruch then carried the scroll into the temple (Jeremiah was so unpopular that he was forbidden to enter the holy place) and read it. Those who heard it considered it inflammatory. It was sent along to King Zedekiah. The king, in a very interesting reaction to prophetic material, had a servant read Jeremiah's words to him as he relaxed by a royal fireplace. When each column of the scroll had been read, the king clipped it out and tossed it on the flames! (chapter 36). (Jeremiah simply dictated the material again.)

The prophet's keen spiritual insight allowed him to predict correctly the course of international affairs, a course that brought the nation of Judah nearer to its date with destruction. As his accuracy increased, his popularity plummeted. He was imprisoned. Once he was thrown into a cistern and left to die.

Not only did Jeremiah speak his message, he also added dramatic twists to his ideas, making them difficult to ignore. On one occasion he put a yoke of straps and bars across his own neck to signify what was about to happen to his people (chapter 27). When he wanted to add a note of hope, he instructed the king to purchase a field as a sign the economy would function again (chapter 32).

When the Babylonian invasion came, and the people and their possessions were taken into captivity, Jeremiah's words were carried away on small scraps of papyrus. He added to these during the time of captivity when he, as part of a small group allowed to remain in Jerusalem, sent letters to those in Babylon. The letters he sent, once the disaster had struck, made him sound like an entirely different person. Now that the people had been punished for their sins, Jeremiah's message turned to one of hope. He promised there would be a time when Babylon would meet the fate of its neighbors. Another, stronger nation would overcome it, and the Jews would be free to return home. That hope was, after Jeremiah's death, fulfilled.

During the exile some of his followers put the prophet's words together in a single scroll. Unfortunately, the book was edited in a way that might have been understood in that time, but is thoroughly confusing to readers today. Poems of woe are set beside accounts of historic events. Threats of doom and expressions of hope reside next to one another. The chronological flow of events is often reversed. The contemporary reader who wishes to make sense of this book would be well advised to read it with a trusted commentary near at hand!

There is no doubt, however, that the work of Jeremiah had great meaning for the faith community during their time of exile. Reading his predictions of gloom helped them understand their predicament. His record of the events just before and during the Babylonian invasions became helpful historical information. Most important, Jeremiah's words of hope sustained the people in their years away from their precious homeland. The people remembered that he had spoken the truth when the truth was painful to hear. A message of hope from this same man could be believed.

Habakkuk

Habakkuk was another of those assigned the title of "minor" prophet. He was minor in the brevity of his writing, but not in his impact. He managed to give a message of major importance in a brief package.

Habakkuk's first chapter is a hymn of praise to the awesome power of the Babylonian armies. They had moved mercilessly across nation after nation. In no way could the suffering they caused be squared with the prophet's sense of God's justice and love. The writer had the courage to challenge the idea that every event in human affairs is the direct will of God. "So the law becomes slack and justice never prevails. The wicked surround the righteous—therefore judgment comes forth perverted" (Habakkuk 1:4).

In his second chapter Habakkuk appoints himself a watchman for the nation and waits for God to answer his complaint. There is, however, no answer. Instead, the prophet hears an invitation to be patient. "Wait for it; it will surely come" (2:3). To this was added one of the most quoted of prophetic texts: "...but the righteous live by their faith." The word *faith* in this context did not mean leaving all matters in God's hands. It meant living by the high standards of Jewish Law in confidence that God would choose the right moment for redemption.

At the close of the book of Habakkuk are found verses that fore-shadow the insights of an even greater poet whose work would be completed several hundred years later. Foreshadowing the book of Job, Habakkuk wrote:

> Though the fig tree does not blossom,
>   and no fruit is on the vines;
> though the produce of the olive fails
>   and the fields yield no food;...
> yet I will rejoice in the LORD;
>   I will exult in the God of my salvation.
>   (3:17–18)

Habakkuk had traveled a long distance from the safe, neat, pre-dictable world of 1 and 2 Kings. In those books history was inter-preted to show that faithfulness brought prosperity and evil actions brought appropriate punishment. This late seventh-century prophet looked at his chaotic world and concluded otherwise. One must sim-ply hold to one's faith though battered by life's ambiguities. In some instances justice fails; the basic provisions that had seemed to be promised by God do not materialize. Habakkuk moved the people from faith *because of* a predictable universe to faith *despite* the unde-served bruises that living inevitably brings.

Lamentations

The book of Lamentations was the first biblical book to be writ-ten in its entirety after the people of Judah went into exile. Its name is a full description. It consists of five poems written by one or more persons (the tradition that it was written by Jeremiah is probably not true since its use of language differs from that of the prophet) to lament the disaster that had occurred.

The third chapter of Lamentations is the one place in the book where a writer allows hope to interrupt the mourning. God's compassion has not failed, the author insists. The Creator continues to grant good things to those who wait in patience.[1] The reader suspects that this section of brighter thoughts was carefully placed at the center of the book.

In their understanding of suffering, the writers of Lamentations took a step backward from Habakkuk. They assumed, as had most of their ancestors, that suffering was a result of breaking the covenant. The second poem (chapter 2) describes the anger that God must have felt to have designed such utter destruction as the Babylonian exile.

Much of Lamentations is written using feminine images. Israel had been raped. Her nakedness had become visible to all the nations. This fact, and the fact that women were the professional mourners in Jewish society, means that there is a strong possibility that the book of Lamentations was written by a woman, or by women.

The book of Lamentations helps the reader understand the enormous sorrow that both the exiles and the remnant remaining behind felt in the early decades of the sixth century B.C.E. It expresses that sorrow with such beauty that some of its verses continue to be used in both Christian and Jewish liturgy:

> Is it nothing to you, all you who pass by?
>   Look and see
> if there is any sorrow like my sorrow.
>   (Lamentations 1:12)

Ezekiel

The book of the prophet Ezekiel was probably organized and preserved during the exile period. It offers the reader a clear date: five years into the exile, this priest was called to become a prophet. (Ezekiel 1:2) As a priest he had been a leader of the public liturgy, an interpreter of the people to God. Now, as a prophet, he becomes a spokesperson for God, an interpreter of God to the people.

By the time Ezekiel began to speak, the people had become thoroughly discouraged. Apathy set in as the community became increasingly uncertain about an early return to their beloved homeland.

The people needed an optimistic word. No comfort came, however, from Ezekiel. He would tell the truth no matter the cost. The early chapters of his book were devoted to a harsh message: The nation received precisely what it deserved. Always the dramatist as

---

[1]The hope offered in Lamentations is concentrated in 3:19–33.

well as the public speaker, Ezekiel took the people, in their imagination, on a walking tour of their nation. He pointed out the sins of the people of Jerusalem (5:5–17), then the sins of the people in the surrounding hills (6:1–14), and then the sins of the remaining, more scattered citizens (7:1–27). He found ways to blame both men and women, prophets and priests, government leaders and common people.

Occasionally a glimmer of light made its way into this landscape of despair. When Ezekiel asked God if there was to be no end to the destruction (11:13), God replied that the exiles would continue to be supported by a divine presence, and that a time would come when the land would be restored. But Ezekiel did not allow his hearers to dwell on such happy thoughts.

This prophet was convinced his task was to defend God's sovereignty and God's actions. If God was truly in charge of creation, then the events of the past decades must be the will of God. Therefore, the next step was clear: Ezekiel must prove that the enormous suffering had been deserved. Thus the blanket condemnations. Indeed, he insisted, had it not been for the mercy of God, such destruction might have taken place far earlier (20:21–24). The nations of Judah and Israel were compared to two sisters who were thoroughly corrupt in their sexual misdeeds (chapter 23).

In the middle chapters of his book Ezekiel allowed his anger to go out to neighboring nations who had been the instrument of Jewish suffering. The intensity of the fury that Ezekiel directed at all whom he believed to be responsible for the fate of his nation seems, at times, overwhelming. It is, however, somewhat easier to understand his foul humor when we encounter the fact that, as the Babylonian invasion was about to begin, Ezekiel's beloved wife died. Given the difficulties of the nation, he felt he could not openly grieve over this personal loss (24:15–18).

Having assigned blame and vented his anger, the prophet shifted toward a message of hope. His, however, was no Pollyanna-like assurance that everything will turn out right in the end. The vision of dry bones, for which this book is famous, was an indication of his view of the future. He asked his readers to imagine that they were looking out from Jerusalem's walls at the scene of a recent battle. There they saw the bones of fallen soldiers, tragically beyond the reach of loved ones who wanted to give them proper burial. Ezekiel, acting in both his roles as priest and prophet, called down the Spirit of God upon the bones. The bones rattled, then came together, gradually mending and receiving flesh. Finally, in a scene that takes us

back to the creation of humankind, divine breath entered the restored bodies (37:1–14).

This vision assured the people that their nation would someday
be restored. It was, however, a restoration that could not be received
lightly. Healing would take place around the scars. New life would
grow out of death.

Significantly, the hope that Ezekiel offered was based on the activity of God, not on the people's good behavior. God had a plan for
Israel, and not even the sinfulness of the nation would ultimately
block its implementation.

As in the case of Jeremiah, the hope offered through Ezekiel was
thoroughly believable. It was believable because it was offered by
one whose general stance was anger and despair. He was, without
doubt, an important element in helping the people cope with their
loss. He gave them a worldview in which to place that loss. We may
overlook the fact that he failed to offer any new perspective for understanding suffering. He had a limited mission, and he performed
that mission with distinction.

Obadiah

The writer of the book of Obadiah left no information about himself. From his manuscript we can surmise that he wrote in the early
years of the exile, when the memory of defeat was fresh.

Obadiah wrote after Babylon had carried off the strongest of
Judah's people. Almost immediately the neighboring Edomites came
to scavenge. They also captured some of the fleeing people of Judah
and turned them over to the Babylonians. Understandably, those
remaining in the city, including Obadiah, were filled with rage at
the Edomites.

Obadiah wrote to vent the anger of the people toward the neighbors who had treated them so shamelessly. He promised the
Edomites that their turn was coming: "As you have done, it shall be
done to you" (Obadiah 15).

Fortunately, Obadiah has the distinction of being the shortest
book of the Hebrew Scripture. It is only twenty-one verses in length.
This brief work helps us understand the emotional state of those
who struggled to keep their culture alive amid the ruins. It is otherwise devoid of spiritual value.

Isaiah 40—55 (Second Isaiah)

To the scroll of Isaiah was added, during the exile years, the work
of another writer. This person of sensitive genius left us no clue to

his identity. It is a genuine loss to know so little about this person, for he (or, possibly, she) contributed greatly to the survival of the faith community and to the expansion of its spiritual understandings.

The matter of divine inspiration in scripture has been widely discussed and debated. A later chapter in this volume will address the topic. Nevertheless, a comment at this point is appropriate. It is more than a truism and more than pure subjectivism to say that one way a reader identifies inspiration is *by that which inspires*. In this sense, many persons of the Christian faith approach Second Isaiah with awe. His insights into the meaning and purpose of suffering, insights later validated by a Christian cross, are remarkable departures from the assumptions of his ancestors.

The opening words of Second Isaiah quickly identify the fact that, in this work, one breathes a spiritual atmosphere quite different from that of other writers of this period. "Comfort, O comfort my people, says your God. Speak tenderly to Jerusalem, and cry to her that she has served her term, that her penalty is paid" (Isaiah 40:1–2).

It is obvious that this poet will not explain the plight of the people in terms constructed from divine anger and retribution. Neither will Second Isaiah deny that God is in charge of creation, including both its joys and sorrows. The first chapter (40), in which most of the themes of the entire work are introduced, is largely a hymn of praise to the one God who rules over all nations. The fact that the descendants of Abraham are experiencing a time of trouble does not mean that they have been separated from their God. On the contrary, God is especially near to those who suffer. "He gives power to the faint, and strengthens the powerless" (v. 29). The tragic exile does not mean that Yahweh has given up on Israel; neither should Israel give up on Yahweh. "Those who wait for the LORD shall renew their strength, they shall mount up with wings like eagles, they shall run and not be weary" (v. 31).

Second Isaiah's most significant contribution was his reinterpretation of suffering. In the view of most of the previous scriptural writers, suffering was a sign of God's displeasure. This popular idea always doubled the impact of pain. The nation (or individual) not only was forced to endure the discomfort involved when disasters occurred, it also was forced to endure the shame that accompanied the assumption of guilt.

Second Isaiah did not deny that much human suffering is self-inflicted, a result of foolish actions. He did deny, however, that suffering is meted out in some just proportion to evil actions. In the case of the exile he was sure the nation was suffering "double for all her sins" (40:2).

The question then arose: why? The prophet's remarkable response to this question was to suggest that *some suffering can be redemptive*. Suffering can be a *gift of* rather than a *punishment from* God. This radical view is given in four passages that have come to be known as Suffering Servant Songs (Isaiah 42:1–4; 49:1–6; 50:4–9; and 52:13—53:12). Students of the Bible debate over whether these poems are about an individual within the exile community, or the community itself, or some future Messiah-like figure (or some combination of the three).

A touch of imagination allows the reader to place a dramatic setting around one of the Suffering Servant songs. During a time of severe oppression, a brave Jewish young man challenged the people to practice their faith despite the dangers. He reminded them of their heritage and the importance of preserving the rituals of their ancestors. This angered the Babylonian captors. They dragged the young man into the public square, pulled out his beard, spat upon him, and creased his back with the marks of a whip. After hours of agony the man died.

The public execution had the opposite effect of that expected by the Babylonians. The man's suffering and death inspired the oppressed people. They determined that if this young man could give his life for his beliefs, they, too, could take whatever risks were involved in remaining faithful to their religious practice.

Later, the writer we know as Second Isaiah looked back to that macabre scene in the public square and reflected on the meaning of suffering. He, like others in the crowd, had at first concluded that God was punishing the man for his impertinence. But from that event had come a good thing—the renewal of the people's faith. Perhaps there are times, the writer concluded, when the suffering of one individual can be redemptive to an entire community. Writing about this later, he gave to the Judeo-Christian tradition one of its most significant ways of understanding suffering:

> Surely he has borne our infirmities
>   and carried our diseases;
> yet we accounted him stricken,
>   struck down by God, and afflicted.
> But he was wounded for our transgressions,
>   crushed for our iniquities;
> upon him was the punishment that

made us whole,
    and by his bruises we are healed. (53:4–5)

As he gave new meaning to their suffering, Second Isaiah also helped his hearers envision the end of their pain. A path would be prepared in the wilderness, suggesting a reenactment of their ancestors' forty-year trek across the desert to the land of promise. This time, however, the trip would be much easier. God would intervene, and the mountain peaks would be brought low, and the uneven places made level, and the rough places a plain. (40:3–4) Having paid double for their sins, they would enter their promised home, this time in gladness.

The contributions of Second Isaiah were many. He helped the people keep the flame of hope burning. He encouraged them to see that their salvation lay not only in the power, but also in the compassion of God. Their suffering was, he assured them, quite possibly not their punishment but their service to the Creator. Because they had experienced divine love in this far country, they became channels through which God's rule could be shared with all peoples. And, finally, he planted an entirely new idea of the coming Messiah. Other writers had promised a leader who would destroy the armies of neighboring peoples; *Second Isaiah helped them consider the possibility of the coming of another suffering servant whose pain might, in a more complete way, make them whole.*

Third Isaiah

Chapters 56–66 of the scroll of Isaiah, and possibly some chapters that were inserted back into First Isaiah, were the product of yet a third era and a third pen. This material was written after the majority of the exiles had returned from captivity. It was composed against the background of the conditions encountered after the return.

The return itself had been nearly as happy as Second Isaiah had predicted. The conditions of ruin they found upon their return, however, quickly overwhelmed their optimism. Third Isaiah warned the people to practice true worship despite their problems. He prayed for God to intervene again on their behalf. When that intervention failed to materialize, the discouraged writer looked forward to a time (he hoped quite soon) when the realities of their current existence would be no more and God would construct an entirely new society. His view of that new age has been a guide for all who work to establish the rule of God in human affairs. The new creation will have no weeping or distress. Children will no longer be born only to die within days. Only those accursed will live less than a hundred years. Justice will reign so that what one builds one may occupy, and what one plants one may harvest. The earlier Isaiah's vision of a nature no longer "red in tooth and claw" is repeated.

> For I am about to create new heavens
> and a new earth;
> the former things shall not be remembered
> or come to mind.[2]

The writing of Third Isaiah ends in ambivalence. He predicted that the people would return to their former, evil ways.

> When I spoke, they did not listen;
> but they did what was evil in my sight. (Isaiah 66:4)

Yet God would not give up on the nation. The promise of divine faithfulness is given in an image remarkably feminine.

> Shall I open the womb and not deliver?
> says the LORD;
> shall I, the one who delivers, shut the womb?
> (Isaiah 66:9)

The impact of Jewish faith will, according to this prophet, be carried to many other lands. They, in turn, will make the promised land their spiritual center. In an especially striking image the writer saw an international collection of people of every social strata. "They shall bring all your kindred from all the nations as an offering to the LORD, on horses, and in chariots, and in litters, and on mules, and on dromedaries, to my holy mountain Jerusalem, says the LORD" (66:20). Thus was the mandate of Israel and its faith fulfilled.

Ezra and Nehemiah

The books of Ezra and Nehemiah are by a single writer (probably Ezra, since he carried the title of "scribe") and deal with a single concept. With the return to the promised land, there was a pressing need to rebuild the wall around the city of Jerusalem. Nehemiah, who had been employed in the royal palace in Babylon, asked permission to return to the city to lead the reconstruction. He went, accompanied by the priest Ezra.

---

[2] The vision of a new creation is in Isaiah 65:17–25. It repeats the concepts given in Isaiah 11:6–9.

The two books that bear the names of this scribe and priest are primarily accounts of the perils of rebuilding. The foundation of the temple had been laid. The response of the people was a study in ambivalence. A few wept for joy that some form of a temple would take its place in the holy city; others wept with grief, contrasting in memory this modest Temple with the splendor of the former structure (Ezra 3:11–13). Despite the interference of neighbors and the lack of resources, construction began.

Ezra and Nehemiah contributed a variety of skills. These two leaders led in the rebuilding of both the wall of fortification around the city and the sacred temple. Ezra, the priest, read the religious Law before the people and challenged them to commit themselves to keep that Law.

Nehemiah and Ezra were confident they knew the reason why the nation experienced difficulty in reconstituting itself. In the time of exile, Jewish men—both those in Babylon and those remaining in Jerusalem—had taken foreign wives. These mixed marriages, the prophets thought, had angered Yahweh. Thus these two leaders forced the Jewish men to send away their non-Jewish wives, including their children. The reader can only imagine the anguish this must have caused.

A sermon could be preached from either of these books about the values of cooperative effort. When everyone pitched in, the wall was constructed. Material for additional sermons or personal meditation is not easily found.

Joel

Joel is difficult to date and to classify. He quoted from Obadiah, which probably means he wrote in the decades just after the return from exile, around 520 B.C.E. He is usually referred to as one of the minor prophets, though the structure of his work is unusual for a prophet. His work is more like a series of oracles designed for temple worship.

Depending on one's point of view, Joel might be considered either a messenger of modified gloom or an instrument of restrained hope.

He began with visions of additional problems. The lack of faithfulness he saw in those who had returned from Babylon made him fear a new time of destruction. Locusts would be the instrument for such ruin. The day of the Lord was coming, and it would be a depressing occurrence:

A day of darkness and gloom,
    a day of clouds and thick darkness. (Joel 2:2)

A beam of light was allowed to penetrate this darkness, however. If the people would repent and renew their covenant, then God would reverse their fortunes. The threatening army of the north would be taken away. God would pour out a divine Spirit upon all flesh:

Your sons and your daughters shall prophesy,
    your old men shall dream dreams,
    and your young men shall see visions.
Even on the male and female slaves,
    in those days, I will pour out my spirit. (vv. 28–29)

The future would not be so bright for the enemies of Judah, however. They would be gathered in the valley of Jehoshaphat (the name means "God will reign"). There they would be victims of God's avenging wrath. The peaceful image of Isaiah was reversed. Nations would "beat [their] plowshares into swords, and [their] pruning hooks into spears" (3:10). In the end "Egypt shall become a desolation, and Edom a desolate wilderness" (3:19) but Judah would be assured of its eternal existence.

Concerning the question of the nature of God, Joel took his place with those who insisted that God was a strong warrior Deity, the God of Judah alone. Yahweh was merely a God among other gods, distinguished only by being of superior strength. Except for those times when other nations must be beaten back to preserve the safety of the chosen people, the God of Joel had no concern for those outside this one ethnic community.

History Revisited: 1 and 2 Chronicles

Following the trauma of the exile, some religious writers felt a need to revisit the history of their nation. The original books of history (which had been edited and put in their final form during the exile) had emphasized the sovereignty of God. Applying the theory of retribution the editors of 1 and 2 Kings and 1 and 2 Samuel had attempted to show that God was in charge of the events of history, and that the divine will was expressed in appropriate rewards and punishments. The nation's kings were judged good or evil according to their strength as military leaders and the degree to which they carried out the laws of justice.

The editors of 1 and 2 Chronicles, writing after the exile, remembered that it was the faithful keeping of the *ritual* laws that had preserved the community through its time of separation from its homeland. Some ritual law, of course, had been impossible to keep away from the temple, but other laws, such as those relating to feasts and rules of ritual cleanliness could, they discovered, be observed in the foreign land. *By keeping those laws, the people had remembered their Jewishness and preserved their community!*

In the years after their return from Babylon an editor or editors wrote another version of the nation's history. The events recounted are the same as those given in the history written earlier in 1 and 2 Kings and 1 and 2 Samuel. This time, however, the ritual practices of the community receive pride of place. King David's talents are rearranged. His skills as a military and political leader are acknowledged, but his skill as a religious leader is put in the forefront. Stories of his sexual transgressions are omitted. The writer assumed that God had rewarded or punished the people for *the degree to which they had been faithful to the rules of temple worship.*

Apart from the difference in emphasis (a shift from prophetic to a priestly understanding of history), the editors of 1 and 2 Chronicles add little to our knowledge of the history of the faith community.

Three Other Prophets: Haggai, Zechariah, Malachi

Three other brief books owe their existence to the problems that followed the return from exile. The first of these is the work of a man named Haggai. He had a single concern: to rebuild the temple in Jerusalem. He reported that the people who returned found only poverty and ruin. They were confronted by drought and poor harvests (Haggai 2:17–19). Nonetheless, Haggai encouraged the returnees to commit their limited resources to the task of constructing a temple. The result was a poor substitute for the magnificent structure that had stood in that place a century earlier. Haggai was confident that once some temple was in place, Yahweh would be pleased, the people would prosper, and the inadequate temple would soon be filled with gold and "be greater than the former" (2:9).

Zechariah was also concerned about rebuilding the former temple. Much like Ezekiel before him, he offered his message in the form of visions. These visions were mediated through an angelic host. God was, for this prophet, too high and lifted up to enter into direct communication with mere humans. Through his visions he reminded the people of God's concern for justice. Perhaps Zechariah saw himself as a counterweight to the priestly editors of 1 and 2 Chronicles. "Render true judgments, show kindness and mercy to one another; do not oppress the widow, the orphan, the alien or the poor" (Zechariah 7:9–10).

Zechariah promised that God would return to Jerusalem and help it become again the holy and happy place of the past. His vision was warm and specific: "Old men and old women shall again sit in the streets of Jerusalem…and the streets of the city shall be full of boys and girls playing" (8:4–5).

This prophet also had a message of hope for a more distant time. A new king would come to the nation. This new king would be different from the triumphant ones of the past. In humility this royal personage would appear riding on a donkey. Despite his humility, or perhaps through his humility, he would establish peace among the nations. The humble and peaceful images become warlike again in a final oracle.

The message of Zechariah was given in affirmative tones. He used the art of positive reinforcement to call the people to their task of rebuilding.

Malachi is the final prophet associated with the time of reconstruction. His words help us understand the heavy depression that must have settled upon the people as they contemplated the enormous task before them. The priests had become lax in their worship leadership, and the people careless in keeping the ritual laws. Where Zechariah had encouraged the people to their task with a vision of hope, Malachi offered them a choice: On the one hand, they could enjoy prosperity if they brought a full tithe to the altar (Malachi 3:10), but on the other hand they would be victims of a fiery final judgment if they failed in this task.

If a final judgment was their choice, it would be ushered in by a special messenger. In contrast to the royal but humble savior figure in Zechariah, Malachi presented his special messenger in aggressive images. The saving person would be like "a refiner's fire and like fullers' soap…he will refine them like gold and silver until they present offerings to the LORD in righteousness" (3:3).

In the Christian version of the Hebraic Scripture, Malachi is the final book. It was not the final book to be written, however. It was probably placed there because of its reference to a figure that might be compared to John the Baptist. This makes it an effective bridge to the Gospel of Matthew that would open the New Testament. In actual chronology, however, several Hebraic books of scripture would be written after Malachi.

Changing Marks of the Community

Traumas are, by definition, events after which no person or community can be the same. The exile was such an event for the Jewish nation.

In the first place, the faith community could no longer assume the absolute protection of God. Times of trouble had occurred before the Babylonian exile, but they had been of much shorter duration and less widespread in their destruction. No other disaster had involved the loss of their homeland. Now the ultimate, the almost unthinkable, had actually happened. Members of the community had lost their land and their possessions. With these commodities had gone their self-esteem and their faith in a God who, they had fervently believed, would protect them against such an ultimate disaster. Many aspects of their life and faith had to be, in those circumstances, reconsidered.

A second change, in response to the exile, brought the people both fear and freedom. No longer was their faith tied to a place. Jerusalem had previously been their sacred spot. In that city had been the altar before which the truest worship could take place. Over the decades of exile they had, nonetheless, survived. Their faith had survived. Children had been born, grown to adulthood, and died as faithful members of the community. On the one hand their success in keeping the community intact in a foreign place was frightening. They had lost the security that had gone with a definable place to mark the presence of God. On the other hand this reality was freeing. They had discovered that Yahweh could not be confined and would go with them to distant places.

The sacred places were still sacred. Yet they had discovered that other spots could be holy also. This startling reality meant that other matters of faith must be reconsidered.

Family Arguments

Several faith family arguments which had previously confronted the faithful were, following the exile, debated with new energy and new focus.

The Nature of God

The exile forced the people to think again about the nature of God. If Yahweh was only a Jewish deity, doing battle with the deities of surrounding peoples, then the defeat by Babylon had proved that the people had chosen a second-rate protector. The former, narrow worldview in which Elijah could sponsor a contest between

Yahweh and the priests of Baal had been shattered. Their vision of God had to be radically broadened or discarded altogether.

As the crisis approached, the prophets had called the people to greater faithfulness. They insisted that, properly worshiped, Yahweh would rise to the occasion and once again expel their enemies. No such miracle occurred. The disaster brought by the Babylonian armies was even more awesome than the most pessimistic prophets had predicted.

A second alternative was considered. Perhaps God was God of *all* nations, able to call upon *any* army to punish or reward the descendants of Abraham. During the same years when they found they could worship, if imperfectly, on the banks of the Euphrates, the exiles were forced to think in larger terms about the breadth of the reign of "their" deity.

Yet another, much more radical, view of God began to emerge from the wreckage of their national life. Perhaps the Creator was not so warlike as they had assumed. Perhaps God achieved the divine purposes by indirection, even by sharing in the suffering of those She/He loved. Second Isaiah's Suffering Servant Songs laid this remarkable possibility before them.

The vision of a suffering deity reopened another family argument.

The Meaning of Suffering

Just as the exile caused the destruction of the temple, so it destroyed one of the nation's most widely held beliefs. No longer could it be argued that *all* suffering is proportional punishment for evil actions, and *all* prosperity a result of religious faithfulness. The people could conceive of no way in which their misdeeds had caused the loss of homeland, of friends, of status, and seemingly of hope itself. How, then, were they to deal with the suffering they did *not* deserve? Could it serve some purpose they had not yet considered?

The Suffering Servant Songs gave a clue. The death of a young man had called them to faithfulness and had helped sustain and renew their faith. Second Isaiah seemed to suggest that the nation of Judah, which had been called into special relationship to God, might have a mission of suffering to help bring the surrounding nations into a saving knowledge of God. This new idea could explain the exile in much more adequate terms.

After the exile, some religious spokespersons tried to turn the clock back. They suggested the old formula be put back in circulation: Faithfulness equals prosperity, sin equals punishment. *Ergo,* suffering is a sure sign of a sinful life and is public proof of divine punishment. Zechariah, however, would not buy into the old argument. Neither would a poet who, some decades later, would compose a dramatic poem about a very good man named Job. The argument contained enough energy to sustain it for many generations to come!

Relating to Other Cultures

The exile forced the community of faith to deal with the question of its relationship to other cultures.

Obadiah and Nahum gave the expected response. After sixty years of defeat and humility it was understandable that many in the faith community had internalized a thoroughgoing hatred for Gentiles. They expected God to design the total destruction of their enemies. Through their wounded eyes, the vision of their antagonists' death was beautiful. Given the enormous suffering of the exile, their thoughts are understandable.

Moving in an opposite direction were Second Isaiah and Zechariah. Both were motivated by a belief that God rules with love over all creation. The Jews, as a chosen nation, would therefore have an obligation to tell other nations about Yahweh and to invite them, in some unspecified manner, into the covenant relationship. In the case of Second Isaiah, the remarkable suggestion is made that Judah may be asked to witness through suffering to those outside its ethnic boundaries. In the view of these prophets, the very fulfillment of Jewish life depended on sharing their vision of God with other nations.

The controversy over relationships to non-Jews carried over to the period of reconstruction. Both Ezra and Nehemiah were confident they knew the key to winning back God's favor. Foreign wives must be put away. Thus, many children and their mothers became human rejects in a social upheaval that left deep wounds. The cruelty of this act would capture the attention of a later short-story writer who composed a tale of a foreign wife who made an invaluable contribution to the total nation. This story will be described in the next chapter.

Visions of the Messiah

Another subject under discussion during and after the exile had its center of gravity in the future. How was the religious community ultimately to be saved? What kind of leader—messiah (literally, "savior")—would lift them above their troubles and ensure a continuing reign of peace and justice?

Since the nation had been overpowered by the Babylonians, it is understandable that some of those who looked to the future dreamed of a leader who, like David, would increase the physical strength of the Jewish community. The savior figure described by Malachi was such a person. With the power of a refiner's fire, he would cause fear in all who understood his mission. Jeremiah looked to a new David whose military skill would ensure that the nation lived in safety (Jeremiah 23:5). Ezekiel had a similar thought. He also spoke of a David figure, tempered by kindness, who, like a shepherd-king, would lead the nation into a new era (Ezekiel 34:23–24). Even the more kindly Zechariah placed his confidence in a new David, a powerful king who would "destroy all the nations that come against Jerusalem" (Zechariah 12:9).

Second Isaiah's vision of a saving person was a radical contrast. This writer's Suffering Servant would not project pain on the nation's enemies, but instead would suffer redemptively for those enemies. "A bruised reed he will not break, and a dimly burning wick he will not quench" (Isaiah 42:3).

The concept of a David-like king who would scatter Judah's enemies continued to be the dominant way of expecting a messiah. Yet the time of exile had forced another view into the open. The nation's defeat at the hands of the Babylonians showed that it was not always possible for tiny Judah to protect itself by military means. Perhaps God was preparing some new and fundamentally different way of lifting the faith community to its fulfillment.

The time of exile had placed many important issues before the offspring of Abraham. It was important to pursue these matters more deeply. Next to have their say on these vital matters would be the artistic community. Their voices are about to be heard.

5

The Community Produces Artists and Philosophers

The location of the island community was an inspiring place for artists to express their creativity. The small community developed an unusual number of poets, musicians, dramatists, and short-story writers.

After their travail on the mainland, the islanders needed to reconsider many of the assumptions about their common life: their unique relationship to the sea, the disruptions that had replaced their former idyllic status, and their relationship to communities on the mainland, to name but a few.

Several artists weighed into these issues, bringing with them their profound insights. A short story writer made a contribution; a poet offered an epic poem; many songwriters contributed to a book of songs that celebrated both the community and the sea; and a dramatist designed an account of an islander whose successful bumbling made the remainder of them grow through laughter. One writer even offered a brief erotic dialogue. A philosopher and a patriotic propagandist shared their thoughts. Of course, these were added to the family album of the island community. These artistic contributions became powerful persuaders in the debates over the important issues before the people.

In the aftermath of the exile a number of Jewish artists and philosophers came forward to participate, in their unique fashion, in the debates taking place within the faith family. Most of these talented individuals had strong opinions about the matters in dispute.

Since all the remaining works of the Hebraic Scripture have a direct bearing on the family arguments already discussed, the books will be classified here under those headings.

Family Arguments

Relationship to Other Cultures

Ordinarily, a people painfully bruised by their contacts with neighboring cultures will tend to withdraw. A normal reaction is to build strong walls that will protect them from similar future wounds. As was pointed out in the previous chapter, many, perhaps a majority, within the faith community favored such separation.

Powerful arguments were needed to persuade the people to consider other options. Two writers determined to use their word skills to convince the community to take a more open stance.

Ruth

The writer of the book of Ruth addressed the issue of foreign wives.

Earlier, Ezra and Nehemiah had insisted that men separate themselves from the foreign spouses they had brought from the exile and from the children these unions had created. Enormous social upheaval and personal pain followed.

The writer of the book of Ruth took the opposite position. This skilled writer, whose name has not been preserved, composed a story based, perhaps, on some historical facts and embellished by the author's creative imagination. The story was designed to encourage the people to revaluate the contribution that foreign wives had made. The drama was set in the time of the Judges (which is why it is placed among the historic materials in scripture). The story opens in a time of famine. A Jewish woman (Naomi) and her husband could not feed themselves and their two sons. Reluctantly they moved to the land of Moab where food was plentiful. They remained long enough for their sons to mature and marry Moabite women. Disaster then struck. Naomi's husband died. Shortly afterward death claimed her two sons. The Jewish widow was left in a distant land with two foreign daughters-in-law. Word then came that her homeland had emerged from famine. Naomi determined to return to her own people. She absolved the two daughters-in-law from any responsibility to her. One of the young women agreed to remain behind (a decision that the writer described as loving and responsible), but the other, a young woman named Ruth, insisted on staying with Naomi. Her pledge of support has become a model of personal commitment:

> Where you go, I will go;
>> where you lodge, I will lodge;
> your people shall be my people,
>> and your God my God. (Ruth 1:16)

Thus they returned, destitute. But they were not without internal resources. Despite the patriarchal structures of the time, these women found ways to redirect their destiny. They went to the fields of Boaz, a kinsman of Naomi, and arranged matters so that Boaz must take note of Ruth. Next they arranged that he must consider marriage. The marriage, despite being the result of clever manipulation, was apparently a happy one. The union produced a son, named Obed. At the end of this tenderly-told tale of human survival and romance was placed a surprise punch line, not unlike the ending of an O. Henry short story. "(Obed) became the father of Jesse, the father of David" (4:17).

The great-grandmother of the mighty David was a Moabite woman!! Adding to the impact of that remarkable disclosure was the fact that Ruth was a woman of intelligence and creativity, capable of making lasting personal commitments. Those who tried to argue for the expulsion of foreign wives suddenly had a much more difficult task. How could they disdain all foreign women when a Moabitess had given her genes to the nation's premier monarch?

Jonah

A second story writer addressed a similar theme: Did the Jewish nation, chosen people of the one true God, have any spiritual obligation toward its neighbors—those who knew nothing of Yahweh or of Yahweh's laws?

The writer of the book of Jonah brought a splendid sense of humor to his task. Readers who do not have their own sense of humor in the "on" position will miss much of the impact of this delightful drama.

The story begins abruptly. Little effort is made to set a scene or establish an atmosphere. The reader simply meets a man named

Jonah. Jonah had heard a call from God to go and preach repentance to the city of Nineveh. Nineveh had been the capital of Assyria, the empire that had destroyed Israel and had posed a constant threat to Judah. Jonah was challenged by God to go and save a group of enemies from their own destructive behavior.

Jonah would have none of this! He quickly went to the docks to board a ship for Tarshish, a city far in the opposite direction from Nineveh.

God, however, was a suitor not easily rejected. Soon after the ship sailed, a strong wind rose, threatening all in the boat. The sailors, suspicious that divine powers were at work and that some passenger was responsible for their plight, cast lots to determine the source of their danger. Jonah drew the short straw. He then confessed that he was running away from a divine assignment. Jonah suggested they solve the problem by throwing him into the sea. Death, at that point, seemed preferable to good deeds in Nineveh. The sailors obliged, and the seas became calm. But Jonah did not die. Instead, he was swallowed by a great fish. He remained inside the fish for three days.[1]

Having discovered that God could play rough, Jonah wisely determined to respond to the original request. The writer of the drama then gives us another of his pithy word pictures: "Then the Lord spoke to the fish, and it spewed Jonah out upon the dry land" (Jonah 2:10).

Poor Jonah then made his way reluctantly to the city of Nineveh. Inside the city gates he made a brief, weak statement warning that the city was about to be destroyed.

At that point the true miracle of the book of Jonah occurs. The people of the city heard the message from this unenthusiastic missionary and responded positively! They determined to change their ways. The king caught word of Jonah and called all his subjects to a time of repentance. God saw their change of heart and determined that the planned destruction would not take place.

Jonah had been successful! He had saved an entire city from destruction! The reader can sense the twinkle in the writer's eyes as

---

[1] Not only is the story of Jonah funny, it produces funny secondary results. Some of those who argue for a literal interpretation of every verse of scripture have said that Jonah was able to remain in the fish's belly for three days because God cut off the beast's digestive juices. If so, this would have been helpful to Jonah; it would, however, have caused the pathetic fish to suffer one of history's most gigantic cases of indigestion! Digestive juices or no, one can hardly imagine a more terrible fate, or a punishment more appropriate for one running away from God, than spending three days and nights in the stinking belly of a fish!!

he penned the next phrases: "But this was very displeasing to Jonah, and he became angry" (4:1). This was precisely what he had feared, Jonah told God, and why he had tried to run away. So unhappy was Jonah that he went outside the city walls and sat down to pout. God graciously allowed a large plant to grow beside him to protect him, so his misery over the salvation of Nineveh would not be complicated by the hot, Mideastern sun. This was far better than Jonah deserved. Thus, the next day, God sent a worm to destroy the plant. Another outburst of complaint was emitted by Jonah. The drama ends, as does the book of Ruth, with a powerful moral:

> Then the Lord said, "You are concerned about the bush, for which you did not labor and which you did not grow; it came into being in a night and perished in a night. And should I not be concerned about Nineveh, that great city, in which there are more than a hundred and twenty thousand persons who do not know their right hand from their left." (4:10–11)

The books of Jonah and Obadiah (see the preceding chapter) are appropriately set next to one another in the Bible. They take opposite views on the issue of how to relate to foreign cultures, including those that have been enemies of Judah. Obadiah offered twenty-one verses of celebration over the destruction and suffering of a neighboring people. The writer of Jonah, by contrast, encouraged the people to laugh at themselves for precisely that attitude. Jonah was depicted as a person who once had the attitude of Obadiah; he, too, would have watched in glee had Nineveh been destroyed. Yet, for himself, Jonah wanted to be protected by a loving God of grace. He enjoyed the status of being part of a chosen people, a people called by the Creator to be a light to the nations. Yet, when challenged to serve this God and to act in his role as beacon to foreigners, Jonah first fled, then reluctantly succeeded, then became angry over his own success. The short-story writer and humorist had made his point with great effectiveness.

The Role of Women

Two artists, in addition to the writer of Ruth, addressed the role of women in the faith community.

Song of Solomon

The first of these two books can be shocking to those of Victorian upbringing. The Song of Solomon is a series of romantic, erotic verbal exchanges between two lovers. It uses explicit language to describe the sexual longings between them.

The writer of these love passages is unknown. The effort to assign it to King Solomon is undoubtedly wrong. Solomon may have been a skilled collector of wives and concubines, but there is no indication in the record that he was an accomplished lover. The language of these poems and their setting belong to another era.

Not a single mention of God or of worship or of anything else usually considered religious occurs in this book. Thus many people have questioned its role in the Bible.

Its legitimacy in the scriptural cannon is easy to justify when one approaches the Bible as a faith family album. The Song of Solomon is included in scripture because this collection of love poems tells us much about our ancestors in faith. It tells us, for one thing, that the people of Israel and Judah were a passionate people. This reality is often missed in the historic record of multiple wives and concubines and of marriages such as Hosea's that were used to teach a moral lesson. Despite the arranged marriages and other social mores that treated women as property, there were men and women who fell deeply in love and whose love included a strong erotic element.

We learn, also, that the Jewish people were not nearly so embarrassed by sex as were their spiritual descendants. To the ancient Jews, sex was a normal and natural part of creation—a reality to be celebrated. Sexual intimacy was, for them, the most profound knowledge of another human being. They had discovered the great power of the sexual drive and devised strong laws to channel this drive into constructive (and procreative) paths. Potentially destructive? yes; dirty or embarrassing? no.

The Song of Solomon also tells us much about the role of women in biblical times. The written Law may have decreed a very restricted role for them, but our faith family album gives us hints that in actual practice women were often strong, heroic individuals who successfully took charge of their own existence. The female partner in these erotic poems does not wait for her lover, but often takes romantic initiatives in pursuing him.

A final explanation may be the strongest reason for the inclusion of this erotic book in the canon. Perhaps the writer wanted to suggest that Yahweh's relationship to her people is like a romantic relationship between passionate young lovers. The writer left no proof of this. If, however, these poems are a symbol of a larger relationship, then the Song of Solomon would lift religion above the level of pure intellect and arid law. Faith, according to this theory, would be a total commitment of God to people and people to God. The erotic adds warmth to the joint search for one another. These love poems affirm that nothing is held back from this defining relationship.

Esther

If additional proof is needed that the Bible's primary focus is on the community and not on the Deity, the book of Esther can supply it. Esther is the story of a woman who managed to use the roles available to females in her day to become a hero and to save a large community of her people. Her story was told with no mention of the Deity. While some references to religious rituals occurred—a fast and the Jewish festival of Purim (this may have been a late addition to the original material)—it is definitely a story whose first concern is the community of faith.

The story-writer who composed this tale brought the reader first into the chambers of King Ahasuerus, ruler of Persia. At a drunken feast, he called for his queen, Vashti, to appear to show how beautiful she was. Just how much beauty she was to reveal is not specified, but Vashti concluded it was more than she could bare. She refused. The king was enraged. He immediately dismissed Vashti and set in motion a contest to replace her with the most beautiful virgin in his kingdom. Esther entered this competition under the sponsorship of her guardian, Mordecai, without disclosing her Jewish identify. Through her beauty and grace she won the devotion of the king and became the new queen. Mordecai, now a frequenter of the palace, discovered a plot to destroy all the area's Jewish residents. At the same time, Mordecai's refusal to do obeisance to one of the king's officials put his own life at risk. Through a series of maneuvers, Esther was able to interrupt the order to kill the Jews, and Mordecai turned the tables on the official who had planned to kill him. The pompous official was hanged from the scaffold built for Mordecai. In celebration of this victory over their potential destroyers, the nation celebrates the festival of Purim each year.

The importance of Esther's tale of survival and victory should be easy to understand. The history of the Jewish people has been often one of scattering (diaspora) and fragile existence in cities where they were less than welcome. This short story is especially important to the women of the faith community. It shows how a woman of strength could transcend the roles open to her in a male-dominated society in order to become, under quite difficult circumstances, a savior for her people.

Neither the Song of Solomon nor Esther makes any mention of God. They are read today not for their spiritual content, but for what they tell us about the faith community's history. The two books are especially helpful in what they tell about gender roles in that history.

Explaining Suffering

How does one explain the amount of pain that exists in a world made by a compassionate God? The standard answer was first suggested in the creation stories, and reinforced by all the material that traced the community's history. Suffering, according to the early theory, was the direct and proportional result of rebellion against God. Eve and Adam were punished for their desire to be like gods. The nation was punished for the behavior of kings who failed to obey the ultimate King. Especially were the people punished for falling into the worship of competing gods.

Yet it was clear that, despite the efforts of the editors of the national history to paint their past in these exact colors, the suffering and the sin did not match. The theory of retribution requires a proportionality and a preciseness that true history never provides.

Second Isaiah (discussed in chapter 4) put another possibility forward. In some instances, suffering might be the call, not the punishment, of God. Individuals, or even the nation itself, might find themselves challenged to suffer so that others may find healing.

Yet, neither of these theories solved the total problem of suffering. It was clear to any observer that pain does not spread itself evenly. As certain psalmists would acknowledge, evil persons do sometimes prosper, and good people are struck down. Nor does suffering always produce redemptive results.

More than a hundred years after the exile, an artist of enormous talent offered his skill and insight in the search for a solution of this vexing problem. He produced a truly epic poem.

Job

The writer of the book of Job apparently had both a negative and a positive purpose. The negative motivation came from good people he had seen who were bruised by tragic circumstances, then had their pain doubled by the cruel assumption that they had, by some secret sin, brought their problems on themselves. So the writer's first purpose was to say, through drama, that *much human suffering has nothing to do with a person's moral behavior. Suffering cannot be explained by blaming the victim.*

The second, more positive statement, was more difficult. If suffering is not caused by sin, then to what can it be attributed? Must we blame it on God's will? Does this not make God into a monster? Here the writer showed his courage, his depth of understanding, and his spiritual sensitivity. He would not pretend to have answers to questions that cannot be answered. So he laid his answer/nonanswer boldly before the reader: *Some suffering takes place in random style, not because God wills it or humans deserve it, but because God refuses to be a puppet on human strings. God does not necessarily run the world the way mere humans think the world should be run!*

The poet presented his case in the form of a carefully-crafted drama. First, he introduced us to his main character, a righteous man named Job. The writer knew that many of his readers would try to make Job responsible for his suffering. So, like a prison builder leaving no loophole for escape, the writer stated that Job fully obeyed the Law himself, had reared children who were faithful, and rose each morning to make sacrifice for his offspring, on the slight possibility that one of them might "have sinned, and cursed God in their hearts" (Job 1:5). Job was truly blameless.

The scene quickly shifted from earth to heaven. God and Satan were engaged in a friendly chat. (This writer, along with the author of Jonah, had a sense of humor!) With a note of teasing in his voice, God asked Satan if he had considered Job, a person who obviously belonged entirely to God.

Satan replied with a question, one that has awesome implications for every religious person: "Does Job fear God for nothing?" In other words, was this upright person religious for anything other than pure self-interest? According to the old formula, faithfulness to the covenant brought prosperity, and rebellion against the Law brought punishment. Job, according to Satan's piercing, mocking question, was simply looking out for his own self-interest. If, Satan continued, Job finds that faithfulness and prosperity are no longer linked, he would join those who curse the very name of God.

Yahweh took the challenge. He allowed Satan to take away all that Job possessed, and to destroy his children. (His wife remained. It is unfortunate, from the point of view of those who yearn to see more positive roles for women, that she would later become an active part of Job's tormented life.) Job, however, accepted his losses with aplomb. He simply pointed out that he was no poorer than on the day of his birth. "The LORD gave, and the LORD has taken away; blessed be the name of the LORD" (1:21).

Satan had lost a battle, but still expected to win the war. His next strategy was to request permission to afflict Job's body. This was granted. Job's skin was infected with "loathsome sores." Job found himself sitting on a dung heap, scraping his sores with a pottery fragment. His wife encouraged him to end his miserable existence by cursing God and dying. But Job's faith remained unshaken. "Shall we receive the good at the hand of God, and not receive the bad?" (2:10)

Strong friendships were among the treasures that had made Job wealthy. Three friends remained. They lived in distant places. Nonetheless, they did (at first) what real friends should do. They set aside their own agendas and traveled the required distance to visit their tormented friend. They wept with him and sat in silence with him. Then, tragically, they began to do what good friends should not do in time of loss: They began to express their opinions! Their opinions were so odious that they put a new phrase into our vocabulary: "Job's comforters"—the kind of comforters no one wants. They attempted to explain instead of trying to heal; they spoke from their heads, ignoring the fact that their friend's pain was in his heart.

For dramatic purposes, Job spoke first. He cursed not God, but the day of his birth. His existence had become intolerable. The three "comforters" then spoke. Each in turn stated a common theme. They defended the old formula of retribution—the structure upon which the history of the nation had been written. Their arguments can be summarized thus: "Faithfulness leads to prosperity, sin leads to suffering. You are suffering, therefore you must have sinned." Day after day, from angle after angle they pressed their case: "Tell us what evil deeds you did, repent and all can be well for you once again," was the burden of their argument. With equal fervor Job defended his integrity. He had done nothing to deserve the disasters that had come to his house. The theory of retribution would not explain his wretched situation.

The three friends were well-meaning sorts. They saw their mission as no less than defending the reputation of God. If God were truly in charge of this world, and if God were compassionate and righteous, then one should be able to make sense of the events of daily life. In the twentieth century Archibald MacLeish rewrote the drama of Job. He stated the dilemma in a pithy couplet:

> If God is God, he is not good;
> If God is good, he is not God.[2]

Job felt he had an equally majestic mission: to make faith true not to some abstract theory, but to reality. The reality of his life was that he had suffered without cause. He would not back away from that truth, even if it seemed to his friends that he was trampling on the integrity of God.

As this debate continued, chapter after chapter, some of the most profound subjects of human life were discussed. The reader feels like a spectator at a wrestling match on Mount Olympus. The topics are gargantuan. What is the meaning of life itself? Where is wisdom to be found? When does self-defense turn to self-righteousness? In the thirty-first chapter Job listed the crimes he had not committed. The passage, with its catalogue of possible moral errors, constitutes a remarkably high ethic. Sexual faithfulness is called for; the equality of slave and slave-owner is affirmed; responsibility to the poor and orphan is prescribed; materialism is denounced.

After the discussion between Job and his first three friends bogged down, a fourth friend was introduced. He tried, with little success, to bridge the wide gap between the antagonists. When this mediation failed, Job requested an opportunity to communicate directly with God.

The request was granted. The result, however, was not what Job had in mind. Instead of speaking to God, he was forced to listen to God. From a whirlwind came the divine voice. In language as soaring as the tornado from which it came the voice asked, in essence, "Who are you to question the ways of the Ultimate?"

> Where were you when I laid
> the foundation of the earth?
> Tell me, if you have
> understanding. (38:4)

Nothing else in literature, sacred or secular, surpasses the thirty-eighth and thirty-ninth chapters of Job in describing the absolute, towering majesty of God. Afterward, Job spoke with much less assurance:

> See, I am of small account; what
> shall I answer you?
> I lay my hand on my mouth. (40:4)

---

[2] Archibald MacLeish, *JB, A Play in Verse* (Boston: Houghton Mifflin Company, 1956).

God then stated the dilemma of evil from the divine perspective:

> Will you even put me in the wrong?
> Will you condemn me that you may be justified?
> (40:8)

The problem had been clearly defined: pain is real; suffering falls unevenly upon both good and evil people. Seemingly blame for this must be placed either upon the victim or upon the Creator. We can either say, with Job's comforters, "You suffer, therefore you must have sinned," or we can say of God, "You created an unjust world."

The players in the drama of Job wrestled mightily with this dilemma, then gave no answer to it. To quote MacLeish again,

> He answered me like the stillness of a star
> That answers nothing.

Yet this non-answer became, strangely, a partial answer. The reader is challenged by this epic poem to be faithful when faith has no guaranteed rewards. Worshipers of Yahweh are to live courageously while carrying unanswered questions and to press on in life even while knowing they will endure pain that has no intelligible explanation.

At the close of the drama Job repented. It is clear, however, that he had still not backed off his previous contention: He had been faithful to the demands of God and thus had not deserved his suffering. He repented, instead, of attempting to understand what human minds cannot comprehend. The reader is reminded of the rebellion of the original man and woman. Their sin had been their attempt to be like gods.

Following Job's repentance comes a prose section that attempts to draw together loose ends. Scholars argue over whether this was a part of the original writing, or whether it was added by some later scribe who could not tolerate leaving the main character in such a low state. In these final verses God verbally spanked Job's comforters for their poor performance. Job's fortunes were restored, indeed doubled. He was again blessed with ten children. (This number is not doubled; the writer was wise enough to know that going from ten to twenty children would not have been a positive step!)

The book of Job, though not easy reading, shows the heights to which inspired literature can rise. Victor Hugo called it "the greatest masterpiece of the human mind." Robert Frost wrote an extended poem about it, and summarized the meaning of the scriptural drama.

("The Deuteronomist" refers to all writers who insisted on the theory of retribution.) In Frost's poem, Yahweh speaks to Job:

> I have no doubt
> You realize by now the part you played
> To stultify the Deuteronomist
> And change the tenor of religious thought.
> My thanks to you for releasing me
> From bondage to the human race.
> The only free will there at first was man's,
> Who could do good or evil as he chose.
> I had no choice but I must follow him
> With forfeits and rewards he understood—
> Unless I liked to suffer loss of worship.
> I had to prosper good and punish evil.
> You changed all that. You set me free to reign.
> You are the Emancipator of your god,
> And as such I promote you to a saint.[3]

Readers may or may not, after traveling through the drama of Job, appreciate the place of arrival. No one can deny, however, that it has been a magnificent journey.

The Nature of God

Almost every writer examined so far has expressed an opinion, directly or indirectly, about the nature of God. Amos understood God as the exacting dispenser of justice. Hosea emphasized divine forgiveness. The writer of one creation story depicted the Creator as distant from the world that was coming into being; the writer of the second story placed before the reader a God who was very much involved in the unfolding human drama. The final four books discussed here sharpen the debate about and deepen the readers' insights into the nature of God.

Proverbs: God the Giver of Wisdom

Almost every family album contains a collection of the wise sayings of its most respected members. In the faith family album the collection is called the book of Proverbs.

Solomon is the designated author. As in other biblical books, his name was used to give status to a work by other hands. Solomon

---

[3] Robert Frost. "A Masque of Reason," from *The Poetry of Robert Frost*, edited by Edward Connery Lathem (New York: Holt, Rinehart and Winston, 1964).

may well have been the first to compose and collect the core of these popular sayings. The majority of the book, however, was recorded at a later time. Some of the material is borrowed from neighboring cultures.

The advice offered in the pages of Proverbs is often proffered in the form of teachings from a parent to a child. In the later chapters this device is abandoned and the wise sayings are simply recorded. The advice touches a variety of subjects: straightforward advice about the normal business of living ("Do not plan harm against your neighbor who lives trustingly beside you" (Proverbs 3:29); admonitions to avoid entanglements with a neighbor's wife and to keep anger in check; advice about controlling one's tongue; encouragement to avoid too much wine, too much food, and too much leisure.

The writer loved the couplet in which a contrast is established between wisdom and foolishness, between good and bad.

> Better is a dry morsel with quiet
> than a house full of feasting with strife. (17:1)

> Better the poor walking in integrity
> than one perverse in speech who is a fool. (19:1)

Many sayings of Proverbs have made their way into current common usage. Speech writers use them, often without awareness of their source: "A soft answer turns away wrath" (15:1), or the Benjamin Franklin-like "Go to the ant, you lazybones" (6:6).

In Proverbs, wisdom is more than a sharp mind. Wisdom is a personified force unto itself, a reality that was present with God in the creation and that helps sustain the world. In Hebrew the word is written with feminine endings. This gender association was possibly the result of influence from surrounding cultures, where goddesses often played significant (and, to the Jewish priests, threatening) roles.

> Does not wisdom call,
> and does not understanding raise her voice? (8:1)

Wisdom, as described in the book of Proverbs, played a role in creation similar to that which the writer of the Gospel of John would later ascribe to the Greek concept of *logos* (word). The following lines sound very much like the famous prologue to the Gospel of John:

> The LORD created me at the beginning of his work,
> the first of his acts of long ago...

> when he marked out the foundations of the earth,
>> ...then I was daily his delight,
>>> rejoicing before him always. (8:22, 29–30)

The secret to a productive life, then, is to listen to and be guided by the advice of this spiritual reality that is a constant companion to both humankind and to God. "Happy are those who keep my ways. Hear instruction and be wise....Happy is the one who listens to me" (8:32–34).

Certain topics consume a large portion of the writer's attention. The relationship between male and female is one of these. It is easy to believe that the editor had made a poor marriage, for he seems threatened by certain behaviors that he felt were typical of women:

> A continual dripping on a rainy day
>> and a contentious wife are alike. (27:15)

A careful reading of the text will disclose that the editor of Proverbs had little trust in the capacity of either male or female to handle their sexuality. In the seventh chapter is a description of a lonely wife whose husband is absent on a business trip and who attempts, as if she were a prostitute, to seduce a neighbor. She is wily and dangerous; he is, by contrast, unable to control his animal hungers and quickly becomes a victim, "like a bird rushing into a snare." So strong is the danger of such entanglements, and so complicating are they when they occur, that the editor earlier suggests that men seek out a prostitute as a lesser evil.

> for a prostitute's fee is only a loaf of bread,
>> but the wife of another stalks a man's very life.
>>> (6:26)

A much more positive view of women is given in the final chapter of Proverbs. Unfortunately, the passage is positive to a fault. It shows the woman carrying on the business of the home, raising and preparing food, buying and selling property (being, that is, an absolute super-mom!), all while her husband sits and trades opinions at the city gates. (This is no doubt accurate. Women are known, historically and cross-culturally, to do much more than their share of the work necessary to sustain human life.) Her spouse can meet other men proudly, for he has made a wise choice for a mate. Unquestionably the woman is very valuable; it is sad that her worth is measured entirely by her value to her husband.

Other bits of advice from this book are equally bound by time and culture. Proponents of corporal punishment of young children can support their views by quoting from Proverbs:

> Those who spare the rod hate their children,
>   but those who love them are
>   diligent to discipline them. (13:24)

Before this practice is assumed to be normative for all in the faith community, it is important to understand the context of child-rearing practices in the post-exilic period. Sons of that era, during their early years, were brought up entirely in the presence of their mothers. The young lads were given, within the ability of the family, whatever they wished (the discipline of daughters was less complicated and, in the value system of the day, much less important). At puberty, however, a radical switch took place. The son became the responsibility of the father. The father immediately had to transform the over-indulged child into one able to deal with the harsh, masculine world. Beatings for the least misbehavior were deemed necessary for this rapid adjustment. Perhaps, then, a new proverb must be constructed lest the old proverbs be abused: One must understand the role of a particular activity within a total culture before that activity can be transferred without danger into another culture.

Most of the book of Proverbs is less culture-bound, and transfers easily to any time and place. Religious language is rare in these discourses. Nonetheless, that which does occur makes clear that the writer believes that religious faith is the foundation on which all other things are built:

> The fear of the LORD is the beginning of wisdom,
>   and the knowledge of the Holy One is insight.
>
>   (9:10)

Wisdom, it was stressed, is not a product of the human mind, but a gift of God.

> Trust in the LORD with all your heart,
>   and do not rely on your own insight. (3:5)

Concerning another faith family debate, the editor of Proverbs took a definite position. Like the writers of the nation's history, he was confident that good behavior would lead to a pleasant and positive life, and that evil behavior would lead to a painful existence. "The LORD does not let the righteous go hungry, but he thwarts the craving of the wicked" (10:3). (Even though both Proverbs and the book of Job are considered wisdom literature, the writers seem not to have read one another's work!)

In Proverbs, God is known primarily as that One who whispers divinely designed wisdom into the souls of those whose religious antennae are tuned to such advice. The good life comes when humans focus their attention on the Creator and learn the skills of spiritual listening. A modern reader is likely to be bothered by the editor's tendency to assign unflattering roles to both male and female, and to oversimplify life by easy good/bad, right/wrong dichotomies. Nonetheless, the book remains a remarkable collection of wise sayings. Its role in scripture is clear and fixed.

Ecclesiastes: Does God's Creation Make Sense?

Through the words of Ecclesiastes a philosopher joined the biblical discussion. The identity of this philosopher cannot be known. He called himself a king, but no king of Judah fits the description of this writer. He probably was a person of the upper social strata, for he seemed to view life from a lofty vantage point. At times he referred to himself as the Teacher; at other points he called himself the Preacher (Koheleth).

This we know: He was a philosopher whose philosophic position is surprising. He could find no meaning in life.

> Vanity of vanities, says the Teacher,
>   vanity of vanities! All is vanity.
> What do people gain from all the toil
>   at which they toil under the sun?
>   (Ecclesiastes 1:2–3)

Since all is vanity, the writer offered a simple prescription for dealing with a meaningless existence. Seven times he urged his readers to enjoy life, for death is coming soon. People are, after all, nothing more than a part of the world of nature. They are no different from animals. "For the fate of humans and the fate of animals is the same; as one dies, so dies the other. They all have the same breath" (3:19). This last phrase seems to deny a vital part of the creation story. In that story the breath of God became part of humankind, thereby distinguishing women and men from other animal species.

The discouraged writer did try to find ways out of his despair. He sought to escape depression by expanding his knowledge. The result was less than satisfactory: "For in much wisdom is much vexation, and those who increase knowledge increase sorrow" (1:18). Like a Jewish Aristotle, he tried to bring order out of jumbled reality. "For everything there is a season, and a time for every matter under heaven" (3:1). At the end of his famous lines concerning the proper time for all activity, however, he returned to despair: "What gain have the workers for their toil?" (3:9) Like the writers of Proverbs, he envisioned a spiritual reality called Wisdom that seemed for a moment to provide hope. But for this teacher, wisdom was far off. "That which is, is far off, and deep, very deep; who can find it out?" (7:24)

Occasional wise statements emerged from Koheleth's gloom. He had his own version of "two heads are better than one." "A threefold cord is not quickly broken." The next verse is advice of a different sort: "Better is a poor but wise youth than an old but foolish king, who will no longer take advice" (4:12–13).

Try as he might, Koheleth could not see reality as did others around him. Neither could he be dishonest. So he shared his opinion, though it contradicted the beliefs of the larger faith family. In a community that insisted that humankind was created to worship and serve God, this writer stated that all human activity was vain. While others said that goodness would be rewarded and evil punished, this teacher said, "Then I saw that wisdom excels folly as light excels darkness…yet I perceived that the same fate befalls all of them" (2:13–14). Later he put the same point more forcefully: "There is a vanity that takes place on earth, that there are righteous people that are treated according to the conduct of the wicked, and there are wicked people who are treated according to the conduct of the righteous" (8:14). And yet again he expressed this sentiment in words that are often echoed in modern speech—occasionally, one assumes, by persons unaware of their source:

> Again I saw that under the sun the race is not to the swift, nor the battle to the strong, nor bread to the wise, nor riches to the intelligent, nor favor to the skillful; but time and chance happen to them all.
> (9:11)

How, then, did this pessimistic statement of despair find its way into the pages of scripture? The book of Ecclesiastes is a part of the faith family album because it carries at least two positive messages.

The book of Ecclesiastes shows that, at least at some important point in their history, the Jewish people were remarkably open and accepting of an opposing point of view. One imagines that Koheleth would not have fared well during the time when the young nation was attempting to establish itself in its promised land, nor in the era when the nation was under attack from Babylon. At some more stable point, however, the people were willing to hear from one who challenged the basis of their faith. Not only did they hear that position, they also preserved it and later canonized it as part of their sacred scriptures. If one is seeking evidence of divine activity in the construction of the Bible, this nearly miraculous fact would definitely stand out.

In addition, the book of Ecclesiastes is in the Bible because it offers a point of entry for those who are about to surrender to life's inevitable wounds. Depressed people are often best reached by other depressed people—by those who understand their agony and share their experience of estrangement. It is easy to believe that many people across the centuries, so discouraged as to be near suicide, might have picked up the writings of this teacher and exclaimed in total surprise: "Here is someone who understands!" Koheleth provides companionship for all who grope their way through the dark night of the soul. Few persons have passed many adult birthdays without thinking:

> It is an unhappy business that God has given to human beings to be busy with. I saw all the deeds that are done under the sun; and see, all is vanity and a chasing after wind. (1:13b–14)

Ecclesiastes is a part of scripture because its concepts both describe and enter an important, though often hidden, aspect of life.

Daniel: God as Protector of the Nation

The book of Daniel is one of the most exciting, yet one of the most frequently misunderstood and abused writings in scripture. It is another dramatic writing, designed to call people to sacrificial faithfulness in a time of testing. Like the patriot Thomas Paine, whose pen became an important weapon in the American Revolution, this writer rallied the people during one of their most challenging times and helped them achieve freedom from a foreign power.

For the faith community, another crisis had arrived from yet another foreign source. This time it was the Greeks, invading more than three hundred years after the Babylonian trauma. Alexander the Great, in a series of remarkable military conquests, spread Greek culture into Egypt to the south and as far as the Indus River in the east. After his death in 323 B.C.E., his realm was divided between his generals. Seleucus took over what had been Mesopotamia and Syria, and Ptolemy took over Egypt. These two men quickly became antagonists. Once again, tiny Judah was caught between powerful forces, one to her north and the other to her south. As long as Ptolemy was their master, however, they could rest easily under his loose rule. He allowed locals full control over their own religious lives.

In 198 B.C.E. the northern king took control of Judah from Ptolemy. He immediately began to impose Greek culture upon the Jewish community. (The king continued the task undertaken by Alexander: spreading what he considered the far superior Greek culture to the "less fortunate" peoples of the surrounding world.) In 167 B.C.E. the Greeks intervened in a dispute over the office of high priest and outlawed the practice of the Jewish religion. The holy temple was desecrated by the erection of an altar to Zeus. In Jewish eyes that was an "abomination of desolation." Most citizens, seeking to save their lives, obeyed the royal order to worship at this new altar. Some refused to bow to a false god and became martyrs.

A resistance movement emerged. The military part of that resistance needed support from the intellectual and religious communities. Such support was the goal of the dramatist who composed the book of Daniel.

Since the Greeks had overwhelming military power, the writer of Daniel felt it his responsibility to call the people to unusual sacrifice, possibly martyrdom. He did so by writing a drama to remind people that God is ultimately in charge of all life and that the values for which the martyrs might have to suffer would not vanish.

Since it was not safe to write directly about the current situation, the writer did a clever thing. He set his drama in the time of a previous national trauma: the Babylonian period. (This is very much like the writers of the television series *M.A.S.H.*, who, in order to make their anti-war statement about events in Vietnam, set their stories in the Korean War.)

Because it was written in code, and because it seemed to foresee the future from its early dramatic setting, it has become what Bernard Anderson calls a "happy hunting ground for those who are fascinated by 'biblical prophecy' and who look for some mysterious blueprint of the future hidden in its pages."[4]

The book opens with a series of miraculous events in which faith

---

[4] Bernard Anderson, *Understanding the Old Testament* (Englewood Cliffs, N.J.: Prentice Hall, 1957).

in God allows people to survive the most trying circumstances. The first story concerns four young men, exiles in Babylon, who were trained to be part of King Nebuchadnezzar's court. They won their way to prominence through the skill of dream interpretation (the same skill Joseph used much earlier to gain power in Egypt). Daniel pleased the king with his interpretation of a royal dream. But when the king later constructed a golden statue and insisted that all fall down and worship it, the Jews refused. In punishment, three of the young men, Shadrach, Meschach, and Abednego were thrown into a very hot furnace (so angry was the king that he insisted the furnace be seven times its normal heat). The three were unharmed. The king, understandably impressed, forgave the Jews and promoted the three furnace survivors. (Daniel 3)

A second story concerns yet another dream of Nebuchadnezzar. In fulfillment of that dream (also interpreted by Daniel) the king became mentally ill for seven years, eating grass like an animal. This was to demonstrate that it is God, not an earthly royal figure, who is ultimately in charge of the earth. (Chapter 4)

A third episode concerns King Belshazzar (confusing, since this is the same Babylonian name given to Daniel), who desecrated the holy vessels stolen from Judah. During a royal banquet in which these vessels were used, a disembodied hand appeared and wrote on the palace walls. Daniel was brought in to interpret the words. He announced that they indicated that the King's reign would be short. That evening the monarch died. (Chapter 5)

Another episode involves Daniel's disobeying a royal decree that all his subjects should refrain from prayer for thirty days. (The entire plot had been designed by Daniel's enemies.) When he was discovered praying despite the command of his friend the king, the sovereign reluctantly had him thrown into a den of lions. The lions were restrained by God, however. When the king discovered that his friend had survived yet another trial, he brought Daniel out and fed the lions with those who had made this effort on Daniel's life. (6:1–24)

The later part of the book of Daniel is made up of four visions that point toward the final consummation of human life. Within these visions are many coded messages that no doubt had to do with life under Greek rule. Beasts are described that arise from the sea; each had unusual, often bizarre, characteristics. The ultimate purpose of these visions is stated clearly: "Understand, O mortal, that the vision is for the time of the end" (8:17). The more immediate purpose is given a few verses later:

> Again one in human form touched me and strength-
> ened me. He said, "Do not fear, greatly beloved, you
> are safe. Be strong and courageous!" When he spoke
> to me, I was strengthened. (10:18–19)

The book of Daniel became a powerful inspirer in the rebellion of the Maccabees that began in the year 167 B.C.E. Through this strange book readers were promised that God would sustain Judah against the most powerful armies and horrid punishments that could be set against it. Individuals may suffer and die, but the nation would endure.

Those who became martyrs against the Greeks could hear another message: God would not forget them. In the final time, when justice shall be meted out to the faithful and the disobedient, "you shall rise for your reward at the end of the days" (12:13).

The message of Daniel, though given in code, was concrete and immediate. It was composed to answer a particular need of a particular moment. Those who want to impose its cryptic symbols on a modern day would do well to heed this clear message: "Go your way, Daniel, for the words are to remain secret and sealed until the time of the end" (12:9).

The book of Daniel established a new category of biblical literature: apocalyptic. The apocalyptic literature, which includes Daniel and the much later book of Revelation, helped people look beyond their moment of suffering to an age of divine fulfillment. The immediate pain was placed in the context of eternity. This, however, was decidedly not escapist. The writer of the drama of Daniel was challenging his people to resist to the death their Greek oppressors. They would be much more likely to do so if they could see their conflict and their sacrifice against a background that extends from everlasting to everlasting.

Psalms: God the Object of Praise

The book of Psalms was both songbook and prayer book of the Jewish people. Quite logically, it was included as part of the family album of the faith community.

The Jewish people defined themselves through their faith. The community was sustained by its acts of worship. The one hundred and fifty psalms of scripture, which have been read by individuals and chanted and sung by choirs and congregations across thousands of years in scattered places, bring the reader into direct contact with a rich, deeply sacred tradition.

Some translations refer to many of these poems as "the Psalms of David." Indeed, David was a musician and may have composed a few of them. It might be said that many were written in David's honor and in his spirit, just as the first five books of scripture were written in the spirit of Moses. Yet the hand of Moses did not write the Pentateuch, and the hand of David wrote but a few, if any, of the psalms. Most belong to another day. Some were written to be used in the coronation of other kings; others are obviously products of the exile and the post-exilic period. They vary both in quality and in theological position.

The psalms address humanity in all its variety. The major emotions of human existence are described: the joy of victory, the awesome weight of royal power, the discouragement of defeat, and the hopelessness of paralyzing depression. All of these human experiences are offered before God.

The psalms are organized into five books, each ending with a statement of divine praise. The earlier poems tend to be prayers for individuals and congregations; later ones tend to emphasize praise of the Almighty. The final psalm is a joyful call for all creation to join in the chorus: Its final words, appropriately, are, "Praise the Lord!"

The psalms are concrete in dealing with the immediate situations in which they were written. Some, therefore, are jarring in their expression of anger. These were composed at times of despair for the nation. The writer of Psalm 139 boasts that he hates the enemies of God "with perfect hatred." He follows that with a declaration of his moral purity: "Search me, O God.... See if there is any wicked way in me" (Psalm 139:23–24). Psalm 137 was written during the exile by a lonely and discouraged individual who wondered if worship could take place in a foreign land. (v. 4) The depth of his anger is then laid out for all to see. He says of those who have taken him from his homeland: "Happy shall they be who take your little ones and dash them against the rock!" (137:9). The sentiments may be understandable, but they are not meant for emulation. Nor are such expressions of anger likely to be found in the liturgy of modern synagogues or churches.

Despite their varied nature, certain general statements can be made about these prayers and songs. First, the psalms as a whole take a definite position on the question of the nature of God. While the Bible, seen in its entirety, is a book about the community of faith, the psalms are centered on the reality of God.

"The Lord reigns" is the central, organizing theme around which this diverse group of psalms evolves. The metaphor is of royalty, yet this is definitely not a projection upon God of what human rulers do. It is, instead, an acknowledgment that God is, in God's own style, the ultimate reality and the ultimate power of the universe.

In this collection of worship resources, one Power apprehends and stands above all. Idolatry has no chance in this atmosphere. The universal rule of Yahweh is unequivocally affirmed in Jewish liturgy. One Creator rules all nations and draws people toward a community of justice. This one Power stands above sin and death. God is sufficiently high and lifted up that people and nations can, by divine power, be lifted from the depths of defeat and depression. The reign of God is above time. It is that toward which all history moves. The psalmists define the holy, the lowly, and the righteous as those who depend on the reign of the Lord.

The psalms declare an unqualified monotheism. Yet they take the reality of other gods seriously. Several psalmists suggest that the gods of other cultures exist, but depend for whatever power they have on Yahweh. "There is none like you among the gods…" sang the writer of the eighty-sixth Psalm (v. 8). The eighty-second Psalm depicts God as taking chief place in the divine council; "in the midst of the gods he holds judgment" (v. 1).

In the psalms, all other questions are addressed against the background of the reality of God. The eighth Psalm is a model. Its theme is the nature of humankind, yet it begins with praise of God. "O LORD, our Sovereign, how majestic is your name in all the earth!" (v. 1). With the centrality of God established, the question of the moment can be put: "When I look at your heavens…what are human beings that you are mindful of them?" (vv. 3–4). Varied as they are in other ways, the psalms take a consistent position on the centrality of God and the power and breadth of divine rule.

To the casual reader, the psalms might seem to modify one of the major characteristics of the Jewish faith. Individualism seems to be introduced. The solitary worshiper appears to be separated out from the larger community. The pronoun "I" occurs in these writings more than in any other book of Hebraic Scripture. The communal nature of the faith appears to have faded into the background.

In a certain sense, individualism *has* been introduced. The individual does speak through the psalms; this aspect of the songs and prayers allows this portion of our faith family album to be a genuine tie to a more individualistic age. It is easy for the person of today to appropriate these acts of worship; the "I" of yesterday becomes the "I" of today. It is important to recall, however, that the personal pronoun was used differently in that day. The "I" of ancient times carried communal overtones. "Out of the depths have I cried to Thee" meant that the entire nation had fallen into a low estate. The pronoun "I" was the way the original readers of these psalms affirmed their place in the congregation. Any modern use of these psalms that separates the individual out of the community (as the modern use of "I" tends to do) is a serious violation of scriptural integrity.

The psalms also took a position on the question of the future salvation of the nation. A messianic figure was envisioned by a few of the writers.

The second Psalm used phrases familiar to the Christian: "You are my son; today I have begotten you" (v. 7). This was not, however, a prediction of Jesus. Kings were known as sons of the Divine, a way of making clear that human kings reign only with the permission of and guidance of the Divine King. The king who would deliver the nation would fit the model of power/exclusion. He would overwhelm the nation's enemies and extend his rule to the ends of the earth.

> You shall break them with a rod of iron,
>> and dash them in pieces like a potter's vessel.
>>> (2:9)

(The second Psalm was probably written to be used at the coronation of a king. At the point in the liturgy quoted above, the new king struck and broke a vessel, scattering its pieces on the floor.)

It is somewhat paradoxical that the psalms, universal in their view of divine rule, envision a messiah in the power/exclusive role. These poets were confident the saving person would belong entirely to the Jews and would lead them in victory over other peoples— this despite the fact that they were confident that Yahweh's rule extended far beyond the borders of the Jewish state.

More than any other one book, the Psalms help scripture to be, in a very concrete way, faith's family album. Written over several hundred years, they grant an especially clear window on the history of our ancestors in faith. They also go far beyond the mere recording of history. They allow us to enter that history. The "I" of the psalmists' prayer can become our "I" as we make those prayers our own. The "we" of other psalms can become our "we" in public worship. Despite the misunderstandings and tragic hostility of the past two thousand years, both Jew and Christian of today can, through the use of the psalms, share a worship activity with one another and with scattered multitudes of the past whose faithfulness has made our faith possible.

The psalms tie Jew and Christian together in yet another way. Any reader of the Gospels will quickly note how readily those writers quoted from their Jewish Bible. Few, however, note that there are in the Gospels more quotations from the psalms than from any other Hebraic source. The psalms were used by Jesus in communal worship; they became building blocks for his own prayer life. So deeply ingrained in his own consciousness were they that, in the moment of his death, he found fellowship with a despairing psalmist who, like Jesus, had felt absolutely abandoned by God.[5]

Conclusion

Thus is closed that part of the faith family album shared by modern-day Jew and Christian alike. It is a remarkable set of documents, comprising many forms of literature, including widely divergent opinions and composed by writers of many styles and forms. The biblical books describe a community held together by several solid assumptions: It was a community of justice. It was also a community of law—law that defined the obligations and privileges of belonging to the community—law that defined the highest ethical standard they knew how to achieve. It was a community in covenant with that God whose name was above every name. Other issues threatened to divide the community. The scriptural writers raised, but gave no definitive answers to, such questions as the nature of God; how humans are to relate to God; the relationship of the Jewish community to its neighbors; and the meaning of suffering. They offered at least two distinct visions of a saving person who would lift the nation above the ambiguities of its troubled existence. The Hebraic Scripture allowed many voices to speak on many sides of each issue. Yet it anchored these questions in the context of faith.

The stage was thus set for a new branch of the faith family to emerge. These new progeny of Abraham and Sarah would be attached to one another not through genes but through common faith commitments. They would wrestle with the same basic questions in an expanded context. Like their ancestors, they would fail to give absolute answers to these basic questions. Their insights, however, would allow the questions to be addressed in new ways, and allow the faith family to be renewed as it was expanded.

---

[5] Matthew 27:46. Jesus was quoting from Psalm 22:1.

6

The Community In Transition: Between Hebrew and Greek

The readers who have made their way through all the Hebrew Scriptures, with all their variety of literature, themes, and varied levels of ethical thought can sing with John Newton:

Through many troubles, snares and toils
I have already come...

The most ominous snare, however, is about to appear. A radical change takes place as readers move from the Hebrew-based part of scripture to the Greek-influenced, uniquely Christian writings. It is easy, in this abrupt transition, to come to false conclusions. It is tempting to decide that one has moved into an entirely different book. It is tempting to conclude that one is dealing with an entirely different subject. It is tempting to believe one is dealing with an entirely different religion.

A Change of Language

A change in original language causes part of the difficulty. Language does more than convey ideas. Language also shapes ideas. Certain languages make it easy to convey certain types of concepts while other languages more easily embody other concepts.

Most of the Bible, from Genesis through Malachi, was written in Hebrew. Hebrew is an earthy language; it is immediate and concrete. It is a language precisely suited to be the instrument of the prophets: "Therefore, thus says the Lord..." Through this medium the prophets could describe the will of God for particular and immediate situations. Hebrew was well suited for writing laws and telling dramatic stories.

Even the devotional material of the earlier part of scripture was shaped by the peculiarities of its Hebrew environment. To say that the book of Psalms, for example, is poetry might suggest, to a descendant of the Greeks, that it is ethereal. On the contrary, the psalms are made up of poetry that is based on the most concrete and universal of human experiences: joy and sadness, problems and depression, bravery and deep fears. The Hebraic, poetic style of psalms enhances the impact of these powerful, immediate, human drives.

Jesus, however, was born into a world of other languages. His family and friends spoke Aramaic—similar to Hebrew, but less literate. Aramaic was fine for communicating day-by-day necessities, but no one would have tried to write a profound poem or a moving drama in Aramaic. These more formal aspects of culture had become dominated by the Greek language. The armies of Alexander, who had carried Greek concepts of thought as surely as they carried weapons of conquest, had long ago withdrawn, but had left behind an assumption of superiority for all things Hellenistic. Thus the people of Jesus' day spoke in Aramaic; they read their scripture in Hebrew; they wrote to friends, especially to friends who lived in distant places, in the international, culturally-ascendant language of Greek.

If Hebrew was the language of prophets, Greek was the language of philosophers. Its words and concepts were more ethereal. Spiritual matters, paradoxes, and closely-reasoned arguments fit well in its structure. Greek had a rich vocabulary, including, for example, three words to describe with precision the concept that English expresses in only one word, "love."

Even in English translations, the echoes of the original scriptural languages can be heard. Bible readers who move from Malachi to Matthew know they have made a significant transition. Culture shock appears. When readers arrive at the Gospel of John, written not only *in* Greek but also *under the influence* of Greek concepts, the differences are even more pronounced.

From Community to Individual

Along with a change of language comes a change of subject matter. Concern for the nation dominates the varied material from the Hebrew Scripture. By contrast, the Christian scriptures, on the surface, seem concerned not with a community but with a person. Jesus, later to be known as the Christ, dominates almost every page. Individualism intrudes. Encouraging individuals to commit to the kingdom of God seems to have replaced the effort to renew the nation of Israel.

The very nature of religious thought seems, in this transition, to have been radically altered. While the Hebrew writers called their readers to keep the sacred Law and to worship Yahweh through proper rituals, New Testament writers seemed concerned only with encouraging people to accept, one by one, the freely-given grace of God.

A Change of Rulers

Part of the change in subject matter is related to the change in political realities. The Jews had lost power over their own government. They were ruled by Rome. Thus no prophet could go to the king and demand justice for all. Neither could the prophets blame the nation's woes on dishonest merchants and self-serving priests. Issues of justice were in the hands of Caesar. Even the priests had to do their work under the surveillance of Roman armies.

The same shift in political power caused a shift from community action to individual action. The Hebrew prophets had called the nation to righteousness; Jesus and John the Baptist called individuals to membership in the kingdom of God. Paul called individuals to repent and be saved. A surface reading of this could lead to the conclusion that a community-based religion had become a religion of the isolated person.

The original questions are thus before us in renewed forms. Is the Bible one book or two? Or is it sixty-six quite disparate books? Is there any organizing theme that holds all this material together? Most important for Christians, is there continuity between our faith and that major part of scripture we know as the Old Testament? Is the vast majority of our Bible—that written in Hebrew—simply an extended and quite confusing introduction to the life of Jesus? Or, to extend the question with a different metaphor, is the Old Testament simply a warm-up of the audience in preparation for the main act?

Implications

The implications for Christians are many. How deep are our religious roots? Do they go only to the first century, to a single man who happened to be Jewish, but who abandoned his Jewishness to set in motion a new religion? Or do our roots sink deeper by fifteen hundred years, making us genuine members of the faith family that began with God's promise to Abraham and continues, without break, to the present day?

The very nature of the Christian faith is at stake. The New Testament acquires a different coloration when it is read as a continuation of and in the context of its Hebrew ancestry. If a new religion begins with Jesus and is clarified by Paul, then followers of Jesus will pay little attention to the ethical insights of the prophets, the moral demands of the Torah, the faith struggles of Job and Koheleth, or the breadth of view of the writers of Ruth and Jonah. If, on the other hand, the major concepts of Judaism are carried over, and the individualism of the New Testament and the Greek concepts applied to Jesus are *simply necessities of the immediate situation*, then new possibilities and meanings emerge.

This volume is committed to the idea that the Bible is organized around a single theme. It is the family album of one family of faith. That family was tragically divided following the life of Jesus. Yet families do divide, without forgetting their common heritage. It is legitimate, following such division, for both to claim the common traditions and to learn to relate to one another as siblings (or, as some might argue, as parent and offspring). The fact that a tree divides into two trunks does not keep it from being a single tree.

In dealing with the New Testament, I will make the following arguments. These arguments show why we can claim continuity of the uniquely Christian scriptures with the Hebraic scriptures. They will show why the Bible is one book, organized around a continuing theme. *That theme continues to be the ongoing life of the community of faith.*

1. Jesus was thoroughly Jewish. He celebrated his Jewishness, lived it with vigor, and never gave the slightest indication he intended that either he or any of his followers would be other than Jewish. His teachings centered around the faith family arguments that had been debated by his own ancestors in faith.

2. The role of Messiah that he embodied was one of the two major messianic roles described in the Jewish Scripture. He rejected the popular role based on power and exclusiveness and lived out the less popular, but still very real, role based on redemptive suffering and inclusiveness.

3. Paul, the evangelist to the Gentiles, was not "converted" to a new faith, but was called to a special mission within his Jewish faith.

4. Paul's chief concern was not to revise the faith, but to open the faith community to persons beyond the Jewish nation. His major problem was how to allow non-Jews to become a part of the continuing community and to do so with no unnecessary barriers and with no sense of being second-class family members.

5. When Paul announced that we are free from the Law, he meant we are no longer obliged to apply every legal requirement in situations where that application can be unloving or destructive. He did not mean to cut followers of Jesus away from their obligation to the high ethical demands of historic Judaism nor to free them from the search for just societies as demanded by the prophets. A careful reading of Paul shows that he was attempting to find creative ways to bring Gentiles into the Jewish tradition. The Law was essential to that tradition. *Paul's concern was to release new converts from a rigid application of the Law, not to set them on uncharted waters where no rules could be found.*

6. Paul's effort to convert the Gentiles was a part of the ongoing drama of his religious community. Paul immersed himself in a long-standing family argument: How is the faith community related to the non-Jew? In the older scripture the narrow, exclusive position had been stated by Obadiah, Ezra, and Nehemiah. The broader, inclusive side had been taken by Second Isaiah, the writer of Ruth, and, preeminently, by the writer of Jonah.

Paul became the Jonah of the New Testament. Both men had been reluctant missionaries. Both had begun with the notion that only ethnic Jews could be members of the faith family. Assertive intervention by God convinced both that the grace of God was sufficient for both Jew and Gentile.

7. The New Testament writers were as committed to a *communal* religion as were the earlier Hebrew writers. While both Paul and Jesus made appeals to individuals, the appeal was to share in the life of a *kingdom*. *Kingdom* is a communal concept, no less so than the concept of *nation*. Circumstances decreed that persons must, one by one, make their commitment to this new society. Once a part of the kingdom, however, the individual was supported and guided by the community, just as individuals had been guided and supported by tribes and nation throughout Jewish history. Christianity has no more place for the spiritual isolate—the individual who limits religion to personal salvation and who attempts to work out the meaning of that salvation apart from the support and corrective input of others—than does its parent Jewish faith.

8. The conflict that finally separated Christianity from Judaism was not, at the outset, a battle between Jews on the one hand and Gentiles on the other. It was at its beginning an in-house struggle, waged between people who were almost exclusively Jews. One party within the Jewish faith was sure that there could be no resurrection of the dead such as that claimed for Jesus. They were also confident that no law of ancient Judaism could be purposely broken, no matter what the circumstances. The followers of Jesus obviously took the opposite side of both issues. The harsh words that were written about "the Jews" must be read with the understanding that they were, in almost every case, penned by other Jews. Otherwise a horrid anti-semitism seems to be present.

If these arguments are correct, and they all can be quite thoroughly documented in New Testament writings, then the faith family that nourishes us has one continuous and very long history. Christian roots reach back a millennium and a half before the time of Christ, drawing nourishment from the soil of Egypt, from the desert sands, and from the blood-soaked promised land. Christians find themselves not as antagonists of Judaism, but as siblings— perhaps, more correctly, as offspring of this parent faith. The anti-Judaism that has poisoned Christianity for all its history is therefore a thing to be thoroughly censured, a grotesque sin for which we must seek both divine and human forgiveness.

A False Approach

Some Christian literature, especially educational materials on the Bible, has attempted to relate the Hebrew Scripture and the New Testament by making over the Jewish faith and its holy writings into a vision created in Christian minds. This takes two forms—forms that are, in the final analysis, contradictory. On the one hand, Judaism is assumed to be an outmoded, rigid religion of laws—laws that even God has now rejected. On the other hand, the Jewish Scriptures are assumed to be filled with cryptic references to the coming of Christ. The writer of Matthew occasionally falls into this latter trap. Luther skated alongside the same pit in his famous comment on the entire Bible, "The scripture is the cradle in which Christ is laid." In its extreme form the argument that the primary purpose of the Hebraic Scripture is to introduce believers to the Christ amounts to telling contemporary Jews that they do not know how to read their own sacred writings.

A genuine connection between the Hebrew Scripture and the New Testament can be established only by respecting the earlier writings in their authentic and original form. The Hebrew Bible is the family album of a strong, vibrant, amazingly resilient tradition that must be confronted on its own terms. Clark M. Williamson, professor at Christian Theological Seminary in Indianapolis, argues this forcefully:

> Another point on which the church needs to come clean is to recognize that its self-understanding is inherently tied up with its understanding of "the other," specifically the Jewish other. The church needs to rid itself of all vestiges of its traditional "teaching and practice of contempt" for Jews and Judaism and in its place put a "teaching of respect" and a theological theory of Jews and Judaism in which Jews can recognize themselves.[1]

Any approach to the Hebraic Scripture that puts those magnificent writings at the service of Christian theology is decidedly not one in which "Jews can recognize themselves."

Another Approach

While it has been traditional in Christian circles to tie the Testaments together by attempting to Christianize the Hebrew writings, this volume proposes to tie them together by recognizing the Jewish nature of the Christian writings. The connective tissue for this is found in the themes already enumerated. However, following these themes through the New Testament books is complicated by the fact that the sequence in which they developed is quite different from the sequence in which the reader confronts them. The first books to be written in their present form were written by Paul. His purpose, as indicated already, was not to tell about Jesus but *to wrestle with the question of who could belong to the community of faith.* As he struggled with this central issue he also found himself interpreting and applying the meaning of Jesus' life. *After* Paul wrote, the four evangelists wrote their accounts of the life of Jesus.

The casual reader of the New Testament, confronting the writings in their present sequence, would certainly conclude that the

---

[1]Clark M. Williamson, *The Christian Century* (October 13, 1993), p. 976.

life of Jesus had been written first, then that same life was interpreted by Paul. Actually, the interpretation—if that is the proper term—was done first. (As the material that follows will point out, Paul was much more concerned with expanding the boundaries of the faith family than with explaining the faith.) The Gospels were penned after, and perhaps somewhat in reaction to, what Paul had written. Despite the order in which they are placed in the Bible, Paul had the first word about the implications of following Jesus. The Gospel writers had, if not the final, certainly a later word. After the Gospels came several other writers, who continued the debate over such issues as Christian responsibility to the Jewish Law and over whether Jesus was primarily human or primarily divine.

Christianity Weakened Without Judaism

When the transition from Hebraic to Christian scripture is made apart from these connecting threads, Christianity is left a weaker religion. It becomes like a tree whose deepest root has been severed.

When the continuity of the two faiths is pushed out of sight, both Judaism and Christianity are in danger of being misunderstood. It then becomes easy for Christians to voice the deadly cliche: "Judaism is a religion of law and Christianity is a religion of grace." In actual fact grace abounds in the Hebraic Scripture. Witness in particular the grace-filled story of Joseph achieving reconciliation with his family, the compassion shown to foreign wives by the writer of the story of Ruth, and the freely-given redemption dramatized by the book of Hosea. On the other hand, the legal code is certainly not dismissed in the New Testament, at least not if the words of Jesus are taken at face value. More will be said on this later.

Without a firm attachment to the Hebraic Scripture, Christianity loses its moral rudder. Some have argued that grace itself places on us a responsibility for moral behavior, but the moral behavior spoken of here is highly individualistic and lacks a social conscience. The evidence is in and it is clear: A religion that fails to define the meaning of moral behavior easily falls prey to all who would keep women in subjection and who would ignore the economic realities that allow the greedy to add "house to house,…field to field." (Isaiah 5:8). Where religion without prophetic voices thrives, the rich soon live atop mounds of conspicuous wealth, and the poor disappear into sinkholes of poverty and despair.

Christian theology often pits law against grace as if these two were opposites. In fact, the opposite of law is anarchy, and the opposite of moral law is moral anarchy. It can be argued that Christianity's rejection of any body of definable, concrete measurements of behavior is associated with the ease with which members of this faith have supported the Inquisition, embraced human slavery, and followed despots such as Hitler.

Without the guidance of the moral law, Christians are easily seduced by the anti-Jewish sentiments that creep into the later writings of the Christian Bible. It will become clear as we examine the New Testament that what began as an intra-family debate about the nature of Jesus quickly became a raging and divisive argument. As the struggle became more heated the followers of Jesus were expelled from Jewish synagogues. Christians, in turn, began to write that the followers of Jesus had taken the mantle of "chosen people" from the Jews and that the Jewish covenant had been annulled. To make themselves look like loyal citizens in the eyes of their Roman persecutors the earliest Christians shifted the blame for the crucifixion from the Romans onto the Jews. From there it was a few short steps to turning Jewish people into objects. They were objects to be converted; failing that, they became "Christ-killers" to be destroyed.

When we draw too far from our Jewish roots we also lose the impact of some of our finest liturgical material. For example, the psalms, as described earlier, are a product of Hebrew language and culture. Because we find that culture awkward, we trivialize the psalms by pretending that they are hiding places for hints about the coming of Christ. Walter Brueggemann suggests that it is only as we allow ourselves to enter the thought-world in which the psalms were originally written that these rich resources can be prayed and sung with authenticity:

> The *stuff* of Jewish suffering and Jewish hope is a unique partner to the *form* of strident, subversive, intense forms of language (in the psalms). That is, this bold *form of speech* peculiarly matches the *Jewish practice* of suffering and hope. It is the interplay of the *stuff of Jewish faith* and the *form of Psalmic speech* which might matter to the spirituality of the Church.[2] (Italics in the original.)

---

[2]Walter Brueggemann, *Praying the Psalms* (Winona, Minnesota: Saint Mary's Press, 1980).

Christianity, then, can be true to itself only as it admits both its debt to and its organic union with its parent Jewish faith. The rewards are great if we can reclaim our Jewish ancestry.

The Bible, then, is our faith's family album. Like all extended families, the family of faith has had disagreements and has argued its central concerns with vigor. After Jesus, the family divided, leaving a Jewish community facing its mostly-Gentile offspring, creating misunderstandings and hostility that have survived two millennia. The bloody results of that hostility can make both sensitive Jew and sensitive Christian weep.

It is important to remember, then, as we turn from the Hebrew language and culture to the thought-world of the Greeks, that the organizing theme of scripture remains unchanged. The Bible is the family album of a community that divides, finally, into two parts, yet shares a troubled but unbroken history.

7

The Community Encounters a Unique Figure

In the island community several generations had been born and died since their exile. In the interim they had repelled other invasions and weathered additional social storms. Recently, another stronger group from the mainland had sent in settlers and begun to exercise financial and political control over the tiny nation.

Then came another major upheaval—to be added to the many that had taken place in the island's extended history. This new crisis was in a quite different form from the former.

A young man appeared among them who was, more than any other individual they had ever known, thoroughly in tune with the ways and rhythms of the sea. He knew, as if by instinct, where to look for fish; he could feel in his bones the coming of storms. He was an excellent boatman, able to bring vessels and passengers through the most difficult waters.

One would think that the other people of the island would have welcomed such skills from one of their number. A few did, and they determined to learn from him. Others, however, kept a distance. They were jealous, especially over the fact that his ways of dealing with the sea seemed superior to some of the old ways. When he demonstrated newer, better methods, people became angry. They felt their own relationship to the sea was being judged harshly and their ancestors' skills dismissed.

Later, reflection helped many of the islanders realize that the young man had never intended to destroy the old ways. In fact, he loved his island and respected all that his ancestors had learned and taught about its special environment. He accepted and built on that ancient knowledge. Whenever he tried to push beyond that knowledge, however, the more rigid members of the community misunderstood.

A second problem emerged. This special young man did not seem to have a proper attitude toward the islanders themselves. He, after some initial hesitation, was willing to share his insights as freely with the mainlanders who had intruded on the island as with the natives. The islanders feared their special way of life would be threatened if too many others learned to live in the same relationship to the sea as they.

Conflicts arose. Soon even the mainlanders began to fear that the young man posed a threat to their power. Perhaps they might be driven away if he used his remarkable skills against them. A plot, involving rare cooperation between leaders of the mainland and leaders of the island, was devised to destroy him. The actual killing was done by mainlanders, for they alone had the power to execute. Thus a unique life was cut short. His only crime was that he did what all islanders had claimed to have done: He lived in relationship to the sea. Yet he did that so well that he became a judgment on the others. The remainder could not tolerate such a life.

Later, many would wish they could recall his exact teachings. Unfortunately, none of his life story or his teachings had been written during his lifetime. This was partly because of the controversy he generated. It was also because of a strong rumor that had begun to circulate. Some who lived near the sea were sure they saw signs that the sea was rising. If so, they knew that their community had a very short future before it. Why write down information that would soon be irrelevant?

The death of this young man caused many of the islanders to reevaluate some of their previous assumptions. They began to recognize that they, too, needed to improve and renew their relationship to the sea. That which had given the community its reason for being had for too long been neglected. A few began to wonder of their nation might be strengthened if they were more open to persons outside their immediate island. If others understood the sea as well as they, could they be received as fellow citizens?

The islanders began to remember and study his example. So many lives were changed that they began to speculate that the special person was somehow still among them, exercising influence. Because it was largely the manner of his unjust execution that caused this reflection, they could say that their way of life had been saved not only by his life, but also by his death.

The Life of Jesus

Much had happened since the writing of the last book of the Hebrew Scripture. Yet many realities remained unchanged.

The Social Setting

The writer of the book of Daniel had so successfully inspired the people to sacrifice that the nation had been temporarily freed from its Greek conquerors. Soon, however, the Romans had followed the Greeks, and once again a foreign power ruled in Jerusalem.

The new conquerors wisely allowed some freedom of worship. Political power, nonetheless, was in the hands of the representative of Caesar. Thus the chief priest was the person in charge of the area of life in which Jews had the largest degree of control. He became the highest native officer of the Hebrew people. In order to achieve as much self-rule as possible, this religious functionary sought and was given authority over many aspects of daily life. Along with the power that flowed into the temple went the possibility of corruption.

The situation was barely tolerable—in some ways, the worst situation a nation can face. When the Greeks, in the time of the writing of Daniel, had attempted to force Greek culture and Greek religion on the Israelites, the situation became so burdensome that rebellion broke out. People took steps to correct the intolerable. Under the Romans, however, their situation was just short of intolerable. The Jews were allowed to keep a semblance of religious freedom while losing their political autonomy. The new situation was evil enough to cause a serious case of national depression, but not quite bad enough to foment a call to arms or to set in motion any form of civil disobedience.

Instead of uniting against the common enemy, the people of Israel tended to project their anger against one another. Various groups sought to identify the major sin that was causing Yahweh to leave them in such a condition. Each group had an idea that it was sure would, if followed, purify the nation and bring the power of God to bear once more against its enemies. Pharisees, Saducees, Essenes, and others vied for public support. It would have been a mistake, at the end of the first century B.C.E., to speak of a normative Judaism. Judaism existed in many, often contradictory, forms.

Jesus

Into this setting came a remarkable religious leader. The circumstances of this man's birth were disputed (though the manner of his birth was not an issue until several decades after his death). What was known was that he seemed to possess more than human power—power that allowed him even to exorcise demons and cure physical disease. Stories circulated indicating that he had even called certain people back from death. Though untrained and without credentials as a teacher, he nonetheless knew well the scripture and traditions of his ancestors. He evidenced great respect for the old ways and the old laws while applying the traditions of his ancestors with dynamic freshness. As a storyteller he was without peer. His parables, taken from the common life of those to whom he spoke, became windows through which people could see the presence of God working in their bruised lives.

The man's given name was Jesus. He came from the town of Nazareth; thus the designation, Jesus of Nazareth. Later generations would give him the title of Christ, a Greek approximation of the Hebrew concept of messiah.

Unfortunately for the generations that came after him, Jesus appeared at a time when many people were expecting an immediate end of the world. This should not be surprising. The power of Rome seemed overwhelming and permanent. The most optimistic Jew could see no way that a new revolt could seize self-governing power again for their nation. How, then, could God's authority be expressed? Only by a consummation of human history. Predictions of the future became a growth industry. Seers insisted they saw signs that a decisive, perhaps violent, action by God would bring human life to a close. Even Jesus himself seemed, in some of his teachings, to share this assumption. At other points he discouraged his followers from investing energy in a search for signs of a divine event that could not be predicted.

One result of this concern for the end of the world was that few people wrote anything down. No scribe followed the Nazarene to record his teachings, for it was assumed that people would remember what he had said for whatever brief time remained. Approximately three decades elapsed before anyone recognized the need for a record of his actions and sayings. By then his followers were trying to define themselves and organize into an ongoing movement. It was easy, at that point, for those who wrote the story of Jesus' life to read back into his thoughts the concerns of the emerging church. In the tenth chapter of Matthew (vv. 28–39), to take one obvious example, Jesus is reported to have predicted the coming persecutions, and to have told his disciples not to fear those who could destroy their bodies but could not harm their souls. This may have been based on something Jesus said; however, it requires no advanced training in biblical studies to recognize that the early church, in recording this material, took some liberties in applying it to their immediate situation. Thus, today, separating out the genuine statements of Jesus from the passions and interests of the young church is a nearly impossible job.

Some facts about Jesus' life are clear. His mighty acts and the incisiveness of his teaching combined to attract a significant following. As Jesus' entourage increased, so did the discomfort of both Jewish religious leaders and Roman officials. The religious leaders, persons of unusual power in that time, wanted no competition. The Romans were even more wary, eager to discourage any group that might develop enough strength to challenge their rule. Conflicts and misunderstandings were inevitable. Two of the things Jesus did seemed designed to increase tensions. One was to include persons outside the Jewish nation in his compassionate ministry and to occasionally include non-Jews as heroes of his parables. The second was to reach beyond those whom his own countrymen had defined as socially acceptable. He made contact with the diseased (assumed to be under curse from God, according to the still-prevalent theory of retribution), spoke openly with prostitutes, and associated with quisling tax collectors. The meal table, that universal symbol of social acceptance, was used to dramatize his embrace of persons that others had marginalized. A near-violent confrontation with those carrying on commercial business at the temple added ammunition to the arguments of those who attempted to label him a radical.

After about two years of public activity, Jesus found himself confronted with three options. He could abandon the mission to which he felt himself called; he could ask his followers to fight violently for his survival; or he could allow the power of Rome to destroy him. Apparently remembering that a former prophet of his people had shown how suffering can be redemptive, he chose the last alternative. He was executed on a Roman cross.

More remarkable even than his life were the events that happened a few days following his death. His closest friends insisted that they had encountered a resurrected Jesus. This experience came first to the women who had been among his followers, then to some of the men who had been his disciples. These friends saw this victory over the grave as confirmation that Jesus had been, as they had come to suspect, the predicted messiah. This seemed to have placed a divine stamp of approval upon all that Jesus had done and said. The disciples determined to continue his activity. They recalled that Jesus had not limited his concern to Jews. Perhaps they also recalled that Second Isaiah's vision of the messiah had embraced the welfare of all nations. For whatever reasons, the disciples determined to spread the news of Jesus to every nation they could reach.

Some General Comments

Despite the problems of identifying Jesus' authentic statements, some general sense of the overall shape of his life and teachings can be seen in those books that were finally written about him.

Thoroughly Jewish

We recognize, in the first place, that *he was thoroughly Jewish*. His life was a continuation of the same faith community that is the central subject of scripture.

As his story was told by those considered to be the most accurate of his biographers,[1] Jesus' adult life was something of a recapitulation of the history of the Jewish community. His father (named, appropriately, Joseph, and much like his earlier namesake, often guided by dreams) took the young Jesus into Egypt. Later, having emerged from Egypt, Jesus spent forty days (to be compared with forty years) in the desert. He chose twelve disciples, paralleling the twelve tribes of Israel. After about two years of public ministry he was drawn to Jerusalem, where other prophets had met their fate. His death and resurrection there could be a way of reenacting the Babylonian captivity and release of the nation.

Although he was willing to adjust some of the ancient laws, he was faithful to those laws (the exception was the body of rules we have called the priestly/individualistic laws; these will be discussed later). He insisted that it would be a most serious sin if anyone broke the laws. He occasionally found himself in controversy over Sabbath activities, such as healing the sick and gathering grain. Even here he remained well within accepted practice of at least the more broadminded of his rabbinical ancestors.[2]

---

[1]This is a reference to Matthew, Mark, and Luke, the so-called Synoptic Gospels.

[2]For a fuller discussion of Jesus' faithfulness to Jewish law, see Geza Vermes, *The Religion of Jesus the Jew* (Minneapolis: Fortress Press, 1993).

He was a practicing Jew. One biographer described the careful way in which his family observed the traditions in his rearing: circumcision at seven days and a family visit to the temple at age twelve. He began his public ministry in his synagogue at Nazareth and ended it by celebrating Passover with his closest friends. The purity of the temple was so important to him that he cleansed it of money-grubbers even though the act probably hastened his death. In one significant moment he was observed by friends in the company of Moses and Elijah. He had many disagreements with particular groups within the Jewish community, but nowhere in the Synoptic Gospels do we find him in conflict with the basic, prophetic/social tradition of his ancestors.

Jesus was Jewish. He never stopped being Jewish. There is no indication that he expected his followers to consider themselves anything other than Jewish.

The Kingdom of God

A second significant feature of his life: He centered his teachings around the concept of *the kingdom of God.*

Because no one took precise notes as he spoke, the exact meaning of the phrase, the kingdom of God, (or the kingdom of Heaven, as it is sometimes called) is impossible to know. Some general observations can be made, however.

The kingdom of God, as Jesus defined it, is not a phenomenon apart from the larger faith community, but is a spiritual fellowship of those who have accepted a particular description of God and a particular quality of human relationship. The reign of God within this kingdom is both present and future. It is slowly evolving, like leaven overtaking dough, yet it is already present in the teachings of Jesus and his relationship to his closest friends.

The kingdom represents a social, not an individualistic, phenomenon. In the stale religious atmosphere of first-century Judaism, Jesus tried to revitalize the faith of his nation. Thus he called individuals to repent and enter the kingdom. One by one persons were challenged to accept that opportunity. Nonetheless, the group consciousness first observed in the prophet Amos was retained. People could come into the kingdom by individual choice, but once there they, like their spiritual ancestors, were in a group setting. Jesus did not intend for any of his followers to stand lonely and naked before God. The unique person had always been surrounded by, supported by, and often judged by brothers and sisters in faith. The kingdom of God would be no different.

The kingdom was also the arena in which justice could grow. Since the nation had lost its independence, the prophetic voice could no longer demand that government pass laws and distribute resources to ensure that every individual would have the wherewithal necessary to live with dignity. Nonetheless, in the spiritual fellowship of the kingdom, people could care for one another, show hospitality to the stranger, and call on the power of God to give sight to the blind, mobility to the lame, and release to the captive.

Both Jew and Gentile

The records also show that Jesus, in renewing the ancient faith, sought *to include both Jew and Gentile in the emerging kingdom.*

The Synoptic Gospels begin with a forerunner of Jesus, a man named John (actually a cousin of Jesus). John was a desert dweller whose clothing was camel-skin. One of John's earliest statements (tactfulness was not one of John's major skills!) was a rebuke to Jewish ethnic pride: "God is able from these stones to raise up children of Abraham." From there the Gospel stories describe how a variety of people—folk who had no genetic claim on Judaism—were offered the opportunity to be part of the faith community that had Abraham as its father. Biological birth had brought Jews into the faith community; but for those outside that community, and for Jews who needed a significant change in life-direction, a rebirth was needed.

Jesus seemed to have gradually come to realize that he had responsibilities beyond his ethnic group. He seemed to have begun with the assumption that his mission was exclusively Jewish. But when he was confronted with Gentiles of unusual faith he quickly changed. Non-Jews were held up as examples of commitment. A Samaritan became an archetype of the true neighbor; an African helped carry his cross. He taught all his followers to pray using a phrase ("hallowed be Thy name") associated in older scripture with the ingathering of the Jews and the sharing of good news with all nations. At the end he sent his disciples out with the charge to carry the good news of the kingdom of God to the ends of the earth.

Jesus, then, was thoroughly Jewish. He saw his mission as renewing his beloved faith community through the leaven of the kingdom of God. He became convinced that this renewal involved breaking the ethnic barriers so that all nations could be gathered into that kingdom.

Faith Family Arguments

It is clear that Jesus of Nazareth took decisive stands on several of the issues that religious leaders of former generations had debated.

The Nature of God

The scriptures as Jesus studied them contained widely varying views about the nature of God. God was sometimes seen as the tribal deity of the Jews, at war with similar deities of neighboring lands. At times God was experienced as the awesome presence who, Moses believed, would immediately destroy any mortal so bold as to look at the holy face. Another view saw God as a compassionate being who could reach out through a prophet to a starving foreign woman and heal the diseased skin of a commander of an opposing army. God was, in the view of some scriptural writers, the powerful being who overwhelmed enemies and consumed the prophets of Baal. God was seen by others as a suffering servant whose weakness overcame evil and was once compared to a cuckolded husband who forgave his wife.

Jesus had a very definite view of the nature of God. In describing God, Jesus often used terms familiar to his hearers, then put those terms into contexts that turned their meanings upside down. He spoke of the kingdom of God, yet the ruler of that domain was hardly an autocrat to be compared with those who sat on human thrones. In human monarchies, the few lord it over the many. Not so in God's kingdom. When God reigns, the status of servant is as high as that of master. Prestige comes not from giving orders, but from giving service. In this strange kingdom the first shall be last and the last shall be first. Jesus taught about a God who was the antithesis of the first-century power broker.

Completely setting aside the idea of God as a violence-prone, blood-thirsty leader of armies, Jesus described God as nurturer. God gives care as a shepherd gives protection to sheep—sometimes going to great lengths to save one wandering lamb. God is also like a parent. To best communicate in his strongly patriarchal society, Jesus used "Father" to describe the care and love of the Creator. The reader should not be fooled, however. This is not the law-giving, emotionally distant, male parent that some patriarchal societies have produced. This is a loving, nurturing parent who knows how to give good gifts to his children.

One particular story told by Jesus shows the radical nature of his concept of God. As has been described in an earlier chapter, child-rearing customs of the day made the male child the responsibility of the male parent from the time of puberty. The father was thus judged in public eyes by the behavior of his adult, male children. Sons who were disrespectful or who behaved in irresponsible ways were a thoroughgoing embarrassment to their fathers. It was not unusual for a father to remove such a social stigma by erasing the name of a rebellious son from the family ledger. Against this background Jesus told a story of a younger son who asked his father for his half of the estate while his father was still quite alive. (This is akin to saying to one's father, "You have not died soon enough to suit me!") Remarkably, the father granted this off-the-wall request. The son set off to pursue his own interests, leaving his father and older brother to care for the family enterprise. The pattern of immaturity continued. The son soon consumed his fortune. In a moment of unaccustomed wisdom, he determined to return home, where he was sure he would no longer be considered a family member, but where he might be allowed to sign on as hired help.

Meanwhile, back at the farm, the father should have, by accepted custom, written this child off, proclaiming that he was no longer part of the family. (This was precisely what the son expected.) How else could he deal with the embarrassment that ensued when asked about this boy by his neighbors? Better to say, "I have no son of that name!" than to admit that the son existed, but had rebelled. Instead, the story implied that the father was constantly looking down the road in hopes of seeing his returning son. One day he saw just that: the son, smelling of swine, beaten down but now much more mature, was returning. The father ran (something else quite beneath the dignity of fathers of that day) to his son, put a ring on his finger (a sign of acceptance into the family), and brought him home. That evening a huge feast was held in honor of the one who had been lost, but had been found. (Luke 15:11–24)

The God of Jesus' teachings was reckless in expressing compassion, yet not infinitely giving or infinitely patient. There came a time when rebellion would no longer be tolerated. God remained God. Yet the emphasis was radically shifted from divine power and human fear to divine love and free human response.

The concept of God as caring shepherd and nurturing parent was not new. The twenty-third Psalm and other Hebraic Scriptures had described the former; the suffering servant passages of Second Isaiah had suggested the latter. Jesus' contribution was to lift this understanding of God from among the many offered by his tradition and to sharpen it by his stories and by the example of his own life.

On How to Respond to God

A second faith family argument of Jesus' time concerned how God should be served. Leading the arguments for one side (the prophetic party) had been the eighth-century prophets. According to them, God is pleased when the community is organized according to structures of justice—when the needs of the weakest members are addressed, when honest scales are used in the marketplace, when the concept of ancestral lands is respected, and when the nation's trust is put less in armies and more in the power of God. Spokespersons for the opposite side (the priestly party) insisted that God was best served by proper attention to the rules of worship. Key among these were the editors of the books of Chronicles who presented David as primarily a religious leader directing the nation to proper practices before the sacred altar. The editor of the book of Leviticus was on the same side, primarily concerned with ritual practices.

Jesus, as depicted by the Synoptic writers, put himself squarely in the prophetic tradition. One of his biographers described the opening of his public ministry in a way that firmly established this tie. Jesus had gone to his hometown and attended Sabbath worship (he obviously, though in the prophetic tradition, considered worship central to his life). During the service he was asked to read from scripture. He choose the following passage from the prophet whom we know as Second Isaiah:

> I have given you as a covenant to the people,
>   a light to the nations,
>   to open the eyes that are blind,
> to bring out the prisoners from the dungeon,
>   from the prison those who sit in darkness.
> (Isaiah 42:6b–7)[3]

From that point on, his public work became a living demonstration of the task of the prophet: redistributing the power and resources of a community so the weak were exalted and those who had abused power were brought down. He turned other values on their heads. In a society that valued the elderly and ignored the young, he pointed

---

[3]The wording differs somewhat in Luke 4:18; this is probably because Luke was quoting from the Septuagint, a then-popular Greek translation of the Hebrew Bible.

to children as a source of wisdom and as prime candidates for his kingdom. He touched and cured the leper. In a patriarchal society he violated the norms by including women among his followers and even accepted financial support from them. (Luke 8:3) He invited the wrath of the traditionalists by eating with tax collectors, people who had much wealth but no social standing. He associated with prostitutes; he lifted the oppression of demon possession; he gave sight to the blind and mobility to the crippled.

Jesus' attitude toward the laws of his ancestors also showed his commitment to prophetic religion. On the surface, his attitude toward those laws seems contradictory. He spoke forcefully of the need to keep the entire legal code.[4] On the other hand, he quite deliberately broke some of those same regulations. Closer examination of this apparent contradiction shows that he kept all those laws that could be called prophetic/social (see the discussion of this distinction in chapter 3), but rebelled against some of the priestly/individualistic laws. The Code of Holiness (a particular form of priestly/individualistic law) prescribed isolation for those with leprosy; Jesus touched victims of this disease and welcomed them back into the human community. The Code of Holiness stated that women during their menstrual period were unclean and not to be touched; Jesus touched and cured a woman of her unceasing menstrual flow. The priestly/individualistic laws were concerned with purity-impurity and cleanliness-uncleanliness—a mind-set that Jesus roundly condemned.

In the ongoing debate between the prophetic and the priestly, absolute positions can be quite destructive. Jesus was not a radical in this regard. He showed proper respect for the basic cultic rituals of his people. He was faithful in Sabbath worship and celebrated the festivals of his ancestors. Yet the central emphasis of his life was the practice of love and not the reform of worship. He had harsh words for those who put major energy into proper dress codes for priests and exact formulas for presenting tithes at the altar. His was a life of doing—doing deeds for the needy and teaching about a loving Creator. He described his authentic family as those who *do* the will of this loving God.

Relationship to the Non-Jew

Among the writers of Jewish Scriptures were some who were sure that Yahweh had made an exclusive covenant with Israel.

---

[4]See especially Matthew 5:17–20.

According to this view, God belonged to the Jews in almost the same sense in which the Jews belonged to God. That view, however, had been battered by many experiences, not the least of which was the Babylonian captivity. The exiles had learned that the rule of God could extend beyond their sacred land. They found that Babylonians might even be instruments of God in distributing punishment and reward to their nation. Their ancient prophets had found high morals and profound faith in many foreign people. Some of those ancient prophets insisted that the nation's restoration would somehow involve more than their own ethnic group: "Then the glory of the LORD shall be revealed, and all people shall see it together" (Isaiah 40:5). Jesus was forced to choose between these two radically different positions.

All who recorded the life of Jesus assume that he began his public work with the idea that it would be confined to those of Jewish ancestry. He could not, however, escape for long the question: What about the Gentile? The issue was pressed on him by a foreign woman (two biographers disagree about her nationality) who begged him to heal her deranged daughter. At first he dismissed her—in a thoroughly discourteous manner. When she persisted and thus revealed an unshakable commitment, he relented.[5] After this event the reader can sense a gradual growth in hostility between Jesus and conservative Jewish groups, accompanied by a larger openness toward Gentiles. The writer Luke, perhaps a Gentile himself, was especially sensitive to the place of non-Jews in Jesus' work. As has already been stated, each of the four Gospel writers report that Jesus sent his disciples out to all the world—to Jew and non-Jew alike. The followers of Jesus were prepared to welcome any who would accept the conditions of the kingdom of God. The prediction of John the Baptist had come true: God had shown an ability to raise up children of Abraham from the most unpromising materials.

It is important to note that neither Jesus nor his immediate followers sought to separate from Judaism. (Indeed, neither can the blame for this tragic split be put on Jewish leaders. The story of how the followers of Jesus became a separate movement—and the misunderstandings and hostility that attended that divorce—is a subject beyond the scope of this writing. "Blame" for the division, if it must be sought, will no doubt be found in abundance on both sides.) Jesus told his disciples to "go into all the world." They chose to go first to Jewish synagogues. As far as the records allow us to see into

---

[5]Compare Mark 7:24–30 and Matthew 15:21–28.

his mind, *Jesus intended to preserve the faith community in essentially its original form, but with its boundaries made permeable.*

The Meaning of Suffering

Jesus personally encountered the fact that pain is an inescapable part of God's good creation. As had his spiritual ancestors, Jesus often addressed this supposedly incongruous reality.

The editors of the historic works of the nation had explained suffering in a way that they felt preserved the integrity of God. Pain was the just punishment that a good and righteous God imposed on a sinful people. Frequently this explanation fit the facts. People often demonstrate their skill at bringing suffering on themselves. At other points this interpretation did not fit at all. A psalmist wondered how long the wicked would be allowed to exult. (Psalm 94:3) Other explanations were ventured. The poet who wrote Job made his case for the fact that some suffering is random, quite beyond explanation. Under this view, suffering is simply the mark of being human in a confusing and ambiguous world. Second Isaiah had an even more radical thought: The suffering of one individual or nation can be healing for another individual or nation. Wounds, then, under some circumstances, are signs of faithfulness.

Jesus seemed to know that all three explanations had, in particular cases, some merit. In an especially telling passage he was asked about people who happened to be at an altar when Roman soldiers attacked. (Luke 13:1–5) These, Jesus insisted, were no worse sinners than any others—only victims of random, inexcusable violence. Nonetheless, he added as a warning, if his hearers would not turn to new ways of living, they, too, might perish. Some suffering is random. Some is self-inflicted.

Otherwise, Jesus put himself in the tradition of Second Isaiah. His teachings reflect this. Pain was to be overcome not in acts of revenge, but in loving embracing of the pain. When struck on one cheek, turn the other, also. In preparing his disciples for persecution (in words that no doubt were sharpened in focus by the young church) Jesus taught them not to fear those who could destroy a human body but who could not damage the soul. For those under persecution, suffering would be a mark of distinction.

Once Jesus was asked what caused a man to be born blind. Assuming, as most people did, that this disability was a punishment, a disciple put the question in an accusing form: "Who sinned, this man or his parents?" Jesus replied that neither had. He then turned the event into an opportunity to express the love and heal-ing power of God. Later, as the prospects of his own suffering came nearer, he expanded his interpretation of pain. His followers were encouraged toward sacrificial living. Only through facing and ac-cepting the suffering that commitment brings could people expect to become members of the kingdom. The wounds of Jesus' hands and feet would become archetypal marks of faithfulness.

The Role of Women

Previous to Jesus, the role of women in the faith community was quite ambiguous. The written rules put women in a decidedly infe-rior role. A lesser value was even quantified: The loss of a woman was worth only sixty percent the loss of a man. In action, however, individual women had penetrated the barriers constructed in the patriarchal society. Athaliah had briefly been queen. Deborah had been both a prophet and a military leader. Esther had saved a com-munity of Jews from the Babylonians, and Ruth had demonstrated the contributions of foreign wives. Many other women had shown themselves to be persons of strength, faith, and courage.

Jesus chose only men as his twelve disciples. Any other arrange-ment would have created a scandal. Nonetheless, women were defi-nitely included among his traveling companions. As noted already, Luke listed several women as close friends and added that these women "provided for them out of their resources" (Luke 8:3). All four Gospels are consistent in reporting that women were the first to discover the empty tomb—a high honor that never would have gone unnoticed by the first-century reader.

Women play other independent, strong roles in the Gospel ac-counts. In one story, already mentioned in another context, a Syrophoenician mother became a heroic character. After asking that her daughter be healed, she endured a harsh retort from Jesus. But she stood her ground and renewed her plea. Jesus recognized her strength. Her daughter was healed, and the ministry of Jesus was lifted from its narrow, nationalistic focus. (Mark 7:25–30)

On the matter of divorce, Jesus' teachings sent a mixed message. Men were urged to avoid exploitative sexual advances to married women. They were told that allowing lust to go unchecked was a serious sin. Women in that time were in constant danger of being discarded by unhappy husbands. Thus any rule that made divorce more difficult was protection for women. Jesus, in the Sermon on the Mount, discouraged divorce. As Luke recorded this same material, Jesus forbade divorce altogether. Matthew's version allowed divorce only on the basis of adultery.[6]

In a story that few scholars accept as historic, yet one that most Christians are certain captures the essence of Jesus' ministry, Jesus was confronted with a woman caught in the act of adultery. She was about to be stoned, according to the Code of Holiness. (The adulterous man was apparently set free, even though the Code of Holiness called for the death penalty for both man and woman.) After a moment of contemplation, Jesus announced that any man (one assumes that only men would have been stone-throwers) without sin should cast the first stone. The stones were laid aside, and the hostile mob departed.

The story of the adulterous woman concerns a very specific form of forgiveness. Jesus' compassion in this account is the foundation for gender justice. By his actions Jesus lifted the onus of sexual sin from the shoulders of a woman, a woman who represents all women who have struggled with patriarchal assumptions. She went free, just as her partner was set free. Jesus had established equality in punishments meted out for sexual misdeeds.

Jesus' overall pattern in regard to gender equality must receive a mixed review from any modern, morally-sensitive audience. Neither his teachings nor his actions are entirely free from sexual bias. Yet he had moved a long way from the harsher laws of the book of Leviticus, or from the days when David and Solomon could fill their palaces with wives and concubines. The measurement here must be in the direction of movement and not the place of arrival.

The Messianic Person and the Messianic Age

The people of Jesus' day looked to a saving person to deliver them from their troubles. There was, however, no agreement on the nature of this messianic individual or the methods he might use to bring the nation its fulfillment.

Two basic models of the messiah had been given by earlier religious writers. One was characterized by exclusiveness and power, the other by inclusiveness and redemptive suffering. The prophet Joel, for example, could foresee a messianic age in which God had gathered all the enemies of Israel together and defeated them. This day of salvation could be celebrated exclusively by those of the Jewish nation. According to Joel, they could prepare for the day by

---

[6] Compare Matthew 5:31–32 with Luke 16:18.

beating their plowshares into swords and their pruning hooks into spears. On the other hand, both First and Second Isaiah had seen visions of peace in the coming age. According to this second vision, the messiah would be a servant whose sacrifice would open the doors to salvation for all nations. For Isaiah this meant a reversal of Joel's move to armaments. Swords would be transformed into plowshares and spears into pruning hooks.

In the first vision the messiah was a person of overwhelming power; in the second vision the messiah was a suffering servant. In the first vision the messiah would set off a cataclysmic event; in the second vision the new age would appear gradually and quietly. In the first vision redemption would be the result of a divine act; in the second vision redemption would be the result of inspired, dedicated people who acted faithfully under the inspiration of God. Jesus lived out the second vision.

The direction of Jesus' work was set early, in the wilderness temptation scenes. Despite their prescientific details—a devil in the drama, the possibility of being rescued by angels after jumping from the temple—these stories have the ring of enduring truth. As Jesus realized he had remarkable abilities to influence people, he must have considered the opportunities these powers offered for self-aggrandizement. In addition, as a loyal Jew, he must have realized the chance he had to gather a band of followers and attack the Romans. Perhaps earthly kingdoms would come under his control. He refused, however, to take the expedient course of manipulation. He would, instead, invite, persuade, encourage; he would even sacrifice his own life to demonstrate another way to overcome evil.

Jesus' rejection of the exclusive/power role for the messiah explains the depth of anger that grew up between him and certain segments of Jewish society. For the Zealots and their friends, who were eager to find someone strong enough to lead them against the Romans, the idea that the kindly Jesus—this wandering preacher whom they must have seen as timid and utterly useless—might be the expected messiah was worse than an abomination. It meant the death of their revolutionary dreams. They thus attacked him with all the vigor they could muster. It is easy to believe that this section of the Jewish community might have encouraged the Roman officials to put him to death.

Those born outside the Jewish community were especially affected by Jesus' choice of the inclusive/suffering messianic role. Had he taken the other way he would have belonged only to his own people. He would have been a Jewish Savior, laboring to restore the prestige and fortunes of the Jewish nation. By choosing the inclusive/suffering model, he made his life a ministry to both Jew and non-Jew. His death was the final, conclusive event that established him as a suffering servant. He had chosen the broader path, opening the community of faith to all who committed themselves to the inclusive kingdom that he had already set in motion. Thus all within the faith family who were born of non-Jewish ancestry can say with conviction: "Upon him was the punishment that made us whole, and by his bruises we are healed" (Isaiah 53:5).

The resurrection stories were a way of affirming that Jesus had, indeed, been the expected messiah. They were also a statement about the power of life over death and the triumph that can come through supposed weakness. The inclusive/suffering messiah might have appeared to his contemporaries as ineffectual. In the longer view of history, his triumph could not be more stunning.

Thus Jesus must be accepted as more than simply another voice adding one more opinion on the issues before the faith community. *The position of Jesus, where it can be known with some assurance, gives us a definitive statement about major questions.* God, the Ultimate Reality, is characterized by love more than power. People who seek to serve God must not be content with proper acts of worship, they must seek loving relationships with their neighbors and just structures in their society. The kingdom into which people are invited is open to all. Faithful living, not ancestry, has been defined as the mark of belonging. Suffering may, at times, be the punishment of an angry God, but on other occasions it is a sign that one has responded to the call of God. Gender roles are redefined, giving new strength and opportunity to both men and women. Finally, the true role of the messiah has been defined. The Savior is not one who uses power to exclude, but is one who suffers in the task of destroying every divisive wall.

Impact

At first the cult of Jesus and his followers was but one more addition to the cacophony of voices that had become the Jewish faith. The followers of Jesus coexisted briefly with Pharisees, Zealots, Essenes, scribes, and others groups. Within a few years those identifying with Jesus began to win a significant number of followers, both in and out of the Jewish community. Then certain questions had to be faced. How, for example, was this new group to be organized? Were the non-Jews properly initiated into the ongoing community of faith—the community that had begun in Abraham and Sarah and nurtured so many religious leaders, survived so many crises, and embraced so many ideals?

To these questions the evolving faith family album turns its attention.

8

Paul Broadens
the Community

The island community was in serious difficulty. Weakened by their divisions, the people knew they could not evict the latest invaders from the mainland. These intruders were as shrewd as they were hostile. Many islanders could foresee a time of near-total destruction, like that which had happened centuries earlier. They fled the island. Islanders settled in a variety of places on the mainland. Among those who went into exile were both followers of the special person who had recently lived among them and others who rejected his insights.

As the islanders fled, some took the documents that described the history of their people and their wisdom concerning the sea. They were confident these writings would help preserve a sense of community among the scattered group.

In each of the cities where islanders took up residence, a few told their neighbors about their special relationship to the sea. Followers of the unique young man were especially inclined to share their views, for they were sure they had superior information. A few of those on the mainland began to show interest in the islanders' way of life, for they recognized that they, too, despite their distance from the sea, were dependent on it.

The newfound interest from mainlanders caused additional disagreements. When people who had lived all their lives on the continent accepted their dependence on the sea and adopted the ways of the islanders, did this make them a part of the exiled island community? Those who followed the old ways insisted that the answer was "no." They contended that only those who had lived on the island and had practiced the ways of the sea in that spot could be considered members of the community. Most of those who were followers of the special young man argued otherwise. They remembered that the young man himself had related comfortably to non-islanders. Their argument was simple. They were sure that by acknowledging their dependency on the sea and by adopting the methods taught by their special teacher, others could become members of the scattered island community. Insisting that such new citizens live on the island was foolish, they argued, because that option had been effectively eliminated.

One person who argued for open entrance into the community traveled from city to city urging islanders to welcome new citizens. He did this in the spirit of the special young man whose teachings he prized. He also instructed the islanders on how to preserve the community and its traditions in their new and more difficult circumstances. Sometimes, after he had visited a city and moved on, he wrote letters back, detailing his advice. These letters were saved, for they were important in helping the islanders adjust to their new style of life.

As often happens in established communities, the cities that received the island exiles were not enthusiastic in their welcome. The new citizens had strange habits; they also posed an economic threat. They might take jobs and land away from longtime residents. When local people began to identify with the immigrants—even joining them—local people became antagonistic. Efforts were made to drive the islanders out. The islanders and their new friends were first insulted, then attacked. Some were killed. Some who had been welcomed as new members of the island community felt they had to keep that fact a secret.

The island community was now effectively divided. Followers of the old ways settled into a survival mode, studying the texts that described the ways of their ancestors and hoping to be able to return to their precious island. Followers of the new ways sought out new people for their community. They grew in number despite the hostility of their neighbors. While those of the old way limited their important texts to those of the distant past, followers of the new way soon added the letters of advice and encouragement that had been written in exile and persecution, and later, stories about the special young man.

Both groups, however, could claim to be authentic descendants of all that had happened on the island. Both could claim to be people of the sea.

Expanding the Faith Community

Was it possible for non-Jews to be followers in good standing of the Jewish Messiah? This question arose because of the latest turn in the drama of the faith community. Jesus, fully Jewish, had performed his public ministry of teaching and healing. Most of that ministry was directed at persons of his own nation. He had shown, however, surprising openness to non-Jews. At the close of his work he sent his disciples out to share his teachings with no regard for national boundaries. Clearly, theirs was a task without ethnic or geographic limits.

The already-divided Jewish community was further split by the impact of Jesus. Some embraced him as the expected Messiah. Most rejected that claim. Nonetheless, the vast majority of the early followers of the Way (as Jesus' followers were soon called) were Jewish.

The followers of Jesus committed their lives to the proposition that he had been the Messiah for whom their people had hoped. He fulfilled that role, however, in his own style. He chose not to overpower the nation's enemies. Quite the contrary, he suffered willingly at their hands. The Messiah taught about a kingdom of God—a phenomenon already present and growing. This kingdom was open to people who were strong in their ethical standards, who were rooted in their commitment to God, and who were willing to share the burdens of life with one another. He demonstrated in a variety of ways that genetic ties to Abraham or Moses were not a requirement for this kingdom.

Jesus' disciples had a clearly-defined assignment: tell all people, both Jew and Gentile, about the new life of the kingdom that Jesus had, by his own life, set in motion.

The disciples' problems were as severe as they were clear. The first problem had to do with the nature of the movement's leaders. Not one of them had either skills or training in human organization. These inexperienced individuals were faced with a second problem: how to bring non-Jews (Gentiles) into the ongoing community of faith on the same level as the Jews who had embraced Jesus.

The first problem, the lack of organizational skills, led to a major development in the early days of the young church. A man who had been trained as a leader by the Roman government became a follower of Jesus. His Jewish name was Saul. When he accepted Jesus as the expected Messiah he changed to his Roman name, Paul. Soon the mantle of leadership was laid on his shoulders.

Paul would need all his organizational skills to confront the problems of his young movement. His major talent was writing. After organizing a new church he would move on to other cities among the scattered Jews. He then wrote long letters (epistles) back to the places he had just left, addressing the myriad growth pains the young congregations encountered. The problems he addressed were more procedural than theological: First, who can belong to the kingdom? and, second, If Gentiles can belong, by what process are they to be included?

In addressing these procedural concerns, Paul evidenced another talent. He knew how to build a theological foundation under the practical decisions he saw as necessary to ensure the movement's growth.

Other controversies were faced in Paul's writings. This early evangelist gave abundant advice about church organization. He argued strongly for his understanding of the meaning of Jesus' life. Even his personal greetings were carefully constructed, telling modern readers much about the early church. Individuals (and sometimes families) were urged to become followers of the Way. Nonetheless, his central issues reminded highly practical.

Paul did not, as one might imagine on first reading, redefine the religion of Jesus. Instead, Paul restructured the community of faith.

A distinction is important for understanding the concerns of Paul's letters. Since Paul was interested in bringing non-Jews into a Jewish fellowship, he wanted to be guided by the religious law. But those laws, especially the one demanding that male converts undergo circumcision, brought serious complications. So he often insisted that faith in Christ releases people from obligations to "the Law." Did he mean by this that all obligation to every law, both priestly/individualistic and prophetic/social had been washed away? Or did he mean that *rigid, legalistic application* of religious law, no matter the impact on the people involved, was to be avoided? Much ambiguity attaches to the use of the term *law,* as was noted in chapter 2.

A review of material first presented in chapter 2 is in order. Jewish people referred to (and continue to refer to) "the Law" in a variety of ways, depending on the context. In its broadest sweep, "the Law" is the total body of rules that tell Jewish people how to conduct almost every aspect of daily life. Some exacting people have claimed to count as many as six hundred and fourteen such rules in the Hebraic scripture. In other situations, "the Law" is a reference to the Torah, the first five books of the Bible, to which Jews have looked for the most important directives for living. In other settings, "the Law" can refer to summaries of the Law, such as the Ten Commandments, or the shorter summary (Shema): "You shall love the Lord your God with all your heart and mind..." When the topic is very specific, "the Law" might refer only to the particular commandment appropriate to that subject. As was indicated earlier, the English language contains similar ambiguity.

It is important to keep in mind these several uses of the phrase "the Law" as we examine the letters of Paul. When Paul, attempting to make membership in the faith community possible for Gentiles, wrote that we are no longer governed by "the Law," he may have intended to release his readers from the entire Hebraic moral code, or *he may have meant merely to free them from the particular commandment of circumcision in its unloving application.* The way this term is read will make an enormous difference in the modern church's understanding of itself and the relationship of the church to the Jewish community from which it emerged.

Paul the Person

More information is available about Paul than almost any other individual of early religious history. Some of these facts come from the letters he wrote. Other information comes from the book of Acts. Acts was written later, after both Paul and the Synoptic Gospel writers had done their work. The book of Acts itself will be discussed in the next chapter, in the chronological order in which it appeared. Some of its information about Paul will be given here, however.

As in the case of Jesus, the most striking thing about Paul is his Jewishness. He told his readers more about this fact than any other aspect of his history or personality.

He was Jewish, yet his background allowed him to stand astride two cultures—the Hebraic on one hand and the Greco-Roman on the other. He had grown up in Tarsus, a Greek-speaking city whose excellent harbor and land routes had made it a center of international trade. His family were Pharisees (Acts 23:6) of the tribe of Benjamin. (Philippians 3:5) Such a background gave him a remarkably broad view of life. He was a citizen of both Israel and Rome; he spoke both Hebrew and Greek (and, perhaps, Aramaic—twice he used the Aramaic term "Abba" to refer to the Deity (Romans 8:15 and Galatians 4:6). Tarsus was ruled by Rome. Viewing the Empire from that vantage point gave him an attitude toward the Empire quite different from that of the Jews of Jerusalem. While Hebrews of Jerusalem were constantly looking for opportunities to rebel, Jewish families in Tarsus experienced the prosperity, the education, the aqueducts and roads that Roman governors provided.

Paul's early life was further enriched when, at about age 20, he went to Jerusalem to study under the famous educator, Gamaliel. (Acts 22:3) While he was in Jerusalem he apparently became a part of an extremist group of anti-Jesus individuals. He participated in the execution of the first recorded Christian martyr, an evangelist named Stephen. (7:54—8:1)

Because Paul had proven his antagonism to the followers of Jesus, the high priest sent him to Damascus in search of other such followers, with instructions to capture them and bring them to Jerusalem. (9:1–2)

The ninth chapter of Acts records one of the significant turning points in religious history. Along the Damascus road, Saul (the Jewish name he used on most occasions of his early life) encountered the voice of Jesus. He heard himself invited into the very movement he had been attempting to destroy.

After some delicate negotiations to win the confidence of an understandably hesitant group of disciples, Saul, now become Paul, was accepted as part of the movement. The change in name of this new follower was symbolic of what was about to happen to the movement. Its Hebrew heritage was soon to be given less emphasis. Its ties with the Greek world were soon to be strengthened.

Many sermons have been preached, and much has been written about Paul's "conversion." He was, indeed, converted from being a persecutor of the Jesus movement to a participant in that movement. He was not, however, converted from his Jewish faith to a new religion.[1] In his letters he continued to refer to himself as a Jew and a Pharisee. He continued to worship in synagogues.

At the end of the book of Acts is a telling passage in which Paul took four Greek men through a purification ceremony to prove to other Jews that he had not forsaken the Law of Moses and was not ignoring the customs. Having guided the men through the process of purification, Paul assumed them to be fully Jewish and took them into the temple. In this passage Paul continued to see himself as Jewish and worked under the assumption that those who wanted to

---

[1] This point, and others for which this writer is indebted, has been made by Krister Stendahl in his book *Paul Among Jews and Gentiles* (Minneapolis: Fortress Press, 1976).

become followers of Jesus must first become Jewish (though without the full, painful, legal ritual of conversion). (21:17–26)

Travels

Three times Paul journeyed around the northeastern end of the Mediterranean. His procedure in each case was this: He would go first to the synagogue, attempting to persuade his fellow Jews that Jesus had been the expected Messiah. This usually produced only limited results (or else brought open, sometimes violent hostility). In response to this rejection, he would turn to the Gentile population where larger numbers of people responded positively. Thus the question: how to bring non-Jewish individuals into the ongoing community of faith—a community that continued to define itself primarily by its ethnic, Jewish background?

Circumcision and Faith Family Continuity

Circumcision was for Jewish men the mark of their heritage— the sign of the covenant. Jewish Law provided for the conversion of Gentiles into Judaism, and circumcision was part of the prescribed process. Unfortunately, circumcision was a painful and even dangerous (this was long before sterile medical instruments) surgery for an adult male. Paul was faced with a troublesome decision. Should he, a Pharisee whose spiritual life had been nourished by the Law, insist that this particular law be imposed on the people to whom he preached?

The continuity of Christianity with its Jewish roots is here expressed in its clearest form. If Christianity were a new religion, then circumcision would have been no issue at all. The new faith could have established its own membership requirements. The original followers of Jesus were in full fellowship with their Jewish ancestors. By their genes they were descendants of Abraham. The new, Gentile folk in the faith community were forced to find a different point of entry. They were a fulfillment of the statement of John the Baptist: God had been able to raise up children of Abraham from unpromising material. But by what procedure, and with what rationalization, were these people to be brought over the previously high barriers of exclusion?

Peter (the acknowledged leader of the Christian movement before the appearance of Paul) had, at first, resisted the idea of accepting Gentiles into the faith community under any circumstances. He changed his mind after a dream in which he saw all manner of food laid before him. When he refused to eat the food prohibited to people of his faith, a heavenly voice assured him that nothing God had made was to be seen as unclean. Peter then approved of the ministry to the Gentiles; yet he also, later, argued forcefully for keeping the requirement of circumcision.

The first major church fight was over this matter. Conferences were held. Paul was forced to develop a rationalization that would allow converts to be brought in without full application of the ancient Law. He spelled out this rationalization in the letters he later wrote to the emerging congregations—letters that would become part of the Christian scriptures. Paul's solution was later received by the young church as theology. His practical arguments, transformed into theology, emerged as central to the life of the Christian church. Paul's justification for this procedure would have far-reaching implications for the relationship of the followers of Jesus to Jews who had rejected the messianic claims.

Paul the Writer

The congregations Paul set in motion were made up largely of the totally uninitiated. New to Judaism, new to the concept of a messiah, most were even new to the idea of religion itself. It is not surprising, therefore, that once organized, they tended to act in ways Paul never expected. They were vulnerable to opposing points of view. They had little idea how to organize themselves for effective witness and work. Internal arguments were epidemic.

Thus, after Paul had left a community and traveled on, he often received word of the problems of a congregation he had left behind. He would then gather his writing equipment and compose a letter. The letters ("epistles" in the more formal, biblical language) were just that: friendly statements from a caring individual to those for whom he felt responsible. When a congregation had been subjected to what Paul felt was false teaching, he argued his own theological position. When organization was a problem, Paul offered practical advice. When a young church was split by internal disputes, Paul chided its members for immature behavior.

Paul was, by his own judgment, an unimposing person.[2] He was less effective as a speechmaker than he wanted to be. But when he took pen in hand, Paul was in his element. Parts of his letters were, as he indicated, weighty—weighed down by the heavy arguments he felt were required by the seriousness of the issues. Other parts of

---

[2] He gave an unflattering evaluation of himself in 2 Corinthians 10:10.

those letters were friendly greetings. The sensitive ear can even hear a rare note of humor. One letter was a short, personal note about how to receive back an escaped slave.

The New Testament contains thirteen letters that have been attributed to Paul. Scholars, however, have disagreed over which actually came from the evangelist himself and which were products of his followers writing in his name. Seven of the letters probably were the work of Paul: First Thessalonians, First and Second Corinthians, Romans, Galatians, Philippians, and Philemon.

Understanding what Paul put in his letters is key to understanding the continuity of the faith community. It is also a key to understanding how the Christian religion has often been set against its Jewish roots.

1 Thessalonians

First Thessalonians is widely accepted as the first New Testament book to be composed in its present form.

Paul's visit to Thessalonica had been tumultuous. This we know from the account given in the book of Acts. (Acts 17:1–9) Nonetheless, from his letter one must conclude that he had only positive feelings about the place and the people who had gathered to make a church. Some continuing persecution was apparently the fate of the followers of Jesus there, and Paul was eager to commend them for their faithfulness.

A positive, complimentary tone pervades this brief letter. Paul was pleased with the reports that his friends brought him of the progress of this struggling community of believers. Since his primary purpose in writing was to express these pleasant sentiments, little argument of a heavy nature is found in the book of First Thessalonians.

The church at Thessalonica demonstrated how the focus on the new converts' relationship to Jesus could cause arguments to break out. One of these arguments concerned the nature of Jesus himself. On one side of this argument were those who understood Jesus as the Jewish Messiah—the very human individual who stood in the prophetic/social tradition and called people to loving and just relationships. This group remembered that Jesus had encouraged monotheistic worship, as had his religious forebears. The other side emphasized Jesus the Christ—a Greek concept that allowed Jesus to be seen as a personal Savior, somewhat in the priestly/individualistic tradition. The second group was soon making Jesus himself an object of worship.

A clue to the way a writer approaches the nature of Jesus can sometimes be found in the name used to refer to him. Speaking of "Jesus" is usually a clue that the writer relates primarily to the historic person whose parents gave him that name. Speaking of "Christ," or a phrase such as "the Lord Jesus" means that the writer relates primarily to the Savior figure whom faith has elevated into a divine being.

Paul, the first writer of New Testament scripture, had a unique opportunity to lay the foundation for Christianity's understanding of its central figure. Yet Paul was hardly unbiased in this matter. He had never known Jesus the person, the physical son of Mary. He had experienced Jesus only as the risen Christ—the Savior figure who, disembodied, intervened to change his life. It is not surprising, then, to find that Paul, from the beginning, referred to Jesus with terms of high respect, such as "Jesus, the Risen Lord." Once, in the first chapter of 1 Thessalonians, he mentions the name "Jesus" without exalting adjectives. He then embraces the practice of referring to Jesus in highly spiritualized ways.

The antagonism between followers of Jesus and the Jews is mentioned in 1 Thessalonians. Persecution of the young church is attributed to "the Jews, who killed both the Lord Jesus and the prophets, and drove us out" (1 Thessalonians 2:14–15). This must be read with an understanding that it was written by a Jew who had not surrendered his native faith. Paul may have carried some anger against a certain group of Hebrew people within Thessalonica who had forcefully shortened his earlier visit. But that anger is not a blanket condemnation of all Jews, and should never be used to label modern-day Jewish people as "Christ-killers." No matter how many such angry statements can be found in the writings of the early Christian community, the historic fact remains that the Romans, not the Jews, had the power to crucify. Also, only the Romans had the power to persecute first-century Jews and Christians.

First Thessalonians also contains interesting statements about the resurrection of the dead. (4:13–18) Paul's advice on this matter indicates that he believed, as did many of those in the young church, that the final judgment and conclusion of human life was imminent. But some followers of Christ had already died. The major question on people's minds was not *whether* people would be resurrected, but *in what order*. Would those continuing to live at the final day take precedence over those already in the grave? The writer gave his own straightforward solution. At the end of the age a divine trumpet would sound and those who had died in Christ would arise. "Then we who are alive" (Paul fully expected to live to see these events) would join in the heavenly reunion. (4:17)

The remainder of the letter consists of good advice for everyday behavior.

Romans

The order in which the remainder of Paul's letters were written is open to debate. We turn next to the book of Romans, not because it can be proven to be next in chronological order, but because much of the theology of the Christian church has been constructed from ideas found in this letter to the Christians in Rome. Some have argued that this epistle has become more important to Christianity than the teachings or actions of Jesus! Turning now to Romans allows us to place Paul's basic arguments clearly before us.

It is important first to describe the situation in which Paul found himself. He was a Jew who had been employed by Rome to stamp out an irritating group who were followers of a Jewish holy man named Jesus. Paul had led an effective campaign against this movement. Later, when a spiritual encounter caused him to change his mind about this group, he experienced painful guilt over what he had done. Afterward, he came to believe that his calling within his Jewish faith was to tell Gentiles about the Messiah who had appeared. He knew that Jesus had embodied the concept of the Messiah that allowed, through his inclusiveness and his suffering, the doors of the faith community to be opened to people of all nations. The cross and resurrection were conclusive statements that Jesus had been the suffering Messiah who would bring the fulfillment of Judaism by opening it to all the people of the earth, just as Isaiah had described. Therefore he could say to his Gentile friends, "Much more surely then, now that we have been justified by his blood, will we be saved through him from the wrath of God" (Romans 5:9).

As a Jew calling people to follow the Jewish Messiah, Paul's first task was to bring new converts into the Jewish faith family. The laws of his religion had provisions for receiving converts. These laws were exacting. They assumed that only a few people would ever want to embrace this demanding faith. The Law insisted that men undergo the surgery of circumcision—the mark of the covenant as given to Abraham.

Paul knew that if he insisted on the total application of the Law, the number of converts would be small indeed. Paul also wanted his new converts to come into the faith community with status equal to those who had entered it by birth. He knew that circumcision was the *sign* of the special relationship to God, not the cause of that relationship. Abraham had, long ago, received an invitation from God to father a special people. Only later was the sign of that relationship put into his flesh. The Law—that carefully-constructed body of instructions about the conduct of daily life—had been composed in *response* to God's love and was in no way the cause of that love. Abraham, and all the descendants of Abraham, had been chosen by God's grace. Each Jewish child born into that faith community was another act of divine grace.

To insist that Gentiles come into the faith community according to exact legal requirements would not only limit the number of converts, it would also imply that human beings were capable of writing, as it were, their own membership cards in the divine kingdom. Enforcing the complete structure of Law upon the new converts would suggest that they had become parts of God's special family by their own manipulation, whereas those with Jewish ancestry could claim their status on the basis of an act of God's freely-given love. Paul would have none of this two-tiered standing. "Or is God the God of Jews only? Is he not the God of Gentiles also? Yes, of Gentiles also, since God is one; and he will justify the circumcised on the ground of faith and the uncircumcised through that same faith" (3:29–30).

How, then, could non-Jews become a part of a faith community that had previously identified almost all its people by their bloodline? *By faith in what Jesus the Messiah (in Greek, "The Christ") had done.* Paul knew that most of his Jewish countrymen had expected a nationalistic savior who would lead an army and drive out the Romans. Jesus had, in contrast, performed a public ministry that reached out to non-Jews, and had, without resistance, died at the hands of the Romans. The Gentiles' faith in this inclusive/suffering Messiah made it possible for them to be "justified" (a legal term describing the fact that a new possibility is acceptable). Both their faith community and they as individuals had therefore found their fulfillment in this suffering servant Messiah.

It is clear, then, how important the suffering and death of Jesus became in Paul's theology. If Jesus had been the kind of Messiah most Jews were expecting—if Jesus had succumbed to the temptation to seek power among the kingdoms of this earth—then neither Paul's mission nor the conversion of Gentiles would have been possible.

By thus coming into the Jewish tradition by faith in the Christ, the new converts were released from the obligation of circumcision. They also came into the faith community at a status equal with those who were there by birth: both had been received by an act of God's loving initiative. Neither had manipulated themselves into relationship to God.

The more conservative among those who had been born into Judaism were less than happy with Paul's way of bringing Gentiles into "their" faith. They insisted that the legal structure was not subject to division. No one, not even Paul, could pick from among the laws those which he wished to keep and those which he might break. (Fundamentalists of every generation have argued similarly: The Bible must be accepted as a whole; if you imply that one part is less than divinely inspired, the authority of the whole evaporates. Conservative Jews argued thus for the application of the Law.)

So Paul was forced from the first to defend himself against the accusation that he believed in no laws at all ("antinomianism," as it was later called in church circles). He stated repeatedly that he was not setting aside the great body of laws by which Jewish life was regulated—the rules that made life civil and decent and just. Paul argued for a very practical position: "It is not the hearers of the law who are righteous in God's sight, but the doers of the law who will be justified" (2:13). He argued, further, that releasing new converts from their obligation to be circumcised simply increased their obligation to the remainder of the law: "So, if those who are uncircumcised keep the requirements of the law, will not their uncircumcision be regarded as circumcision?" (v. 26). Finally, in one statement, Paul made absolutely clear that his task was not to make a new religion, but to bring Gentile followers of Jesus into the tradition of his own ancestors: "Rather, a person is a Jew who is one inwardly, and real circumcision is a matter of the heart—it is spiritual and not literal" (v. 29).

Paul continually argued his point: A free gift of God had allowed Gentiles to be justified as Jews apart from the full legal requirements. To this point he returned in letter after letter. (His zeal was understandable, for this argument made his entire work possible, and all his Gentile conversions possible.) To those who insisted on the total application of every rule, Paul proclaimed that law kills while the spirit gives life. In the moving argument recorded in the eighth chapter of Romans he began with a statement that theologians have often used as bedrock of their beliefs: "For the law of the Spirit of life in Christ Jesus has set you free from the law of sin and of death"

(8:2). Such statements lead some to conclude that Paul was releasing followers of the Christ from any obligation to the Law as well as from the guilt that follows any breaking of the Law. Such an interpretation has led to the belief that Paul was addressing himself to what Krister Stendahl has called "the introspective conscience of the west."[3]

A more careful and balanced reading of Paul, however, shows that his purpose was not nearly so theological (and certainly not so psychological). His purpose was quite practical: How can Gentiles be brought into the ongoing faith community on an equal plane with those who were born into that community and in a way that will not impose the cruel requirement of circumcision?

The law in this context—the law from which Christians have been set free, is *the specific law applicable to this specific situation.* Setting people free from the law of circumcision does not release them from, for example, the demands of the Ten Commandments! Neither does this freedom sever followers of Christ from other ties to their Jewish background.

Those who wish to separate followers of Christ from the Jewish law are fond of quoting Romans 10:4. In most translations, this is given as "Christ is the end of the law." But "end" is certainly not the only possible translation of the *telos* of the Greek manuscript. The phrase takes on an entirely different coloration when translated, "Christ is the *fulfillment* of the law." In the context of Paul's argument, this second interpretation makes much more sense.

The popular misinterpretation of Paul has been tragic for both Judaism and Christianity. When Paul's task has been seen as theological and psychological, the result has been a radical dichotomy between a supposedly rigid, unfeeling, legalistic Judaism on the one hand, and a free, spirit-filled, gracious Christianity on the other. Neither is an accurate picture.

Judaism is a religion of prophets and laws. It is not, however, necessarily rigid or legalistic. (Some rigid and legalistic individuals appear in every branch of every faith, no less so in Judaism than in Christianity.) It was, after all, Jeremiah who first spoke of a covenant that is written on people's hearts. Second Isaiah described a saving figure who would overcome evil not through angry confrontation but through freely-chosen suffering. When Jesus said that the Sabbath was made for people and not people for the Sabbath, he was

---

[3] Krister Stendahl, *Paul Among Jews and Gentiles*, p. 78.

reflecting the better part of his Jewish tradition.[4] Likewise, his summaries of the Law are lifted, for the most part, from Jewish Scriptures.

Jesus was a reformer who changed the pattern of Judaism without tearing its fabric. As one Jewish interpreter of Jesus has written, "What is characteristic of Jesus is the supreme emphasis he lays on ideas which are present, but less absolutely attested, in ancient Jewish piety."[5]

A similar misinterpretation of Paul can lead to another tragic result. It can lead the Christian to embrace the concept that the Jewish religion, and, by implication, Jewish people, are legalistic and unfeeling. In fact, Judaism has never embraced an unfeeling application of rigid rules. Paul the Pharisee knew this. Jesus knew this. Neither is Christianity a faith without law. Paul argued that the loving thing was to set aside a particular rule *as it pertained to new converts to the Jewish faith.* As any reading of his letters will attest, Paul never released followers of Jesus from the demands of decency, or of the honest behavior and mutual respect that is the basis of the Jewish legal system. At points, such as releasing new converts from the burden of circumcision, Paul lifted the general law of love above some other, more particular law. But many other commandments remain in effect—a point that is especially clear in the middle verses of the thirteenth chapter of Romans.

Judaism and Christianity have become, across the centuries, two different religions. One continues to wait for a messiah who will restore the fortunes of Israel; the other insists that the messiah has already come in an entirely different form from that originally predicted. Their differences, however, are not nearly so radical as has often been trumpeted from Christian pulpits. A careful reading of the total Bible shows that Judaism is not nearly so bound by rules, nor Christianity so free from rules, as has often been assumed.

Paul's defense of his ministry to the Gentiles consumed the first eleven chapters of his monumental letter to the Romans. At that point he altered course and began to give encouragement and advice.

A part of the advice he offered his readers in Rome was that they should obey the secular government, for the government officials were God's agents in establishing social harmony. (13:1–2) This advice—written, in part, to assure Roman authorities that Christians could be model citizens—has become an added burden to modern Christians who live under oppressive dictators. The verse is a clear

---

[4]See Geza Vermes, *The Religion of Jesus the Jew.*
[5]Ibid., p. 35.

example of why it is important to remember the original setting of biblical teachings. This teaching, wed to the devaluing of Judaism that can come from a misreading of Paul, became a deadly instrument in the hands of Adolph Hitler.

As was explained earlier in this chapter, Paul's experience with the Roman government had been quite different from the experience of the Jews living in Jerusalem. No Jerusalem Jew would have advised unrestrained obedience to the government that had engaged in countless acts of cruelty to the Jewish nation.

It is important, therefore, to read any particular teaching of Paul against the background of his larger advice. The law of love must stand above the particular law. Being subject to governing authorities may be the best advice in most situations. There are other situations, however, in which the call of justice is to oppose a government devoid of concern for basic human rights. This principle is very biblical. The prophets made the point with vigor. So, too, did the writer of the book of Daniel, and, much later, the writer of the book of Revelation.

Accepting the Bible as our faith's family album allows modern readers the freedom to make such choices. Paul is accepted as part of our ancestry in faith. Current Christians do not force inerrancy upon him, but insist that his particular advice be judged against the better angels of his merciful side.

The final chapter of Romans consists of greetings to a surprising number of persons in Rome whom Paul knew by name. The last verses consists of a benediction that has echoed through Christian churches across two millennia. (16:27)

1 Corinthians

The church in Corinth was quite different from the church in Rome. Paul felt he had to defend and explain his views to the church leaders that had gravitated toward the Roman capital. He simply had to enforce discipline on an immature congregation in this Greek seaport.

Paul had visited Corinth and helped establish its congregation. Then he went away. Though distances were great, communication in that time was surprisingly effective. Paul, in a new location, received bleak news of the young congregation. Disputes had broken out. Some members of the congregation claimed to be disciples not so much of Jesus but of various early church leaders. These false messiahs, the evangelist was distressed to learn, included Paul himself!

Thus the letter that Paul composed and sent back to Corinth began with a minimum of personal greetings. It moved immediately into a scolding mode. Congregational leaders, he insisted, should focus on Jesus, not on lesser individuals. Paul had not been crucified for anyone! Neither should any other of the early church leaders be subjects of adoration.

The leaders of the early church were common folk. Indeed, the argument proceeded, God had often chosen the weak and humble to put to shame the strong and proud. So the people of the congregation should not be so bold as to think they knew enough to cause divisions.

An incident of sexual immorality captured the writer's attention. (1 Corinthians 5:1–11) He advised discipline: Do not associate with such a one! (One assumes that Paul knew that the rather cruel practice of shunning, still practiced by some sects, was contrary to the life and teachings of Jesus. He must have assumed that the Corinthian congregation, still learning the most elementary facts of faith, was too fragile to try to heal those who had broken the sexual codes. It was another bit of Pauline advice addressed to a very specific situation.)

In the faith family argument over the nature of humankind, Paul came down on the side of human weakness over against those who would proclaim human strength. (1:25–31) He believed all humankind to be in a state of disarray until faith in the risen Christ makes each one right with God. But he never stated this so brutally as did the later church. Those who look to Paul for a doctrine of total depravity will look in vain.

In the fifth chapter, Paul referred to Jesus as "our paschal lamb" (5:7). Here is the first hint that the death of Jesus could be interpreted as part of the system of sacrifices of the priestly tradition of Judaism. The idea will, as we shall see, grow apace.

Instructions in other, more immediate matters followed. In part of these instructions Paul showed that he shared the patriarchal assumptions of his time. He also assumed that Jesus would return shortly and bring human life to a triumphant close. Together these factors caused him to argue, first that women should be submissive to their husbands (even had he been otherwise inclined to do so, he was not interested in working for gender justice in a society that was, he was sure, near its end), and to advise those unmarried to remain in that state unless their sexual drives were unbearable.[6]

---

[6] Teachings about gender issues are found in 1 Corinthians 7 and 11.

The background of Paul's teachings on sexual matters is important. Corinth was a port city. Like most seaports, it supported a thriving trade in prostitution. Prostitutes were identified by their gaudy clothing and often loud demeanors. In advising women to be modest and quiet he was saying, in essence, "Do not be like prostitutes." Against a backdrop of open immorality, Paul was calling the followers of Jesus to a higher sexual ethic. There is no evidence that he intended to design cultural behavior for women for the next two millennia.

One problem that followers of Jesus faced in Corinth concerned meat that had been offered on the altars of idols, then placed in the marketplace for public consumption. Some members of the congregation refused to eat such meat, seeing this as an act of idolatry. Others disagreed. Paul, while agreeing with the second group, advised that all refrain from such meat lest its consumption cause someone to stumble. It was another example of Paul's practicality and his elevation of the law of love.

The unruly Corinthian congregation needed better organization to prevent further disputes. In the twelfth chapter of this letter Paul encouraged them to a division of labor, a division he compared with the various organs of the body working together for the common good. Otherwise, all would compete for the more glamorous tasks. Competition and wrangling had no place in the congregation; instead, he wrote, "I will show you a still more excellent way" (12:31).

The "more excellent way" was the way of love. In thirteen brief verses that make up the famous thirteenth chapter of 1 Corinthians, Paul gave a stunning definition of the spiritual force that binds people to one another. The frequent use of these words in weddings and other romantic settings has given them an ethereal ring. To the contrary, the ideas were composed in response to a very messy situation: a feuding church! Nonetheless, the use of these words in weddings is quite appropriate, for marriages are also very earthly realities! The practical side of this advice, however, must not be lost in the romance.

One chapter later the subject becomes much less romantic. "Women should be silent in the church" (14:34), Paul wrote. This seems to come from nowhere, and completely contradicts the earlier positive things the writer had said about the contribution of women to the life of the congregation. Biblical scholars continue to search for a plausible explanation of words that, if enforced, would place an intolerable burden on women and rob the church of more than half its effective leadership. Jouette Bassler argues persuasively that these words were a "marginal gloss"—comments written into the margins by a member of the Corinthian church and later added to the manuscript.[7] John Bristow points out that the church women of Corinth were likely to be persons who had no experience of group life. The common etiquette of a committee meeting would have been altogether foreign to these formerly housebound individuals. When they came to worship or to church meetings, chaos resulted. To avoid social confusion Paul instructed them to be silent in church and to ask their husbands about procedure when they returned home.[8] For whatever reasons, this advice is obviously tied to a particular time and place.

The final chapters of 1 Corinthians are concerned with advice about speaking in tongues (a practice not helpful to the church, Paul wrote, since no one knows what the speaker is saying!). Other advice concerned the resurrection from the dead (those already dead will be given an imperishable body; those still living when Jesus returns—again, Paul expected to be one of those—will be transformed). Paul finally made an appeal for a collection for the needy in other congregations and closed with an uncharacteristically brief benediction.

2 Corinthians

Paul's second letter to the church in Corinth (most scholars believe there may have been a third that has been lost) has played a lesser role in the development of the faith community.

A significant amount of time had elapsed since the first letter was sent. The scolding of the former epistle must have been effective, for this one was more conciliatory. Paul had moved into his mode of positive reinforcement. He found much to commend in the Corinthian church.

The reader senses that hostility had been growing between followers of Jesus and the Jews who could not believe that Jesus was the expected messiah. Paul compared the Christian hope with what he saw as a lack of hope in Judaism, "not like Moses who put a veil over his face...Indeed, to this very day, whenever Moses is read, a veil lies over their minds" (2 Corinthians 3:13–14). It was the first of what would be many unfortunate efforts by Christian leaders to insist that Jews understood neither their tradition nor their scripture!

---

[7] Jouette Bassler, *The Women's Bible Commentary*. Eds. Carol Newsom and Sharon Ringe (London: SPCK, 1992).

[8] John Bristow, *What Paul Really Said About Women* (San Francisco: HarperSanFrancisco, 1988).

Paul gave a great deal of helpful biographical information in this letter. It was here that he admitted to being unimpressive in his physical being. (10:10) He also reminded the congregation that, by practicing his trade of tentmaking, he had made no financial demands on them. (11:9) He included a list of all the suffering he had endured on their behalf. (vv. 2–28) Without any information about the specific nature of the affliction, he mentioned an illness, a "thorn in the flesh" that he could not cure and that he felt was given to keep him humble. (12:7) He closed with the usual exhortations and expressions of personal concern.

Galatians

The book of Galatians was written not to an individual congregation, but to a group of churches in the area of Galatia. It was designed as a group message to be passed around among the congregations. Thus it lacks some of the personal comments that begin most of Paul's epistles.

Apparently some of the young churches that Paul had helped launch had been visited by other evangelists. These other preachers insisted that all males undergo circumcision as evidence of their conversion into the Jesus branch of the Jewish community. Paul was incensed. He reiterated the basic arguments contained in the letter to the Romans. (Or, perhaps, the letter to Rome was a return to arguments made to Galatia; it is not clear which letter came first.)

To buttress his arguments, he first had to establish his authority. The message he preached had been received not from other humans, but from God, he insisted. His only contact with other apostles had been with Cephas (Peter), who had told him the story of Jesus.

The depth of the dispute over keeping the full Law of the Jews is revealed in the letter to Galatia. Paul had taken the role of missionary to the Gentiles (the uncircumcised). Peter was chief missionary to the Jews (the circumcised). Peter continued to believe that all males who became followers of the Christ (and thus became Jews) should undergo circumcision. To the Galatian churches Paul wrote: "When Cephas (Peter) came to Antioch, I opposed him to his face, because he stood self-condemned...so that even Barnabas was led astray by their hypocrisy" (Galatians 2:11, 13). Strong words, these, among followers of the gentle Jesus!

Two concepts are emphasized more strongly in the letter to the Galatians than in the letter to Romans. One is freedom; the other is maturity. The two are closely connected. Using a familiar metaphor,

Paul insisted that the Galatians had been adopted into the faith family. The converts had been brought into the family as children. As they grew in faith, they would receive the privileges of adulthood. The laws of Moses had been, to use another metaphor, like a child's custodian whose task was to keep the child safe and to deliver her to the security of her schoolroom. Maturity meant freedom from this custodian; it meant the ability to make moral decisions on one's own.

Paul was convinced that those who preached the necessity of circumcision were quite immature, unable to moderate the demand of Law with the more tender prompting of love. They failed to understand that the door to the community of faith had been opened by Christ's role as a universal suffering servant. Mature people, in contrast, were free to set aside the rigid application of the Law *in that particular circumstance* and to receive persons on the basis of Jesus' death. He could write: "For freedom Christ has set us free" (5:1).

But to what degree had this freedom been granted? The old question was again before the reader. Did this mean that the follower of Christ had no obligation at all to the Ten Commandments, or to the laws concerning treatment of strangers, or to the prophets' call for justice? Not at all. Maturity always meant willingness to accept appropriate rules and to abide by necessary restraints. Paul played his hand in this regard by his comment: "Once again I testify to every man who lets himself be circumcised that he is obliged to obey the entire law" (v. 3). Refusal to undergo circumcision was, then, a declaration of freedom. A few sentences later the writer insisted that the reader not use this freedom for self-indulgence. Just afterward he gave a list of those practices that the free individual, the one led by the Spirit, will avoid. This is not absolute freedom from rules; this is responsible freedom in applying rules.

Often in church history Paul has been interpreted as if he dealt in extremes: Either we are slaves to all the Hebrew rules, or else we are entirely free from all of them. Dealing in absolutes was not Paul's weakness; this was the immaturity he saw in his opponents. They wanted to apply rules no matter the cost. Paul had no desire to abolish the body of Law that had nourished him in his growth and guided him through adulthood. He wanted to moderate it and apply it with loving discretion. As the book of Acts would later make clear, Paul remained a Jew and a Pharisee until the end of his life. He argued in his letters for responsible freedom exercised within a supportive body of believers. Sadly, he has often been interpreted as if he were the apostle of an unrestrained license that could lead to an attitude attributed to Voltaire: "God will forgive me; that's His business." Absolute freedom, no matter how much it is couched in terms of grace and love, leads eventually to a breakdown of discipline and to ever new inquisitions and holocausts. Absolute freedom from the Law is also freedom from any social conscience. Paul the Jew—Paul the apostle of responsible freedom—knew this well.

The book of Galatians ends with some practical advice, one more swipe at the hypocrisy of those who insist on circumcision for all, and a concise benediction.

Philippians

This letter was written from prison. Just which prison he was in at the time is not clear, since Paul, over the course of his ministry, inhabited several.

Some themes from other letters were further developed in this comparatively brief effort. Like the church in Corinth, this congregation seemed to have had more than its share of conflicts. Thus unity became a central theme. As in other letters, Paul felt compelled to defend himself against those who preached the keeping of the total Law, thus dividing the congregation.

Redemptive suffering was another theme that received special attention. This was much on Paul's mind as he spent his days in jail. What had happened to him had been beneficial. "My imprisonment is for Christ; and most of the brothers and sisters, having been made confident in the Lord by my imprisonment, dare to speak the word with greater boldness" (Philippians 1:13–14). Somewhat later, the writer, apparently using a hymn or early statement of faith, instructed his readers to share in the sacrifice made by their Savior.

> Let the same mind be in you that was in Christ Jesus,
>   who, though he was in the form of God,
>   did not regard equality with God
>   as something to be exploited,
>   but emptied himself. (2:5–7a)

In these words a "higher" christology was developing. Actually, one uses the word "developed" here with some caution, since the chronological order of this letter is difficult or impossible to establish. In some of his writings Paul seems quite aware of the humanity of Jesus. In other writings Paul depicts Jesus as the eternal Christ, already present with God before his short sojourn on earth. In which order Paul developed these themes is not clear.

The level of anger at those who preach circumcision had increased. Circumcision was no longer simply a rite that every Jew should have accepted as normal; it was now a way to "mutilate the flesh" (3:2).

The letter ended with thanks for the support Paul had received from the church in Philippi. His words of encouragement were phrased with unusual beauty: "Finally, beloved, whatever is true, whatever is honorable...think about these things" (4:8). Personal appreciation was expressed for the work of two women who "have struggled beside me in the work of the gospel" (vv. 2–3). One suspects from hints such as this that women were quite important in the leadership of the early movement. The social setting and Paul's own patriarchal thinking combined to discourage too strong an acknowledgment of this crucial role for women.

Philemon

The final of the seven letters that probably came from Paul is only twenty-five verses in length. It manages, nonetheless, to generate a great amount of interest.

Again, Paul wrote from prison. He addressed the words to an old friend, Philemon. Philemon was a wealthy Christian and an owner of slaves. One of his slaves, Onesimus (the word means "useful") had escaped, been captured, and placed in the same jail as Paul. Two significant things happened between Paul and his fellow prisoner. First, Paul learned that Onesimus had escaped from his friend, Philemon; second, he told Onesimus about Jesus, prompting Onesimus to convert. Since he had also been the instrument of Philemon's conversion, Paul considered himself the father in faith of both men—which, of course, made Onesimus and Philemon brothers in faith!

Onesimus then agreed to return to Philemon (a brave thing to do, since the punishment for escaped slaves could be severe). Paul sought to lessen the danger by sending along a letter. The letter told of Onesimus' commitment to the faith and of Paul's personal fondness for him. "I am sending him, that is, my own heart, back to you" (v. 12). Legally, Onesimus returned still as Philemon's slave. In Paul's mind, however, Onesimus' acceptance of the faith radically changed the relationship. "No longer as a slave but more than a slave, a beloved brother—especially to me but how much more to you" (v. 16).

Not a word of judgment had been said about the institution of slavery. This fact raises an interesting point. One of the reasons it is often difficult for people to identify the continuity of the Bible story is the near total absence of any discussion of social justice from the last Hebraic prophet to the writing of the Synoptic Gospels. In Paul's letters, concern for the structures of the larger community seems to receive no attention at all. It is not surprising, then, that Paul is sometimes misinterpreted as starting a new religion, an individualistic one with little relation to the justice-centered tradition that had come before.

The absence of social witness in Paul is explained, as discussed earlier, by the fact that Paul's purpose was practical, not theological. In dealing with Onesimus, however, Paul, perhaps inadvertently, took a prophetic role. He did so in an oblique, yet highly effective way. A slave was returned in a new role—as a brother in Christ. Philemon, in a secular setting, may have been able to justify the idea of owning another human being. But Paul changed the context. How, now that both were followers of Jesus, could one claim ownership of one's brother?

Paul had struck a powerful blow against the entire institution of slavery! The fact that he may have done so unintentionally may be a further indication that a divine Spirit intrudes in unexpected ways into the pages of scripture.

Other Letter Writers

Six other New Testament epistles are attributed in some translations to Paul. Intense study of these letters, however, suggests that they were the work of later writers who were followers of Paul and who wanted to extend his influence. Writing in the name of a more famous person was common practice at the time. Those six letters, mostly elaborations on the themes of Paul, were written later, after the four Gospel accounts of Jesus had been put into circulation. They will be discussed in chapter 10.

Summary

Paul, the apostle to the Gentiles—the Jew sent to convert the non-Jew—is responsible for at least seven books of the New Testament. When the context in which they were written is ignored, and when they are read as treaties on theology and psychology, these letters can appear to have created a new religion—a religion quite unconnected to its Jewish roots. Ironically, this new faith would also have had little relationship with Jesus of Nazareth. When the letters are taken in their larger context, however, it becomes clear that Paul was dealing with a thoroughly practical matter within the continuing story of Judaism: how to bring non-Jews into a new branch of the Jewish community. To accomplish this goal Paul called for a mature and flexible application of the Jewish Law. Thus these letters continue the unbroken story of the faith community. Jesus, the inclusive/suffering Messiah, destroyed the walls that had previously surrounded the faith family so that people of all nations could enter. Paul wanted to ensure that these new faith family members entered not by some formula of human design but in the same way that Abraham had earlier entered: through an act of God's grace. The dividing wall of hostility had been broken. New children of Abraham had been created by a nonbiological route. The fulfillment of Israel's promise had been glimpsed in a now borderless community of God's people.

9

The Community Records the Stories of Jesus

As indicated in an earlier chapter, a special young man had lived in the island community. His skills, the effective way he had taught those skills, and finally the manner of his death had caused many extensive changes in the community.

Because of an unusual set of circumstances, however, no one had written down any of his teachings or anything about his life. After people of the island community had been scattered across cities of the mainland, letters which seemed to interpret the young man's life circulated. But the stories of the man himself continued to exist only in brief, written fragments, or in accounts transmitted by word of mouth. As explained earlier, this was largely because many people expected the ocean would rise and wipe out their community. No one was motivated to write down anything.

Several decades went by. The sea had not risen as expected. Many people had fled to other cities, but the basic community was still intact. The island itself was occupied by mainlanders and under constant threat of destruction.

Some of those who had known the special young man began to die. Others who had known him, or who were close friends of people who had known him, determined that the time had come to record the story of his life and his major teachings.

The first person to write composed a brief overview of his life and teach-ings. This seemed satisfactory for a few years. But new questions arose about the meaning of that life. Some persons wanted to modify or correct impressions left by the letters that had circulated concerning the special individual. Additional fragments of stories and sayings appeared. A sec-ond, then a third writer told the story, each using the work of the first and adding the unique material he had been able to gather. These three manu-scripts were similar; their differences simply enriched the impression that a reader could receive of that special person.

Additional decades passed. Then, on another part of the island, a fourth writer began to work. He lived closer to the mainland and was strongly influenced by the way mainlanders wrote and the way they framed their ideas. By the time this man took his pen in hand the oral stories about the special person had begun to change. The newer stories presented him as less an earthly person and more a person of the sea. His relationship to the sea had taken on a mysterious, spiritual quality. This fourth writer made use of some of the information used by the first three; his interpretation of that material, however, was quite different.

Taken together, these four writers gave a fascinating, but sometimes con-fusing, picture of the special person who had lived in their unique community.

Those who considered themselves followers of the young man were espe-cially delighted to have this written information even though the informa-tion left many questions unanswered.

The followers of Jesus were nearly overwhelmed by success. Their growth had begun to strain their organizational resources. Peter had encouraged Jews to accept Jesus as the expected Messiah. Paul had, in the name of this same Messiah, converted thousands of Gen-tiles into the faith community. The movement had gone international. As Paul's letters attest, it was also bruised by controversy.

But who was this Jesus, the Christ, to whom so many were giv-ing their allegiance and for whom some were giving their lives? Paul had written his version of what that life meant, giving almost no information about the person, Jesus, and the companions and events that, woven together, made up that life. Yet interest in the details of Jesus' activity remained high. People told their friends about Jesus, and circulated the few stories and collections of teachings that had been written. Yet no organized account of his life and death existed.

This relative vacuum of information created fertile soil for serious disputes.

Mark

Approximately thirty years elapsed after the death of Jesus before a person—one whose identity has been quite lost to history—accepted the task of giving an account of the life of Jesus. Church tradition has said that the person was named Mark, a friend of Peter's, who learned most of his information from Peter himself. However, the negative light in which Peter is shown in several passages of the book makes this an unlikely explanation. Nonetheless, it is helpful to be able to refer to this writer by a name: Mark.

Mark's short name was appropriate. He had a habit of brevity. His description of Jesus was designed to give basic information. The stories are told in a rapid, almost breathless, fashion. "Immediately" ("straightway," in the poetic language of the King James Version) is one of Mark's favorite words. One event is described and "immediately" another event follows.

Central Themes

The writer of Mark began his account when Jesus was an adult. Neither the manner of his birth nor the progress of his growth through childhood was considered important enough to record. What was important was a central theme. That central theme was announced in the first sentence: This is $\tau o \upsilon \ \epsilon \upsilon \alpha \gamma \gamma \epsilon \lambda \iota o \upsilon$, the good news! Mark then established the continuity of his account with what had come earlier in Jewish history. John the Baptist, forerunner of Jesus, fulfilled a role described much earlier by Isaiah.

Jesus was baptized and *immediately* he was driven into the wilderness to be tempted by Satan. (The particular events of the temptations are not described by Mark. Matthew and Luke would later add additional detail.) Jesus returned to call his first disciples; quickly he was teaching, preaching, and healing. The reader hardly has time to settle into one scene before the landscape changes.

Another important theme is announced early. "The kingdom of God has come near" (Mark 1:15). Twenty more times in this brief biography the phrase "kingdom of God" occurs.

The phrase "kingdom of God" implies royalty and organizational power that moves from top to bottom. Not so, as Jesus, in the book of Mark, described the divine kingdom. The will of God is to be obeyed by those in the kingdom. Obedience, in the kingdom of God, is to be absolute. This obedience, however, is motivated not by fear but from choice. When two disciples applied for positions of authority in the emerging kingdom, Jesus brought them up short. Where God rules, matters of human, tyrannical power will be set aside. Those who wish to be great must learn to be servants of all. Jesus is the example: He "came not to be served but to serve" (10:41–45). People whose primary concern is pushing others around make poor candidates for the kingdom. The better way to enter is with the attitude of a child. (vv. 13–16)

Half the book of Mark has elapsed before any mention of the Messiah is made. Peter confessed that he believed Jesus to be the Expected One. Jesus instructed all present to keep this a secret. He immediately indicated that his understanding of this role was one of suffering. (8:27–33) Again, the kingdom was not to be built by force from the top down; it was to be built by compassion and by self-chosen suffering.

The energy of Jesus and his disciples was at first directed only at people who shared his ethnic identity. A significant turning point came when Jesus was confronted by a Gentile woman whose daughter was mentally ill ("possessed by a demon," in the first-century worldview). Jesus at first brusquely dismissed this non-Jew, insisting he had no mission to her. But when she persisted with admirable humility, he could no longer resist. The daughter was healed. The ethnic walls that had defined the kingdom of God had been lowered.

The walls of the kingdom were lowered further by other conflicts. A disagreement with the Jewish leadership allowed Mark to alert the reader that Jesus would reach beyond Israel. Parables such as that of a vineyard owner (12:1–12) whose tenants reject even his own son are clear references to the Jewish nation. (Some of the parables of conflict were probably edited and made stronger by the later church in its struggle with particular Jewish leaders.) Note, however, that the conflict that Mark describes is always with a group *within* Judaism, never with Judaism itself.

The Law and the Kingdom

Remembering that the Gospel of Mark was written *after* Paul's letters, it is important to see where Jesus (as Mark described him) stood on the issue of obeying the Jewish Law. Paul had seemed to lessen the force of those commands. Yet Jesus, when approached by someone asking how eternal life might be inherited, referred the questioner to the Ten Commandments. Only when the man affirmed his faithfulness to these did Jesus push him further. Assured that the questioner had kept the basic Law, Jesus then insisted that he give his wealth to the poor. This was more than the man wished to pay, even for eternal life. (17–22) This story was typical of Jesus' attitude toward the ancient rules. He did not set them aside, but pushed them deeper and made their application broader. In an earlier situation Jesus' attention had been called to blood relatives who were nearby; Jesus replied that his real family was made up of those who *do* the will of God. (3:31–35)

Mark's writing can be seen as a clarification of the message of Paul. In his letters, Paul said almost nothing about Jesus the person or of Jesus' moral guidance. Mark filled a significant part of this gap. In doing so, Mark addressed potentially serious misunderstandings. As was pointed out in the previous chapter, Paul's concern was highly practical: how to bring non-Jews into the faith community without putting the males through the indignity and pain of circumcision. To accomplish this goal he found himself arguing for a softening of a legal system that many wanted to apply with rigidity. The evangelist had wanted a mature and compassionate application of the Law. What is found in the Gospel of Mark strongly supports and clarifies this point. Jesus, as Mark described him, taught his followers that they had an enduring obligation to the Law, lovingly applied.

The Nature of the Messiah

In Mark the reader finds a strong interest in Jesus the human being. Nonetheless, the supernatural was not ignored. Jesus' mighty works and his penetrating wisdom leave no doubt that this was a unique person on a unique mission. But he was a person, nonetheless intimately tied to a very earthly existence.

The reader encounters in Mark a strange ambivalence about the uniqueness of Jesus. Time after time Jesus, after some mighty act that would lead his friends to suspect that he was the special person expected from God, told those friends to stay quiet about what they had seen.[1] The reason for this secrecy should be clear to those who recall that the Jewish scripture writers had disagreed over the nature of the expected savior. The word "messiah" carried heavy baggage for the first-century Jew. The majority expected a new King

---

[1] See, for example, Mark 7:36, or Mark 8:30.

David whose military strength would rid the nation of their Roman captors. Jesus clearly did not want his followers to think in those terms. Only after the crucifixion could these friends say "Messiah" and know they were speaking not of a new all-conquering king, but of a new Suffering Servant. Therefore, any hint of Jesus as Messiah was to be kept quiet until that time.

In contrast to the spiritualized messiah we meet in some other New Testament writings, Mark presented Jesus as a very earthly, completely human individual. Mark did not hesitate to depict Jesus as driven by the engine of human emotion. Later, the writer named John would depict Jesus as if he were a puppet whose strings were manipulated by God. Not so in this first Gospel story. In Mark's Jesus we encounter human nature that is motivated and controlled by internal forces, both mental and emotional.

Mark's emphasis on the internal life of Jesus in no way diminishes Jesus' strength. Unfortunately, a cultural norm of modern life is that emotions are somehow inferior motivations. Yet we know, also, that a lack of emotions leads to a mechanical, colorless existence. One outstanding psychiatrist has described the emotion-free existence as "the pattern of noncommitment."[2] No one who reads the story of Jesus as told by Mark would say that Jesus reflected in any sense a pattern of noncommitment. On the contrary, his was a life of *full emotional commitment to the realities he valued.* More than any other Gospel writer, Mark lays open the raw humanity of Jesus. When some rigid individuals attempted to prevent him from curing a person's withered hand on the Sabbath, he "looked around at them with anger; he was grieved at their hardness of heart" (3:5). Perhaps because people of faith are unaccustomed to the idea of a Jesus influenced by emotion, the translation at this point is weaker than in its original form. The Greek for *anger* is ὀργή, which, every other time it appears in the New Testament, is translated "wrath." Here Jesus is pushed by two of the strongest emotions known: wrath at their hardness of heart and grief over their lack of the milk of human kindness. Another time Mark records that a work of healing was motivated by pity (1:41), and on yet another occasion Jesus "began to be very distressed and troubled" (14:32).

Emotions are only part of what Mark tells about the complexity that was Jesus of Nazareth. The Gospel writer was dedicated to the fact that Jesus was unique, the promised Messiah. Some have

---

[2] Andras Angyal. *Neurosis and Treatment: A Holistic Theory* (New York: The Viking Press, 1982).

calculated that Peter's identification of Jesus as the expected one is at the exact center of the work, the fulcrum on which all else is balanced. (8:29) Pushing this simile further, Mark manages a precise balance on the two sides of this fulcrum. On the one side was the Messiah. This Messiah possessed special powers of persuasion and healing—powers to change human existence. On the other side, this same Jesus participated fully in human life. No puppet on divine strings, this Jesus of Nazareth was a person sent from God to share in the struggle and the ambiguity of earthly existence.

Crucifixion and Resurrection

Mark's account of the crucifixion and resurrection are characteristically pithy. After increasing conflict with those who would make Judaism rigid and unfeeling, Jesus was turned over to the Roman authorities. He was crucified in complete disgrace, with a common criminal on each side. Even in his agony he reached back in memory to the liturgy of the temple that had nourished his life. He identified with one of the psalmists who had cried out: "My God, my God, why have you forsaken me?" (15:34). Jesus died and was buried in the tomb of a wealthy follower. On the morning after the Sabbath three women arrived at the tomb and found it empty. They were assured that death had been unable to hold him. Understandably terrified, the women rushed to tell the disciples. The original ending of Mark was quite brief: Jesus sent his followers to both east and west with news of eternal salvation. The early church probably added the longer ending used in many modern translations.

Matthew

Another decade passed. Mark's work was, during this period, the only written account of the life of Jesus. Peter and other disciples were busily encouraging Jews to accept Jesus as their promised Messiah. Gentiles were joining the movement in large numbers.

Jews had many questions. What was the evidence that Jesus was the one they were to expect? Obviously this saving person had not driven the Romans out of the Holy Land. The fortunes of Israel remained in a pitiful state. What kind of Messiah was this, after all?

To address the questions raised by the Jewish audience, a person that church tradition has known as Matthew wrote another account of the life of Jesus. Matthew was, without question, a Jew himself. In his writing he addressed the questions raised by those who shared his ancestry.

Sources

A comparison of the material in the Synoptic Gospels[3] leaves little doubt that Matthew had the Gospel of Mark before him as he wrote. He quoted almost all of it, occasionally making editorial changes. In addition he seemed to have taken advantage of another scroll that contained teachings and stories. This added material (which Luke would also use) has been dubbed the "Q Document." Finally, he seemed to have had some unique information from yet another source, which has come to be known as the "M Document." Matthew alone would consult this third source. With these materials at hand, he began to write to his Jewish friends.

Jesus as Messiah

His first and most important task was to establish a basis for the claim that Jesus was the Messiah expected by the Jewish people. Matthew attacked the problem in his opening words: "An account of the genealogy of Jesus the Messiah" (Matthew 1:1). Traced through Joseph, the genealogy was given in three sets of fourteen generations. Since both seven and three are sacred numbers (doubling the seven still leaves it sacred), a message is clear. Jesus held a special place among the chosen people.

Genealogies are part of what makes scripture reading difficult for many people. No count has ever been made of the people who have come enthusiastically to the New Testament determined to read it from cover to cover, only to turn away when they find themselves confronted with sixteen verses of "so-and-so was the father of such-and-such." Indeed, these long sections are hardly appropriate for public or bedtime reading. Yet they serve a very real purpose. When the Bible is seen through the metaphor of a family album, the genealogies become the sinews that hold the drama together. Dry though they are, they identify the entire Bible for what it is: the story of a community.

Having established the Jewish ancestry of Jesus, the writer (or editor: the first two chapters of Matthew may have been a later addition to the work) turned to establishing the uniqueness of Jesus. He recounted how Jesus was born of a divine father and a human mother. In order to make the virgin birth a fulfillment of an ancient

---

[3] A book of Gospel parallels is helpful in establishing the relationship between the first three Gospel writers.

prediction he lifted a quotation from Isaiah, taking the passage out of context,[4] and used the Greek translation of Isaiah (from a Greek translation known as the Septuagint), since the term "virgin" is not in the original Hebrew. Such sleight of hand would be judged ethically questionable today; it was considered quite acceptable in the first century.

Of the four Gospel writers, only Matthew tells of the holy family's flight into Egypt to escape the murderous fury of Herod. Any Jewish reader would recognize the significance of this event. Matthew's story of Jesus was recapitulating the story of a Jewish nation that once had endured slavery in Egypt. Jesus' later forty-day stay in the wilderness was a reminder of the forty years the Hebrews spent as nomads in the desert. In the fourth chapter Matthew carefully established that Jesus' first mission was to the offspring of Abraham. The place-names given there were a clear signal to all who knew the region. Jesus carried on his work of teaching, preaching, and healing in the historic promised land. Peter, probably the disciple most known and trusted among the Jewish people, identified Jesus as the expected one. (16:16)

Throughout the material, the writer quotes verse after verse of ancient scripture to establish the authenticity of Jesus as the expected Messiah. His thoroughness in making this tie with the past probably earned his book the place of honor at the beginning of the New Testament.

One of the questions Jews must have been asking at that time was why so many Gentiles were becoming followers of Jesus. Most of Matthew's readers expected that the Messiah would belong exclusively to the people of Israel, would restore their fortune and prestige, and would drive away their enemies. The followers of Jesus seemed to be quite unconcerned with fortune and prestige, and they were bringing outsiders into the community of faith in unorthodox ways. No wonder many Jews rejected the Messianic claims of the early church!

Jesus and Non-Jews

The question of how the message of Jesus was related to people of other nations was faced early by Matthew. According to this second Gospel writer, Jesus, from the very beginning, belonged to more

---

[4] See the discussion of this passage in chapter 4.

than the Jews. The first people to recognize the importance of the birth of Jesus—the first to pay him homage—were a group of Gentile astronomers. The writer of Matthew quoted John the Baptist scolding the Jews who felt that their genetic inheritance was enough to win a special place in the concern of God: "God is able from these stones to raise up children to Abraham" (3:9). A major theme of the remainder of the book is the evolutionary shift from exclusive attention to the Jewish community to a challenge to go to all the world with the gospel message. Important motivators of that shift included a military man of Capernaum who evidenced a remarkable trust in Jesus. (8:5–13) A few chapters later Jesus confronted equal persistence and faith in a Canaanite woman. Four times in the latter chapters of his work, Matthew uses the phrase "the nations" when describing those who might receive Jesus' message.

Along with the positive pull of the faith-potential he found among the Gentiles, Jesus experienced the negative push of rejection from many Jewish people. By the time the book of Matthew was written, deep hostility and serious anger had developed between Gentiles and Jews over the significance of Jesus. Matthew reflected that unpleasant relationship. Jesus was depicted as exasperated by the intransigence he encountered in certain sects of Judaism. Scribes and Pharisees were shown as rigid in their application of Jewish tradition and Jewish Law. Jesus' anger spilled out in uncharacteristically harsh language.[5] It is important to note, however, that this anger was directed at overly-structured groups within Judaism. Matthew never suggested that Jesus engaged in any blanket condemnation of Jewish people. Quite the contrary, Jesus described his mission as one of renewal of Jewish faith, and he offered membership to Jews in the imminent kingdom of God.

Keeping the Law

Matthew established a clear position concerning some of the new family arguments that had arisen in the faith community. One such argument was over a question that many followers of Jesus were asking at the time: to what degree was the follower of Jesus obligated to keep the Jewish Law?

Paul had spoken: The Law could, he insisted, be modified to allow Gentiles to join without circumcision. Mark had reminded his readers that the Law, as a whole, had not been nullified. Matthew

---

[5] See especially chapters 19, and 21—23.

put the question in an ever broader form: what is the relationship of the followers of Jesus to their Jewish heritage?

Matthew, as has already been noted, saw the life of Jesus as a recapitulation of the history of the nation. The continuity of the Jesus movement with Jewish heritage was not in doubt. In the matter of the Law itself, Matthew left no question about where Jesus stood on this issue, or where he as a writer stood. The Sermon on the Mount, a collection of Jesus' sayings that described the values and moral duty of the citizen of God's kingdom, interpreted several of the Ten Commandments, affirming each and driving it deeper into the human psyche. Murder and adultery were seen as evils of such magnitude that they must be attacked in the motivational stage, before action had become a possibility. Swearing falsely was forbidden, but so, too, was swearing of any sort. "Do not think that I have come to abolish the law or the prophets; I have come not to abolish but to fulfill" (5:17). No clearer statement could have been made to those who had misinterpreted Paul!

The argument was pursued in other passages. Whereas Paul and his followers had implied that simply by calling on the name of Jesus one could be saved, Matthew quoted Jesus: "Not everyone who says to me, 'Lord, Lord,' will enter the kingdom of heaven, but only the one who does the will of my Father in heaven" (7:21). Lifted from Mark was the quotation about Jesus' family: "For whoever *does* the will of my Father in heaven is my brother and sister and mother" (12:50, italics mine). In another story shared with Mark, Jesus was approached by a man who asked what he must do to have eternal life. Jesus' first answer was disarmingly clear: "If you wish to enter into life, keep the commandments" (19:17).

Jesus and the Marginalized

On another matter in which some corrective of Paul may have been taking place, Jesus associated freely with those whom the remainder of society had rejected. Paul and those who wrote epistles in his name had encouraged the young church to rid itself of undesirables, fearing that the immature Christians would be contaminated by the evil of a few. Jesus, however, risked loss of his own social standing by eating with "tax collectors and sinners" (9:10). When criticized about this, Jesus simply replied that those who are well have no need of a physician.

Another issue that Paul had left in a state of confusion was the role of women in the life of the growing church. At one point he had seemed to abolish all distinctions between the roles of male and female; at another point he apparently attempted to silence women altogether.

Matthew argued for gender roles more just than those of his patriarchal society, yet not fully equal. He included story after story in which women were strong, self-reliant individuals. Peter's mother-in-law was healed, then rose immediately from her sick bed to give compassionate service to Jesus. (8:14–15) A woman suffering from a long-standing hemorrhage was shown to be a model of faith. (9:20–22) In one parable, a woman took the role of God, mixing leaven in a lump of dough until all was leavened. (13:33) In the drama of crucifixion and resurrection, the only persons who embodied persistent bravery and commitment were women. (27:55—28:10) Yet, in most of these situations, the women expressed their strength in roles defined by men. Full gender equality had not yet been envisioned.

Human or Divine?

The most pressing faith family argument at the time of Matthew's writing was the question of the nature of Jesus himself. Was Jesus the fully human servant of God that the Jews had expected as their Messiah, or was Jesus' humanity an illusion? If he was other than human, did that make him the spiritual being that the later church would worship as the second person in the Trinity?

As has already been noted, Paul had little interest in the historic person named Jesus. Envisioning Jesus, the Christ, as the way through which Gentiles could be brought to a saving knowledge of God gave the evangelist a decided bias toward a spiritual nature for the Christ. Mark, in contrast, had told of a very human individual who could be moved by the emotions of compassion, anger, or grief.

Matthew's view of Jesus was much closer to Mark's than to Paul's; yet a decided shift had taken place in the decade that elapsed between the composition of the two Gospels. The shift is subtle; less emphasis is given to Jesus as the earthy man of strong emotion. On the other hand, Matthew makes little effort to spiritualize Jesus.

Matthew's primary purpose was to show that Jesus had been the Messiah promised to the Jews. To achieve this goal he turned to external things. He showed little interest in Jesus' inward experiences. One incident was particularly telling. As Mark described Jesus healing a leper, he recorded that Jesus acted out of pity.[6] Matthew, however, edited the story so that all emotion was wiped away. It

---

[6] Compare Mark 1:41 with Matthew 8:2–4.

was simply a mighty act to show the power of God working in the Messiah. In another telling shift of emphasis, Mark had recorded that Jesus had been powerless to perform mighty acts in the face of faithlessness and hostility. In Matthew's editing of the same story Jesus was no longer powerless, but *chose* not to perform miracles among those whose beliefs were weak.[7] The foundation for a later spiritualizing of Jesus was being systematically laid.

In Matthew the word "worship" was used for the first time in relation to Jesus. The wise men of the birth story do more than show their respect: they "fell down and worshiped Him" (2:11, NKJV). After Jesus was seen walking on water and calming a storm, "those in the boat worshiped him" (14:33). The writer thus tossed an explosive word into an already-simmering situation. The Jewish establishment was by then quite disturbed by the Jesus movement. Matthew was writing to Jews. The strong Jewish emphasis on the oneness of God would never have allowed them to worship anything other than the one Creator. In using the word *worship* in relation to Jesus, Matthew was telling his Jewish audience that they must make a significant change in their understanding of God if they were to become followers of Jesus. A turning point had been reached.

Luke

Matthew had written to address questions raised by Jews. A few years later someone undertook the same task on behalf of the Gentiles. Tradition says this person was a physician (because the healing stories are told with knowledgeable detail). His name, again according to tradition, was Luke, a Gentile friend of Paul mentioned in some of the epistles. The same person wrote both the Gospel of Luke and the book of Acts.

Sources

This third Gospel writer had before him all of Mark (almost all of which he used), the "Q document" (which he shared with Matthew), and some unique information that has come to be known simply as the "L document." In this later manuscript are some of the Gospel's most beloved parables, including the good Samaritan, the prodigal son, and the unjust judge.

---

[7] Compare Mark 6:1–6 with Matthew 13:54–58.

Destruction of Barriers

Luke's major task was to assure Gentiles that they had a legitimate claim to a place in the kingdom of God. Yet he was clear about the fact that Gentiles were joining a faith community that previously had been exclusively Jewish. Jesus' ministry was portrayed as a continuation of the prophetic tradition of his own people. As Luke presented it, another major part of Jesus' effort, however, was to lean upon the ethnic barriers until they fell open, admitting all God's people to the banquet which God had prepared.

Social barriers in general, and not just ethnic barriers, fell in the wake of Jesus' potent love. Luke included women in his accounts, not just as objects of Jesus' concern but as movers and shakers of the new movement.[8] Others who had been excluded by society, such as the poor, lepers, tax collectors, prostitutes, and other sinners were welcome in the company of the Master.

Luke's primary task was to show that Jesus, the faithful Jew and the expected Messiah, was the one who opened the door of the kingdom to non-Jews. A secondary, but still crucial goal, was to show his friend Theophilus, probably a Roman official, that Christians were law-abiding citizens from whom Rome had nothing to fear.

The birth stories[9] set the tone. Both John the Baptist and Jesus were shown to stand in the prophet tradition. Both would have a role in restoring the former strength (a spiritual strength) of Israel. John was destined to "turn many of the people of Israel to the Lord their God" (Luke 1:16); God would, through Mary's son, "[bring] down the powerful from their thrones, and [lift] up the lowly" (1:52). The theme of justice was clear. All Jewish rituals concerning the birth—and later his visit to the temple at age twelve—were carefully observed. Yet Gentiles as well as Jews were to be embraced within the expanding circle of justice. When the elderly Simeon saw the infant in the temple he joyfully announced that he had lived to see "a light for revelation to the Gentiles and for glory to your people Israel" (2:32).

Whereas Matthew had traced Jesus' ancestry back to Abraham, father of the Jewish nation, Luke traced it back through a genealogy that extended to Adam, father of humanity. (3:23–38) In introducing

---

[8] For a different view of the role of women in the book of Luke, see Mary Rose D'Angelo, "Women in Luke-Acts: A Redactional View," *Journal of Biblical Literature,* 109 (1990), pp. 441–461.

[9] As in the case of Matthew, the birth stories of Luke might be argued to be an addition by another editor.

John the Baptist, Luke gave a longer quotation from Isaiah than had Matthew, ending with the words, "and all flesh shall see the salvation of God" (3:6). Thus the stage was set for inclusion of all people in Jesus' ministry.

Prophetic Role

Events in chapter 4 of Luke again establish that the roots of the Jesus movement are firmly in Jewish soil while its branches reach far beyond the nation's boundaries. To enforce this point Luke carefully set the stage for the story of Jesus' return to his home in Nazareth, just as the editor of a family album might place an impressive frame around a pivotal event. As described in chapter 7, Jesus, having completed his preparations, was ready to begin his public ministry. He returned to his hometown, to the people who had watched him come to maturity, to announce his life work. During worship he was handed the scroll of Isaiah and invited to read from it. He chose a passage of beauty and power:

> The Spirit of the Lord is upon me,
> because he has anointed me
>   to bring good news to the poor.
> He has sent me to proclaim release
>   to the captives
>   and recovery of sight to the blind,
>   to let the oppressed go free,
> to proclaim the year of the Lord's favor.
>   (Luke 4:18–19)[10]

"Today," he added, "this scripture is fulfilled in your hearing." It was a remarkable thing for a young man from an obscure village to say. Jesus had placed himself in the unique tradition of the prophets of Israel—those who had challenged the power of kings and insisted on justice for all. He expected that his ministry would have special concern for those who had been pushed to the margins of existence.

The townspeople were at first impressed—pleased with the sense of mission possessed by this young man they had helped form. Jesus, seeing that they continued to have little understanding of what he was about, began to speak more forcefully. His task was not to make his former neighbors feel good. Indeed, his task, as Luke would allow it to unfold, was not limited to the wounds of his own nation.

---

[10] The quotation is from Isaiah 61:1, 2; and 58:6.

Jesus reminded his townspeople of the times in their Hebraic Scriptures when God reached beyond the national boundaries to feed a hungry widow in Sidon and to cure a Syrian leader. The people were not fond of such talk. Like others of their nation, they wanted a messiah who would focus exclusively on their own troubles. His former neighbors tried to push him off a cliff. But Jesus apparently stared them down: "He passed through the midst of them and went on his way" (4:23–30).

The parable of the good Samaritan, which only Luke recorded, established as did no other single story the legitimate role of all people in the kingdom of God. Like Mark and Matthew, Luke missed no opportunity to stress that membership in the kingdom is reserved for those who *do* the will of God. The context of the story was a question raised by a lawyer (a passage that Mark and Matthew also included): how might he inherit eternal life? A favorite Jewish summary of the Law was suggested: "Love the Lord your God with all your heart, and with all your soul, and with all your strength, and with all your mind; and your neighbor as yourself."[11] Jesus commended this answer, only to hear himself challenged again. "Who is my neighbor?" To this second question Jesus responded with a story of a member of a rejected group, a Samaritan, who stopped and gave aid to a badly wounded traveler. The traveler's nationality was not identified; he was simply a member of the human race. The action of the Samaritan was contrasted with that of two Jewish religious functionaries who passed by on the other side of the road, perhaps fearing defilement by a dead body.

The remarkable part of Jesus' story is not the insight that true neighborliness can be measured in kindly deeds—a definition that might have been given by any compassionate teacher. The remarkable fact was that Jesus, himself a member of an occupied nation, would lift up as role model a member of an even more oppressed group. Even in this setting, people were to be judged not by the source of their genes but by the nature of their compassionate actions. (10:30–37)

Samaritans would become role models in another story related by Luke. Jesus encountered ten lepers who pleaded from a distance for mercy. Mercy was all they could ask, for lepers were forbidden from any contact with noninfected people. Jesus sent them to the

---

[11]The Shema, taken, as noted earlier, from Deuteronomy 6:4, and quoted in Luke 10:27.

priest, but they found themselves cured on the way. One returned to express appreciation. He was a Samaritan. "Was none of them found to return and give praise to God except this foreigner?" (17:18)

The Gospel of Luke closes with the risen Christ sending his disciples out to preach "repentance and forgiveness of sins" to "all nations" (24:47). Clearly, the writer of this Gospel wanted to show that all people are candidates for places in the kingdom of God.

The Role of Women

Luke similarly attacked the social traditions that left women in subservient roles. The drama of Jesus' birth provided both Elizabeth and Mary with leading parts. When Jesus was brought to the temple as a baby he was witnessed by two elderly people, one male, one female, whose lives had been extended so they could see the Savior. Simeon was simply "righteous and devout," but Anna had the high status of a prophet (2:25–38). Both recognized the importance of the child in Mary's arms. Likewise, only Luke told of a grateful woman who anointed Jesus with expensive oils. (7:36–50) Most remarkable of all, Luke mentioned, almost as an afterthought, that women were not only among his close followers, but were a significant part of the movement's financial support. (8:1–3) As in the other Synoptic Gospels, only women showed enough courage to be a consistent presence at the cross. These same women had, next to Jesus himself, the place of honor in the drama of resurrection. They were the first to discover that death had failed to have its usual, final word.

Other Marginalized Persons

The poor were also, in Luke's account, provided a special place of honor in the kingdom. Whereas in Matthew one of the Beatitudes read, "Blessed are the poor in spirit," Luke simplified it to "Blessed are you who are poor" (6:20). Luke expressed special interest in Jesus' relationship to a disabled beggar (18:35–43); he included Jesus' teaching that banquets should not be given for those who can invite you in return, but for those such as the poor, the crippled, and the blind, who cannot reciprocate. (14:12–14)

Estrangement from "The Jews"

Concerning one group, however, Luke was less compassionate. The Jews themselves were the target of the writer's anger. The growing estrangement between Jew and Gentile by the latter third of the first century is evident in Luke's Gospel. Since he was writing after the Romans had destroyed much of Jerusalem in 70 C.E. he could insist that this was divine retaliation for the Jews' rejection of Jesus. (19:41–44) This put Luke in the unfortunate role of Job's friends—placing the blame on the victim. The story of the crucifixion was told in a way that placed minimum blame on the Romans (who alone had the authority to crucify) and maximum blame on Jewish authorities. While Mark and Matthew had located the conflict more precisely between Jesus and subgroups within Jewish culture, Luke laid blame indiscriminately on "the Jews."[12] Twice Luke put into Jesus' mouth words about Jews being people who slay their prophets (11:47 and 13:34), which, with some reinforcement from later church writers, could easily lead people hostile to Jews to label them "Christ-killers."[13]

The situation of the Christians at the time of Luke's writing helps us understand why he wrote about Jews as he did. The persecutions were beginning, and every follower of Jesus was in serious danger from Roman authorities. Writing to "most excellent Theophilus," likely a person of some political contacts and power, Luke sought to minimize any sign of conflict between Jesus and the Roman authorities. Blaming the crucifixion on the Jewish people suited Luke's purpose (although one wonders if Theophilus, who must have known the legal code, was convinced).

Yet Luke did record one event that casts a more pleasant light on a part of the Jewish community. Through all four gospel stories the hostility between Jesus and the Pharisees seems unrelenting. Once, however, a Pharisee, having learned that Herod was trying to find Jesus to do him harm, warned him in time to allow him to escape a dangerous region. (13:31)

The occasional blanket condemnation of Jews is a tragic flaw in a writer who otherwise gave the world a picture of Jesus who was entirely open to all and compassionate toward those most in need of love.

---

[12] The writer of the Gospel of John would later adopt this same stance and expand upon it.

[13] In actuality, few nations have shown much patience toward those people who challenged them to high moral standards. The Jewish people have a remarkably tolerant record in this regard, including extraordinary tolerance of the prophets who insisted that even the monarch live up to the nation's highest principles.

Other Family Arguments

Jesus, as portrayed by Luke, took stands on other issues which his ancestors in faith had debated. One was the nature of God. The reader of this Gospel is exposed to a view of God that is warm and compassionate in the extreme.

"Compassionate" does not equal "soft." Luke repeated some parables of Matthew, such as the parable of the talents, which implied that God expected people to respond appropriately to divine love. Discipleship would be hard, Jesus assured his followers. (12:4–12) But the difficulties were not the fault of God. When told about a group of believers who were attacked and killed by Pilate's men during a service of worship, Jesus took the opportunity to assure them that God would not set such an event in motion to cause punishment. Be on guard that you do not bring such things on yourselves, he warned them, but also avoid blaming such tragedies on a loving Creator. (13:1–5)

God is, in Luke's account, generous. Though people must suffer for their allegiance to Jesus, God will care for them, even more than God cares for birds and plants. (12:22–31) Citizens of the kingdom are obliged to do acts of compassion, yet the kingdom itself is not something people can build; it is a gift of God. (v. 32)

The parable of the prodigal son gives the clearest view of the warmth of Jesus' understanding of God. As explained in chapter 7, this story is a dramatization of a father who is reckless in generosity and willing to forgive at considerable cost to himself. This kindly man, whose concern for his wayward son far outweighed his concern for his own reputation, was Jesus' (and Luke's) vision of the divine nature. Many Israelites continued to insist that God was an autocratic Being whose dignity was easily bruised. Both Sadducees and Pharisees envisioned God as a rigid taskmaster for whom the least bending of a sacred law would bring instant punishment. But Jesus, in this story that only Luke records, laid before us a God with a very different character and agenda. That vision of God was one of Luke's major contributions to the faith community.

Another family argument, one that had intensified with the effort to bring Gentiles into the faith community, concerned the obligation of Jesus' followers to the legal code of Judaism. Paul, as has been pointed out previously, had loosened but not lifted that obligation. Both Mark and Matthew had written more favorably of the legal code.

The Jesus of Luke's Gospel, like Paul, would reject any idea of a God who insisted on rigid application of rules. Nonetheless, Luke recorded incident after incident in which Jesus affirmed a commitment to ethical living. John the Baptist was the first to address the issue. Those baptized asked what they should then do. John replied that the newly baptized should practice generosity, honesty, and other forms of basic justice. (3:10–14) To a question about how to achieve eternal life, Jesus first referred to a summary of the Law, then to the practice of compassion. (10:25–37) When a voice from a crowd shouted blessings on his mother, Jesus responded that blessings were more appropriate to those who *do* the will of God. (11:27–28) In one strange passage, Jesus seemed to release his friends from the Law, only to reinstate a particular law in the next breath. (16:16–17) Actually, these seemingly contradictory sentences simply amplify previous comments about the kingdom being a gift. People cannot force their way into the kingdom through moral behavior; once in, however, they cannot escape their ethical responsibilities.

The Nature of Jesus

On the matter of the nature of Jesus, Luke's view differed little from that of Matthew. Despite the tenderness of stories such as the prodigal son and the good Samaritan, Luke treated the emotions of Jesus with great restraint. He gave few clues to Jesus' feelings about those who came to him for healing; neither did he describe the inner reaction of Jesus toward the characters who populated his parables. While Matthew and Mark told of Jesus' being "distressed and troubled" in Gethsemane, Luke described only the surface events.

While Luke decreased slightly the emphasis on Jesus as human, he made no effort to match this by an increase in Jesus' unique, divine nature. The birth stories of Luke are no more miraculous than those of Matthew. The shepherds who come to the manger do not worship the baby as did the wise men. Instead, they return to their fields praising God. (Luke 2:20)

Summary

Luke had been guided by the purposes established in his opening sentences. He had written to a Gentile, one "most excellent Theophilus." To this Gentile, and all other non-Jews who read this document, he gave assurance that no one was more welcome in the kingdom of God than they. God had revealed, through the Messiah named Jesus, that God was the creator and sustainer of all people and that the love of God was biased toward those whom society had marginalized. The second implicit purpose in writing to Theophilus was to assure him and others of the Roman government that followers of Jesus were not a political threat.

In the second purpose, Luke was apparently less than fully successful. The writer soon found himself composing a second document written to the same Theophilus. The second book described the activities of those who became followers of Jesus. It was named, appropriately, The Acts of the Apostles.

The Acts of the Apostles (The Book of Acts)

The book of Acts was written by the same person who composed the book of Luke. Comparing the first verses of the two volumes makes this clear. The second story picks up after the account of Jesus' life. The disciples watched as the resurrected Jesus was taken away from them (this story is repeated at the end of Luke and the beginning of Acts, like the highlights of the previous episode in a television series are repeated to reorient the viewer).

The disciples then returned to Jerusalem, to an upper room (similar to that in which they had celebrated Passover with Jesus before his death). In that meeting they chose a successor for the betrayer, Judas, and were about to discuss their next actions. All this took place on the fiftieth day following the resurrection; thus the name, Pentecost. Significant in the eyes of Jewish believers, it was also essentially fifty days after the celebration of Passover.

With no warning at all, their next action was thrust upon them. They experienced the presence of God so vividly that they could describe it only with phrases such as "tongues of fire." They began to communicate with one another in ways which, a few minutes earlier, would have been incomprehensible.

They immediately recognized the impact of this strange event. They would not be alone in their special mission. A divine Spirit would be their companion and guide. In response to this marvelous knowledge they rushed into the streets of Jerusalem and began to tell anyone who would listen about their experience.

Jerusalem was an international city, with traders passing through from many nations. Many of the foreign visitors were Jews, part of the scattering of the nation that had taken place over the past centuries. An unusual number of foreign-born Jews were in the streets at that time. They had come to celebrate the Feast of Weeks, a one-day Jewish festival that closed the harvest season (see Exodus 34:22). (Even Pentecost, which most followers of Jesus assume to be a uniquely Christian celebration, has deep Jewish roots!) The disciples thus found themselves speaking to a polyglot group—"Jews from every nation under heaven." The writer described a miracle in which they were able to speak the languages of all those in the streets that day.[14] Peter spoke for the group. He quoted the scriptures that predicted the coming of the Messiah. Some three thousand people became the church's first membership class!

Luke very carefully described the street scene on this Pentecost. When he wrote, the disciples of Jesus still saw themselves as a Jewish group, and were not ready to tackle the question of non-Jews. Yet the task before them was to create a community that had no national boundaries. Luke cleverly accomplished his task through an international group of Jews. This was both historically likely and symbolically powerful. A new reality was born. The direction was set. The faith community had broken out of its former walls.

Mission and Conflict

The other early chapters of Acts were written to affirm that the disciples were authentic carriers of the mission of Jesus. They had the power to heal. They preached with effectiveness. The writer made another point about the followers of Jesus: they were not a collection of isolated individuals, despite the fact that they had made solitary decisions to join the movement. They were a community, bound by strong bonds of commitment and concern. So strongly were they linked that they pooled all their material possessions, distributing those possessions to each member according to need. The communal system broke down quickly when one couple tried to cheat, but the point had been made: the followers of Jesus were in this together. The social justice concern of the prophets was still operative. The new Christians were committed to one another's welfare, and by their fellowship witnessed to the realities of justice and peace.

The compassionate works of the disciples naturally drew public attention. Fearing that such power as these people possessed might

---

[14] Persons of the scientific age might prefer to think that the emotions of the disciples became an international language, communicating the importance of what they had encountered.

be put to destructive use, officials imprisoned some of the leaders. This simply gave them an opportunity to witness in a different setting.

Not all survived their captivity. A disciple named Stephen refused to be cowed by his arrest. He defended himself vigorously. He was convicted, nonetheless, and was stoned. Watching the execution with approval was a Roman official of Jewish ancestry named Saul.

Jesus and Non-Jews

Telling the story of Stephen gave Luke an opportunity to reestablish the Jewish roots of the new movement. When accused of blasphemy, Stephen gave a long sermon that traced the roots of the Christian movement from "Abraham our ancestor" through the entire history of the Jewish people. Clearly, Luke, in writing the book of Acts, was not attempting to establish a new faith but was claiming the high ground of the ongoing community of faith.

After Stephen's death the church in Jerusalem came under persecution and the followers of Jesus were further scattered.

The first non-Jewish convert to be recorded in Acts was an Ethiopian eunuch. The disciple Philip interpreted the scriptures to him, and the eunuch accepted Jesus as Messiah. He was baptized and sent on his way—the only time in the New Testament when someone is brought into the faith without immediately being attached to a community of faith. Nonetheless, two important truths had been announced: First, the new movement would have no racial barriers; and, second, it was possible to allow non-Jews to become part of the faith tradition that had produced Jesus without forcing those people to undergo all the legal requirements of conversion.

A Lighthearted Story

Not all scripture is as sober-sided as most readers assume. Occasionally the writer of the book of Acts evidenced a surprising sense of humor. The preaching of Jesus as Messiah had brought conflict with that part of the Jewish community that expected a nationalistic, powerful leader in that role. Thus, hostility sometimes followed Peter's preaching. He had occasional, extended stays in local jails. On one such occasion (in Antioch) the local church began to pray for Peter's release. While they prayed an angel visited the evangelist and brought him out of prison. Peter immediately went to the house where the faithful were praying for his release. When he presented himself at the door, the people could not believe it could be he. Peter was in jail, they insisted. The person pounding at the door must be some supernatural being. They then went back to praying for Peter's release! (Acts 12:1–17) Thus did the writer poke fun at early Christians who prayed fervently but expected no results. Another funny story concerned a sermon by Paul in a crowded room. One individual had to climb into the frame of an open window to have a place to see and hear. The sermon went on too long! "Eutychus, who was sitting in the window, began to sink off into a deep sleep while Paul talked still longer" (20:7–12). (Was this the first worshiper to sleep through a Christian sermon?) The unfortunate Eutychus fell three stories to his death, but was quickly revived by the power of the disciples.

From Peter to Paul

The action in the early chapters of the book of Acts takes place in Jerusalem. The leading character is Peter, who had become the acknowledged leader of the disciples. At the beginning of the ninth chapter, a rather abrupt shift takes place. Saul, soon to be renamed Paul, takes center stage. The action leaves Jerusalem and moves into the world of Greek people and Greek thoughts. Peter and the Jerusalem disciples fade into the background after chapter 12. The remainder of the book is concerned with Paul and his journeys around the Mediterranean.

The middle chapters of the book of Acts give a vivid, blow-by-blow description of the first significant church fight. That fight was over the question of how to bring non-Jews into the previously all-Jewish community of faith. Two men of enormous stature led this struggle. Peter, the leader of the mission to Jews, first insisted that non-Jews should be excluded altogether. Later he would allow them in, but only after the males had been circumcised. Paul, who had been given the leadership of the mission to Gentiles, argued persuasively that not only should Gentiles be admitted, but that they should admitted without undergoing circumcision.

Peter was brought halfway to the view of Paul by a dream recorded in the tenth chapter of Acts. In that dream an array of foods was placed before him. He refused to eat those that his tradition had declared unclean. A divine voice rebuked him; "What God has made clean, you must not call profane" (10:15).

The dream convinced Peter that Gentiles were legitimate candidates for membership in the faith community. No human being, created in the image of God, could be labeled "unclean." The matter of circumcision, however, remained in dispute.

Peter's dream related to an ancient concern. In the book of Leviticus certain laws had labeled people who behaved in what was perceived as unacceptable ways as "unclean." The dream was a way of saying that in the new faith family that had been touched by Jesus, *people could not be dismissed from divine concern because of anything in their essential nature*. The dream, then, took a very different position from that of the Code of Holiness. The Code of Holiness, a series of laws beginning in the seventeenth chapter of Leviticus, was described in chapter 3. In these laws, people were either acceptable or unacceptable. No middle ground existed. Women during their menstrual cycle were said to be unclean, as were men who touched them. Lepers were described as unclean. Certain sexual practices caused people to be unclean. As Third Isaiah pointed out, people who were unclean were helpless to do anything to restore themselves to relationship with God. (Isaiah 64:6–7)

Peter's dream implied that followers of Jesus are released *from those laws relating to cleanliness and uncleanliness, and from the system of sacrifices needed to restore the unclean*. The legalities from which we are released are priestly/individualistic. This, however, leaves fully intact the body of prophetic/social laws—those that call for decent individual behavior and communities constructed in justice.

Travels

The remainder of the book of Acts describes the travels of Paul the missionary. Near the end of the book, he returned to Jerusalem, partly to use that setting to prove his status as a Jew in good standing. As the book of Acts ends, Paul was imprisoned once more. Using his status as a Roman citizen, he appealed to Caesar. This meant a trip to Rome. The trip was an adventure, complete with storm, a winter stop on a remote island, and an opportunity to witness to the crew and other passengers. Luke, the writer, leaves Paul in Rome, where for two years he celebrated his relative freedom in fellowship with others followers of Jesus. The book of Acts has an unfinished feel at its end. This is appropriate, for the story of the Acts of the Apostles is still being composed.

John

Many Differences

Moving to the Gospel of John means breathing a different atmosphere. What had been immediate and earthy in the three previous descriptions of Jesus becomes, in John's account, eternal and spiritual.

John was the last of the four Gospel writers whose work was accepted into the biblical canon. Much had changed in the twenty years or more that had elapsed since Luke's Gospel began to circulate. Two unpleasant problems that Luke had faced had, in the intervening time, become worse. One was persecution; the other was the estrangement between the followers of Jesus, who were by the time of John mostly Gentiles, and the leaders of the Jews.

Another shift was occurring. Those who had known Jesus in the flesh were either dead or elderly. Those who knew him only through reports of his mighty works and his resurrection were moving into positions of church leadership. Thus a gradual but persistent transformation was taking place: the church was moving from remembering Jesus as a human being, the expected Jewish Messiah, to seeing him as the Christ. The Christ was the one in whom the Eternal Spirit lived uniquely and who was thus able, through his sacrificial death, to be the Lamb of God who took away the sins of the world. In other words, we see in John the completion of a process in which Jesus the Jewish Messiah is transformed into the Christ, the second person of the Trinity. The human being of Mark's account, compelled by human thoughts and passions, had become the divine messenger, motivated only through the promptings of divine guidance.

Moreover, by the time of John's writing, the followers of Jesus were primarily Gentile. Most Gentiles lived and had their being in the world of Greek thought and language. Hebrew concepts and Hebrew language belonged primarily in the past.

These two realities, a shift from the historical Jesus to the spiritualized Christ, and the movement from Hebrew to Greek concepts ensured that the estrangement between Jews and Gentiles would be exacerbated.

John seemed to have worked with different sources than did the other three Gospel writers. He included some of the same stories as did the others, but in a radically different order. The Synoptic writers put the cleansing of the temple in the final week of Jesus' life; John placed it near the beginning of Jesus' ministry. (John 2:13–22) John included other events, such as Jesus' attendance at a wedding (2:1–11), and the washing of the disciples' feet. (13:1–16) The Synoptic writers described Jesus' public ministry as taking place outside Jerusalem, with his only adult visit to that holy city occurring the week of his death. John, on the other hand, depicted Jesus as making several visits to Jerusalem.

One other difference is found in the Gospel of John: storytelling is less important. Matthew, Mark, and Luke filled their scrolls with the parables of Jesus. John, by contrast, emphasized more formal teaching.

Prologue

It is fitting, then, that the Gospel of John began not with story but with poetry. The famous prologue (1:1–18) set the mood of the work and established its important themes.

First, Jesus was described as an eternal being. Completely disembodied at first, he shared with God in the work of creation. This Word—this Logos—this means of divine communication—took on flesh and lived among us. The Synoptic Gospels tended to see Jesus as the leader who pointed his followers toward God. In John, Jesus was a divine presence who was himself an object of worship. It was a small step for the early church to say that John's Christ, having completed his brief time on earth, had returned to be with God as the second person in the Holy Trinity.[15] Accompanying this different understanding of Jesus came a shift in the locus of salvation. No longer were people saved within this present world. Salvation, in John's view, meant being transformed into a realm of eternity.

The second of John's themes to appear in the prologue was the increasing hostility between Jew and Gentile. "He came to what was his own, and his own people did not accept him" (v. 11). Others did accept him, and were given "power to become children of God" (v. 12).

A third clear message of the prologue was that membership in the community of faith was no longer associated with blood lines, but was a free gift of God offered to all who accepted the saving power of Christ. "But to all who received him, who believed in his name, he gave power to become children of God, who were born, not of blood or of the will of the flesh or of the will of man, but of God" (vv. 12–13). Later in John's writing Jesus would tell a Pharisee named Nicodemus that he must be born from above, this time of the water and the spirit. Obviously his first birth counted for nothing in

---

[15] This claim was made by the early church after the writing of scripture. The doctrine of the Trinity is not described in any systematic way in the Bible.

getting him into the kingdom of God. Spiritual rebirth, not ancestry, would win divine approval. (3:1–5)

A fourth theme grew naturally from the third. The Law—the group of commandments that define the way of life of the Jewish people—had been set aside. On this the prologue took the same position as the more extreme followers of Paul (whose writings will be examined in the next chapter). John perceived a radical separation between the former way of the Law and the new way of accepting the saving power of Christ. "The law indeed was given through Moses; grace and truth came through Jesus Christ" (1:17). Ethical living played an insignificant role in the Gospel of John. This is not to imply that John invited his readers to dissolute living. Morality was simply outside his purpose.

The remainder of the Gospel of John is largely an elaboration of these four themes.

The Christ

In dealing with the nature of Jesus, John wrote and thought much more like a Greek than a Jew. John carefully developed the idea that Jesus was the Christ. In John's view Jesus was more than a Jewish Messiah; he was a divine being who was an appropriate object of worship. Unlike the first three Gospels, John keeps no secret about Jesus' special mission; from the beginning Jesus himself described his role as the one who was coming to "proclaim all things to us" (4:26). Again in contrast to the Synoptics, the Jesus of John's Gospel did not wait for someone else to recognize his role, but claimed that role from the beginning in bold ways. "Before Abraham was, I am," he declared to a questioning group of Jews. (8:58)

Scattered throughout the Gospel of John are texts in which Jesus used similes to describe his mission. In these "I am" proclamations Jesus made claims such as, "I am the bread of life...I am the gate...I am the good shepherd...I am the resurrection and the life... I am the true vine" (in order, 6:35; 10:9; 10:11; 11:25; 15:1). No Jewish Messiah would have made such claims for himself: the concept of Messiah was of one who pointed beyond himself to the reality of God. The Christ of John's Gospel points to *himself* as a carrier of the divine nature. Two summary statements of the role of Christ in John's Gospel are disarming in their simplicity, yet absolute in their impact: "The Father and I are one" (10:30), and "No one comes to the Father except through me" (14:6).

The trend already noted, away from Jesus as an earthly person driven by human emotion and toward one who responded only to divine commands, gathered speed and continued in the Gospel of John. One story is an exception: Jesus was motivated by inner feelings when his friend Lazarus died. In this account Jesus was described as loving Martha; her sister, Mary; and their brother, Lazarus. When he was confronted with Lazarus' death, he wept. Apart from these two brief glimpses into an inner life, Jesus' emotional life, as depicted by John, is flat. One can note the steady movement away from the moral demands of an earthly Jesus toward a spiritualized Christ who would become the Lamb of God taking away the sins of the world. From a Jesus who challenges us, the train of biblical thought moves relentlessly toward a Christ whose suffering saves us apart from any effort of our own.

From Prophet to Priest

Comparing the opening chapters of John with the opening chapters of Luke shows the radically different direction in which John is taking the reader. Following the introductory material, Luke took Jesus into the wilderness where Jesus wrestled with the temptation to allow his miraculous powers to become the basis on which people were won to the kingdom. In particular, he resisted the temptation to turn stones into bread. In John, by contrast, Jesus opened his public ministry by attending a wedding where his miraculous powers *do* become the basis on which his reputation spread. In particular, he transformed water into wine. In Luke, the temptation story was followed by Jesus' return to Nazareth, where he attended worship and read from the prophet Isaiah. Thus he placed himself in the prophetic tradition. In John's Gospel the wedding scene at Cana was followed by a story of Jesus' cleansing the temple. This concern for proper temple behavior placed him in the priestly tradition. Clearly John had in mind a corrective to, if not a radical reorientation of, the view of Jesus given by the Synoptic writers.

Tensions with Jews

The shift to Jesus as an object of worship guaranteed that the second theme would appear: the increased tension between the followers of Jesus and the leadership of the Jewish community.

The Jewish concept of monotheism was deeply offended by Jesus' claim of oneness with God. Adding fuel to this already-raging fire,

Paul had released Gentiles from any obligation to circumcision—
the sign of the Jewish covenant. Either of these would have been
sufficient to incense traditionalists within the Jewish community.
Tensions rose. It is easy to imagine the way misunderstanding piled
on misunderstanding, and hostility was added to hostility in a vicious cycle of tragic proportions.

In the Gospel of John one of the first signs of conflict came with
a Sabbath healing—a story taken from the Synoptic Gospels. In the
discussion that surrounded this event the Jews (note the lack of any
distinction: all Jews seem implicated) took issue with Jesus' use of
the term "Father" for the deity, stating that this made Jesus equal
with God. (5:1–18)[16]

Conflict with Jews was also commonplace in the Synoptic Gospels. Yet in John a different level of hostility is reached. Mark, Matthew, and (to a lesser extent) Luke usually were careful to point out
that Jesus had disagreements with particular groups within the Jewish community—especially the more rigid scribes and Pharisees. In
John, however, the conflict was with Jews in general. Also, the conflicts were much more intense. In the first incident recorded, a simple
disagreement over whether it was appropriate to heal on the Sabbath became cause for capital punishment. "For this reason the Jews
were seeking all the more to kill him" (5:18). Even the Jews who
were followers of Jesus were painted with the same angry brush:
"Then Jesus said to the Jews who had believed in him...'I know that
you are descendants of Abraham; yet you look for an opportunity
to kill me'" (8:31, 37).

John seemed to miss no opportunity to show that Jews in general hated Jesus. One situation seems especially forced. Jesus told
his disciples that he would not attend a sacred Jewish celebration—
the Festival of Booths—because "the Jews" were trying to kill him.
He went, later, incognito, and listened as people discussed him. "Yet
no one would speak openly about him for fear of the Jews." But
who were these people discussing him at a Festival of Booths, if not
Jews? (7:1–13) In another case Jesus was quoted in a way that seemed
to make the Jews the source of Christian persecution. "They will put
you out of the synagogues. Indeed, an hour is coming when those

---

[16] It could be argued that this encounter is manufactured, since it is unlikely
that Jews would object to Jesus' use of this term. No conflict over this term is recorded in the Synoptics; Psalm 103:13 and Jeremiah 31:9, along with other Hebraic
Scriptures, refer to God as a male parent.

who kill you will think that by doing so they are offering worship to God" (16:2). The blame for the crucifixion was placed entirely on the Jews. "Then he [Pilate] handed him over to them [the Jews] to be crucified" (19:16). All this, despite the fact that the Jews were not, at the time, in control of their own political destiny and had neither the power to persecute another group nor the legal right to administer crucifixion.

Increased anger moved in both directions. Jesus, also, was depicted in John as an irate combatant. Though a Jew himself, he spoke of the Jewish faith as if it were impotent in bringing genuine salvation. "*Your* ancestors [note how Jesus here seemed to separate himself out from his Jewish lineage] ate the manna in the wilderness, and they died" (6:49, italics mine). In another place Jesus was quoted as saying of his own spiritual ancestors: "All who came before me are thieves and bandits" (10:8). In a confrontation in the synagogue, Jesus insisted to his hearers, "unless you eat the flesh of the Son of Man and drink his blood you have no life in you" (6:53). No words could have been designed that were more offensive to a Jewish audience than these, given the Hebraic aversion for touching dead bodies and drinking blood in any form.

Yet, despite this growing separation between the followers of Jesus and their Jewish ancestors in faith, John could not hide the fact that Jesus was Jewish and remained so until his death. Jesus was faithful to the celebrations that were central to his people's liturgical life: Passover (2:13–25), the Festival of Booths (7:1–13), and the Festival of the Dedication. (10:22–30) In one remarkable phrase that runs counter to the sentiment of much of the remainder of the book, Jesus said to a needy woman, "for salvation is from the Jews" (4:22).

John was writing to a young church that had already become largely Gentile in membership. New rituals of the church were emerging—rituals quite different from the former Jewish festivals. The split in the faith community had caused numerous wounds. In explaining those wounds John left material that must be read in its context, as otherwise it offers fuel for continuing Christian hostility toward brothers and sisters of the family of faith.

Included by Grace

Two other issues were less developed in John, yet had major significance for followers of Jesus. On one issue John fully agreed with the material already written by Paul; on the other John went considerably beyond Paul.

In the first of these, John seemed to agree with Paul that all who were accepted into the family of God (John seldom uses the term "the kingdom of God") entered only as a result of God's gracious love. People cannot earn their way into divine favor. Neither can one claim a place in the family simply because of genealogy. Biological birth counts for nothing. One must be "born from above" to enter the company of the saved (3:3). Nor does the manner of one's life, the degree of one's ethical faithfulness matter. "True worshipers will worship the Father in spirit and truth" (4:23).

Thus an important debate within the faith community continued. The prophets would not have been pleased with John's position; they had insisted that seeking justice was more important than proper worship. The writers of Chronicles, Ezra, and Nehemiah, however, would have applauded!

On a closely related issue, that of the process of salvation, John moved beyond Paul. He made a radical separation between salvation by the grace of God on the one hand, and any ethical considerations on the other. Paul had relaxed the Law pertaining to bringing individuals into the faith community. John not only stressed that salvation is always a result of the grace of God, he seemed to have set ethics aside altogether.

Only the prologue deals with the issue of morality directly, and it has already been quoted: "The Law indeed was given through Moses; grace and truth came through Jesus Christ." John includes no other discussions around this dichotomy, and that lack of material is a telling point. In the Gospel of John, Jesus makes no ethical demands on his followers. The one possible exception is in the washing of the disciples' feet: "I have set you an example, that you also should do as I have done to you" (13:15). Except for this call to humble service, nothing is asked of those who accept the salvation offered in Christ.[17]

Thus, a particularly severe family argument continued to move back and forth. Paul had relaxed the Jewish Law in regard to a specific situation. The Synoptic Gospel writers then pulled the young movement back toward its Jewish roots with reminders from Jesus

---

[17] Some interpreters have argued that the entire passion story in John is an invitation to Jesus' followers to become equally self-giving. If so, John contains the highest ethic possible. This interpretation, however, while interesting and appealing, is just that: an interpretation. As John describes it, Jesus' sacrifice seems a unique event, impossible to duplicate. The writer of the book of Hebrews would definitely interpret the death of Jesus in such an individualistic, nonchallenging way.

that members of his true family were those who "do the will of my father." John then cast his vote for a position in some ways more radical than that of Paul. Later followers of Paul, especially the writer of Ephesians, would side with John.

Summary

Reading the four Gospel stories, plus Acts, encountered in the order in which they were written, shows how the faith community began taking a radical new shape. The Jewish Messiah, a human being driven by passions of anger, grief, and love, was transformed into a divine being, motivated only by the will of God. A faith that made demands on people, called them to obey both the letter and the deeper meanings of the Law, a faith that challenged its adherents to take up a cross, was transformed into a faith in which being born from above was the only key necessary to open the door to divine acceptance. A Jewish milieu gave way to a Greek way of thought; a Jewish movement became a Gentile church.

The movement from Messiah to the Christ had enormous implications for the future of the church. The Messiah was a Jewish concept, a man chosen by God for a redemptive mission; he pointed beyond himself to God. The Christ was a concept more at home in the Greek world; he was more than a pointer toward God; he was the very presence of God. The Jewish Messiah, in one ancient interpretation, was crucified as the final act in the role of suffering/inclusive Savior; by accepting this role, Jesus opened the faith community to all people. His resurrection was God's stamp of approval on what Jesus had done. The Greek Christ, by contrast, died as God's sacrifice for humankind—the Lamb of God that takes away the sins of the world. His resurrection, in this second view, opened the gates of eternal life to all people. The Messiah's suffering was an invitation to others to take up their cross and follow. The Christ's sacrifice was a onetime event that cannot be duplicated. The Messiah's death was a challenge. The Christ's death was a gift. The Messiah entered completely into the messy ambiguities of human life. The Christ touched human life but was not soiled by its necessary compromises. The human Messiah was driven by internal forces, grief, compassion, and anger. The Christ was driven exclusively by the will of God.

Life does not offer human beings pure choices between light and darkness, as the dualism of the Gospel of John implies. True human life is lived by making choices between degrees of twilight. The Messiah, as understood in the Jewish Scripture, can enter into the ambiguity and painful options of actual life. He can make those choices that leave him tainted but not corrupted. On the other hand, the Christ can touch this life at its edges, but cannot enter it fully, else the purity of God will be compromised. The idea that there was once a human being who was totally without sin is a statement that can be made in faith, but cannot be supported in reality.

The church has attempted to embrace both Messiah and Christ in the one person, Jesus Christ. The contradictions are covered by the term "paradox." Yet, even an appealing term such as paradox cannot paper over certain problems. Either Jesus was a man, pushed and pulled by the engines of inner experience, battered between imperfect and often painful choices, or else he was fully God, near enough to touch this life but not able to share it fully. The first option is a Jewish, earthy one; the second is a Greek, philosophic one. Even the effort to combine the two concepts into one who is "Very God of Very God...incarnate...And was made man..."[18] is a triumph of Greek philosophy over Jewish religion. The church continues today to struggle with the pull of these opposing poles.

On one fact the four Gospel writers fully agree. In Jesus of Nazareth something ultimate was introduced into human history. Whether one puts an emphasis on Jesus the person or Christ the object of worship, it is clear that his story is not a collection of normal events. Jesus of Nazareth defined, as has no other person, what it means to be human as the Creator intended. God was also revealed through this person in a unique manner. A Scottish saying is accurate: "In Jesus Christ we see the 'hither side' of God." The suffering of this individual had universal implications. The resurrection stories also had infinite implications in the struggle between light and darkness, good and evil, life and death.

The family arguments were far from settled. Additional writers would add their views to the faith family album. It is important to move to the final set of these writers.

---

[18] Taken from the Nicene Creed.

10

The Community Copes with Persecution

The island community was no more. It was dispersed among a variety of cities on the mainland. It was also effectively divided. Those who had accepted the teachings of the special young man had little to do with those who rejected his insights.

As the number of followers of the special person grew, so did the perceived threat to the traditionalists in the cities where they resided. Followers of the old ways feared that those committed to the ways of the special young man would take control of what remained of the island community. Hostility developed also from a second source. Their mainland neighbors saw all former islanders as another kind of threat; they feared the ways of their new neighbors would overwhelm their own ways of living.

The alien government from the mainland was especially concerned about the followers of the special young man. Like many governments, it demanded absolute loyalty from its constituents. The exiled islanders seemed much more committed to the ways of the sea as interpreted by their recent leader than they were to the central government. The government found ways to blame this group of people for problems they had not caused. Having blamed them, it was easy to try to eliminate them through torture, death, and other forms of intimidation.

Most followers of the special young man stood firm. They supported one another by continuing the practice of exchanging letters. One individual wrote a tract calling people to courage and wrote it in a code that only the ousted islanders could comprehend.

Despite the hostility between the two groups of islanders, one letter that circulated reminded the special young man's followers of their debt to the history that they shared with the other expatriates.

Even under these difficult circumstances, the followers of the special person continued to examine the issues that had caused controversy in the past. These included the nature of the special young man, their relationship to the other exiled islanders, and ways they might continue to practice the ways of the sea in their scattered condition. They also produced insightful materials advising one another on ways to endure the persecution.

Background

More than half a century had gone by since the crucifixion of Jesus. Most of those who had known him in the flesh had died. A military rebellion in Jerusalem had failed. Instead of driving the Roman armies out of the Holy City, the rebellion had angered Roman officials. They had driven Jews out of their homeland and leveled their temple. Jewish families took up residence in major cities around the Mediterranean in a Diaspora that would last nearly two thousand years.

Rome continued to see the followers of Jesus as a Jewish sect. Naturally, then, part of the hostility that followed the Jewish rebellion fell on Christian heads.

The scattering of Jews—a genuine tragedy for that people—became an occasion for Christian growth. Paul and other missionaries used the synagogues of distant cities as launching points for their evangelism. They usually found a few converts among the Jews, then turned their attention to the Gentiles. The Gentiles usually responded in larger numbers. Thus, small but vibrant congregations developed.

As the first century closed, several important factors faced these new followers of Jesus. In the first place, it was clear that the division between the Jewish community and the followers of Jesus had become permanent. Most Jews wanted and fervently believed in a messiah who would belong exclusively to them, and who would restore the fortunes of their nation. Jesus, the Suffering Servant who invited Gentiles into his kingdom and who allowed himself to die at the hands of the nation's invaders, was entirely too far from this image. Other sources of misunderstanding and conflict sealed a sad condition of separation. These included Paul, with his flexible attitude toward the Torah; the increasing emphasis on a eucharist in which the body and blood of Jesus were symbolically ingested; Christian writings that seemed to make Jesus an equal with Yahweh; and the efforts of Christians to place the blame of the crucifixion on the Jews. Thus followers of Jesus found it increasingly difficult to continue as a movement within Judaism. One matter that remained unclear was whether Christians would remember their Jewish roots or reject those roots as inappropriate to their new circumstances.

As the conflict with the Jews intensified, so did that with Rome. Relations between the Empire and the followers of Jesus were never entirely smooth. Roman officials had ordered the crucifixion. Christians had been associated in Roman minds with the Jewish rebellion.

One can understand, then, that when Rome burned in July of the year 64 C.E., Nero, slightly deranged and possibly responsible for the fire himself, could choose a small, misunderstood sect of Christians as his scapegoat. Many Christians in and around the city of Rome were executed.

Full-scale persecution did not come until the reign of Domitian (81–96 C.E.). He was the first of the emperors to claim divine status for himself. He insisted on being called "Lord and God," and at least one shrine for his worship was established outside Rome. The Jewish faith absolutely forbade such worship of a mortal, and the followers of Jesus still saw themselves as Jewish enough to remain under this ban. The stage was set for deadly conflict between the emerging church and its Roman governors.

With the persecutions came a need for organizational structure. Faced with severe suffering, people reached for authority that was strong, clearly defined, and closely associated with the power and love of God. Suddenly those who wished to build the church on hierarchical patterns had the upper hand. Also, as the church debated the nature of Jesus—to what degree was he human and to what degree was he divine—those arguing for divinity were strengthened by the shadow of persecution. One will die much more readily for a savior of whom it can be said, "I and the Father are one," and who invites one into paradise from a position at the right hand of God, than for one who can claim mostly human credentials.

Other factors pushed toward clear definition of doctrine. With the death of those who had known Jesus, some clarity of belief was needed. The original apostles could quote Jesus and thus establish correct belief. As they vanished, various other persons took advantage of the situation to push new interpretations of the faith. People who had been strongly influenced by Greek doctrines made their way into the leadership of the churches. One doctrine that was lifted up was gnosticism, a belief in dualism. The Gnostics were convinced that the power of God existed over against an almost equal power of evil. They believed further that human souls participated in divinity, but human bodies were of the devil. They believed that God was too pure to have created the world, but performed the act of creation through intermediaries. The idea that God would live in human flesh was abhorrent to the Gnostics; they preached that the human body in which Jesus had supposedly been seen was only an illusion. The followers of Jesus who remembered their Jewish roots knew that God had created the world and had called it good. They labeled gnosticism a heresy. These conflicts are all seen in the final books of scripture.

All the books discussed in this chapter were written within a few years of each other at the close of the first century. The precise order in which they were written is impossible to establish.

Conflicts within the Churches

Internal tensions are the price of growth. For the followers of Jesus, both their numbers and their diversity were growing. Conflicts were inevitable. Several of the later books of the Bible were written to keep the impact of these tensions to a minimum.

The Pastoral Epistles: 1 and 2 Timothy, and Titus

The three "pastoral letters" of the New Testament may not have been letters at all, but general writings addressing the problems of the growing church. They surely were not written by Paul, for they address issues that arose after his death. The idea of writing in the name of Paul, as if to young pastors, may have been a literary device to allow the airing of what the writer felt were important concepts. The advanced structure of the congregations, with their assigned offices and other division of labor, indicate that the letters were among the last of the New Testament to be written. Placing them just after the opening of the second century would probably be accurate.

In contrast to the sentiments of some of the followers of Paul, the writer of the pastoral letters called for a return to respect for the

Law. "Now we know that the law is good, if one uses it legitimately" (1 Timothy 1:8). The use to which this writer would put the Law was to create communities of defined structure. Men and women were given assigned roles in the leadership of worship (to the detriment of women—men were given the more visible positions). Bishops and deacons were required to meet certain standards of moral behavior (including being married to only one wife: polygamy had not yet been entirely eliminated!). (1 Timothy 2:2, 12)[1] Specific instructions were given to the young and the old. Slaves were instructed to be obedient to and worshipful of their masters.

The advice given here about structure may be judged, by current standards, overly rigid and hierarchical. The context, again, becomes important. The church, by the late date of this writing, was under heavy persecution. Filled with persons entirely new to the faith, congregations needed clear structure and clear lines of authority.

While giving advice about clear lines of authority, the writer also included personal advice about pastoral duties. In addition, he gave suggestions about ecclesiastical organization that have influenced the church through its history. False teachings were among his strongest concerns. To protect purity of belief he made an often-quoted comment about the nature of scripture: "All scripture is inspired by God and is useful for teaching, for reproof, for correction, and for training in righteousness" (2 Timothy 3:16). The reference, of course, was to scripture as the writer knew it: the Hebraic Scripture which is sometimes called the Old Testament. The writer had no idea that his own words would someday be included in an expanded sacred canon! Just what "inspired" implied was not spelled out. More will be said about this verse in this book's final chapter.

The letter entitled "Titus" revealed the state of the churches in this period of time. The writer (probably the same as that of 1 and 2 Timothy) was especially concerned with proper doctrine: "But as for you, teach what is consistent with sound doctrine" (Titus 2:1). Tensions with the Jewish members of the church were evident. One comment made about the Jews of Crete is a boorish generalization. Quoting from another source, the writer remarked, "'Cretans are always liars, vicious brutes, lazy gluttons.' That testimony is true" (Titus 1:12–13). In addition, the writer wanted to build solid

---

[1] 1 Timothy 2:2 and 12. The common translation, "married only once," implies a restriction on divorce. The Greek says, instead, "Be husbands of only one wife."

hierarchical structures to give security in the time of testing. He advised appointment of elders in every church in every town. He also instructed women to be submissive to their husbands, and all citizens to be submissive to public authorities.

The epistle begins and ends with the usual personal greetings.

2 Thessalonians

Apparently the church in Thessalonica had misinterpreted Paul's earlier letter, believing that he said the day of judgment had already occurred. Thus the warning: "We beg you, brothers and sisters, not to be quickly shaken in mind or alarmed, either by spirit or by word or by letter, as though from us, to the effect that the day of the Lord is already here" (2 Thessalonians 2:1b–2). One immediate problem of this belief was that some of the new converts had determined that, since the day of judgment was already here, they did not have to continue to work! Thus this brief letter was written by a later disciple of Paul to counter this false doctrine and to tell the people to get on with the business of living. The message is given forcefully—even harshly. "Anyone unwilling to work should not eat" (3:10).

The letter quotes extensively from the first letter to the church in Thessalonica. Otherwise it uses a different style, creating the probability that this material, much in the spirit of Paul, was not written by him.

2 Peter and Jude

Two brief letters, 2 Peter and Jude, are concerned about particular false teachings that had damaged the life of the young congregations.

One of the letters was written in the name of Jude, the brother of Jesus. However, the writer spoke of the apostles in the past tense and referred to rather well-developed heresies, indicating a date for the material after the life of Jesus' siblings. Likewise, the writer of 2 Peter used concepts that were not abroad until after Peter's death. Both writers claimed authorship by early church leaders to give credibility to their ideas.

Jude seems to have been the first to be written, and 2 Peter was largely copied from it. In angry tones the first of these writers described those who turn the faith, with its lack of rigid laws, into an opportunity for licentiousness. Other false teachings undermined the authority of church officials. The writer reminded his readers of what the anger of God had accomplished in the past and threatened similar vengeance if they did not reject those who sought to lead them astray.

The brief book of Jude contains an interesting insight into the way inspiration occurs. For twenty-three verses the writer described the darkened, uneven landscape over which his readers were moving. He mentioned a multitude of ways in which their feet could misstep, along with another multitude of ways God could punish them. The reader can, at this point, visualize the original scene. The writer had accomplished his purpose and was ready to close. For a moment he lifted his pen and reviewed what he had written. "Have I been too negative? Have I dwelt so much on the problems that I have given them nothing to which to cling, no reason to hope?" There was a pause, then a flood of words as if from outside him. A secular writer might describe such a moment as a visitation of the muse; a religious writer is more precise about its source. The pen returned to paper, and a writing style that had been angry and wooden was transformed:

> Now to the One who is able to keep you from falling
> and set you in the presence of his glory, jubilant and
> above reproach, to the only God our Savior, be glory
> and majesty, might and authority...now and for
> evermore. (Jude 24–25 NEB)

Perhaps inadvertently, meaning only to put a standard benediction to his harsh words, the writer had assured the people that God was interested in more than correct dogma and just punishment. A divine Spirit was available to help them in their time of trouble. God would prevent them from ultimate failure, and would forgive them when the inevitable, momentary mistakes occurred. In such moments, when a burst of inspiration comes, as it were, from no identifiable source, readers know they are being addressed by more than human sources.

The writer of 2 Peter uses much of the same language to address many of the same issues.

1, 2, and 3 John

These three letters, very much in the spirit of (but with important differences from) the Gospel of John, were written to counter several beliefs that the writer defined as dangerous heresies. Enough similarities exist between these three letters to assume they came from the same hand.

The disputes seem to have been over a proper interpretation of the Gospel of John. As seen in the previous chapter, that Gospel includes almost no ethical content. Thus the writer of the epistle of John took care to say that people cannot "come to the light" (a favorite figure of all biblical writers who call themselves "John") unless they learn to love one another (1 John 2:8–10). Repetition of the love theme is a way of ensuring that no one misunderstands this truth: It is not enough simply to be born from above and to accept proper doctrines. One must also relate to other people in loving ways, since the God who invites us into the light is the essence of love. Another heresy, this one associated with gnosticism, said that Jesus had no real physical body and thus did not truly suffer. This is corrected with a vigorous statement: "By this you know the Spirit of God: every spirit that confesses that Jesus Christ has come *in the flesh* is from God" (1 John 4:2, italics mine).

Another possible heresy of the emerging church was individualism. Since people had come into the faith community by individual choice, it was easy for them to assume that each of them could, like an only child, remain as an isolated person relishing a unique relationship to God. The family images throughout these three letters press home the idea that the church, even though increasingly divided from its Jewish neighbors, continued the Jewish tradition of group cohesiveness. Converts to the faith are repeatedly addressed as "little children" who have a sibling relationship to one another.

Individualism was not rejected entirely. The community was present for support and discipline; individuals, nonetheless, could not escape responsibility for their actions. The brief third letter of John gave two examples of the faith community's interacting with its individual members. In one case it gave positive reinforcement to one (Gaius) who had acted in exemplary fashion; in a second it offered discipline to a person named Diotrephes who sinned by pushing himself forward too aggressively.

The writer closes with the hope that personal contact will soon take the place of impersonal letters.

An Effort to Make Peace

Most biblical writers of the time attempted to secure the new church by defining proper doctrine. This was a necessary activity. Doctrine, nonetheless, tended to exacerbate the growing division between followers of Jesus and the Jews who rejected the claims that he was the Messiah. Two writers, in contrast, made efforts to heal this growing schism.

Ephesians and Colossians

Ephesians and Colossians can be discussed together, since they seem to have come from the pen of a common author.

While these letters are based on the thoughts of Paul, especially on the first letter to Corinth, several differences from Paul can be detected. The issues discussed are from a time after Paul's death.

The central purpose of both these letters was to bring harmony to squabbling congregations. The writer gave special attention to the problems between Jews and Gentiles. The Gentile members of the congregations were reminded that they had received free admission to the ongoing community of faith. The suffering of Christ accomplished this. Referring to the wall in the temple, beyond which no non-Jew could proceed, he said, "For he is our peace; in his flesh he has made both groups into one and has broken down the dividing wall, that is, the hostility between us" (Ephesians 2:14). The warm greeting given the people in Colossae and the positive statements about their sharing in the work of the larger community was no doubt written to achieve the same purpose. Again, the death of Jesus was seen as overcoming division: "And you who were once estranged and hostile in mind, doing evil deeds, he has now reconciled in his fleshly body" (Colossians 1:21–22). In regard to reconciliation, the writer of these two books definitely understood the meaning of the suffering/inclusive Messiah.

The peace sought was not, however, to be at the price of false doctrine. Thus some realities were clearly defined. In order to ensure proper doctrine, the writer was willing to risk widening the schisms he wanted to overcome. In regard to the nature of Christ, we see further evidence of movement away from the earthy, Jewish Messiah to a spiritualized and eternal heavenly being. "God, who is rich in mercy…raised us up with him and seated us with him in the heavenly places" (Ephesians 2:4–6). "So if you have been raised with Christ, seek the things that are above, where Christ is, seated at the right hand of God" (Colossians 3:1). Yet the writer does not adopt the view of the Gnostics: Jesus had a real body, and divine-human reconciliation is based, as indicated above, on that "fleshly body" (Colossians 1:22).

Not only had Christ been spiritualized, but so also had the life lived in obedience to him. The writer advised his readers to give attention not to things of this world, but to the realities of the heavenly kingdom. "Set your minds on things that are above, not on things that are on earth" (Colossians 3:2).

One debate was entered from a more radical position. While Paul had argued that followers of Jesus were free to apply the Law with compassion and maturity, the writer of Ephesians gave permission to ignore the Law altogether. "He has abolished the law with its commandments" (Ephesians 2:15). This was a blanket statement that Paul, the Pharisee, never would have made. If the view of the writer of Ephesians were to prevail (indeed, it has prevailed in many later interpretations by the church), then Christians would be cut off entirely from their Jewish roots.[2]

Even if the writer intended to separate followers of Jesus from the Jewish Law, he apparently did not mean to separate them from the traditions of the Jewish faith community. Earlier in this section the writer of Ephesians made it clear that he, along with Paul, saw Christ and Christ's crucifixion as bringing Gentiles into the continuing tradition of Judaism. "Remember that you were at that time [previous to following Jesus] without Christ, being aliens from the commonwealth of Israel, and strangers to the covenants of promise" (Ephesians 2:12). The outcome of Jesus' reconciling work is this: "In him the whole structure is joined together and grows into a holy temple in the Lord" (v. 21).

In a seeming contradiction, the writer of these two letters listed quite a large number of laws to which the Christian was still subject.[3] The writer also stressed one other tie to Jewish roots: the communal nature of the religious life. Just as the individual Jew was always a part of a community, so too was the Christian individual inseparable from the congregation. "Above all, clothe yourselves with love, which binds everything together in perfect harmony. And let the peace of Christ rule in your hearts, to which indeed you were called in the one body" (Colossians 3:14–15).

The books of Ephesians and Colossians were efforts to achieve a cease-fire in the churches' internal debates. The cease-fire, however, was to be based on proper doctrine as the writer understood it. Fortunately, he was convinced that proper doctrine included peace itself. Christ had died to break all dividing walls of hostility.

---

[2] Perhaps even this passage is not the absolute dismissal of law that most English translations imply. The phrases in the fifteenth verse of chapter 2 do not transfer easily from Greek to English. The New Jerusalem Bible insists that it is the *hostility,* not the *law,* that had been abolished: "...by destroying in his own person the hostility, that is, the Law of commandments with its decrees." This very different reading is much more the tenor of Paul's arguments, and fits the theme of the immediate context.

[3] See especially Ephesians 4:25–32 and Colossians 3:5–11.

Conflict with Rome

Additional stress came to the young church via persecution from Rome. Three of the later books of the New Testament were efforts to prepare people to suffer and to interpret this suffering. Two rather different approaches to this task were taken.

1 Peter

The writer of 1 Peter felt called to an enormous responsibility. He attempted to prepare a congregation for suffering and possible death. Apparently written to a Jewish congregation (meaning that not all Jews had left the Christian fold), it began with general admonitions to be prepared.

Interestingly, the writer helped prepare the people for their trial by reminding them of their heritage. They continued the tradition as God's chosen people—a tradition that reached back to their ancestor Abraham. "But you are a chosen race, a royal priesthood, a holy nation, God's own people" (1 Peter 2:9). *Their first defense against persecution was to embrace this role and to act it out through moral living.*

They were to make themselves unique through their high ethical standards. On the other hand, they were to live within their normal social structure as much as possible, lest they call attention to themselves and make the persecutions more severe. Three forms of submission were advised: the people were to "Accept the authority of every human institution" (1 Peter 2:13); slaves were to accept the authority of their masters (v. 18); and wives were to accept the authority of their husbands. (3:1)

It is important to see these admonitions in context. The writer was certainly not giving his stamp of approval to a government that was attempting to destroy his faith. Nor was he approving either the institution of slavery or a pattern of marriage that made wives the property of their husbands. *Submission was, in this case, both a technique for survival and a means of resistance.* The writer was advising people to turn the other cheek in evil situations until the unjust structures exhausted themselves in their demonic activity. A wide gap exists between passive acceptance and passive resistance. The writer of 1 Peter was advising passive resistance. Accepting the humble role in their situation, he advised, would bring them exaltation "in due time" (1 Peter 5:6).

The writer of 1 Peter prepared his people for persecution in one more way. He reopened the old faith family argument about the meaning of suffering. In the dispute between those who saw suffering as an embarrassing sign of God's displeasure and those who believed that suffering could be the will of God for human redemption, this writer came down decisively on the side of the latter. Their pain would put them in fellowship with Christ. (3:18) They could accomplish something of the same result as he: "Since therefore Christ suffered in the flesh, arm yourselves also with the same intention" (4:1).

A promise of an early end to such persecution concludes this letter.

Hebrews

The writer of Hebrews prepared his readers for persecution in three ways. He attempted to strengthen their faith; he reinterpreted the meaning of suffering; and he reminded them of their obligation to the ongoing faith community.

In older translations this book is called "The Letter of Paul to the Hebrews." It was, however, as new information has shown, written well after the death of Paul. In addition, the name of the letter is misleading. The evidence that this was written to a congregation of Jews is weak. Probably this was not a letter at all, but a sermon written for general distribution in churches faced with the possibility of severe suffering.

A firmly-grounded faith was the first defense against Roman persecution, the writer insisted. Thus his first sentences introduced his understanding of Jesus. Jesus carried "the imprint of God's very being." He had become "much superior to angels" (Hebrews 1:3,4). Yet the writer would not fall into the gnostic trap of assuming that Jesus' body had been as angelic as his spirit. In order to relate to people in their suffering, "he had to become like his brothers and sisters in every respect" (2:17).

To explain the role that Jesus had in human redemption, the writer of Hebrews chose the metaphor of the high priest. Many of the early chapters of the book are an extended (and, some might feel, labored) effort to show how Jesus could take this role and why he filled it with such effectiveness. Since Jesus was not born of the priestly bloodline (Levites had a corner on this sacred role), the writer found a reference to an ancient priest named Melchizedek[4] who had an authentic priestly role outside the tribe of Levi. (5:10) The writer of Hebrews placed Jesus in the line of Melchizedek. Jesus was also

---

[4] See Genesis 14 and Psalm 110.

superior to all the old high priests of the Jewish community. While other priests offered sacrifices of animals, Jesus offered himself. "He entered once for all into the Holy Place, not with the blood of goats and calves, but with his own blood" (9:12). Here was a new interpretation of the meaning of Jesus' suffering. Jesus had become the sin sacrifice for the entire community. This idea had been suggested before, but never so clearly stated.

Faith, according to the writer, offered genuine power to cope with persecution. In the often-quoted eleventh chapter, the writer listed his major ancestors in faith, beginning with Abel, moving through such giants as Abraham and Moses, reciting their achievements—achievements made possible by faith.

It is important to note that the word *faith* (the Greek πισ′τος, "pistos") does not translate easily from Greek to English. It can be translated "faith" in the sense of proper beliefs. It can also mean "trust." In the second meaning it implies a commitment of one's total life to that in which one has trust. The writer of Hebrews was confident that proper dogma was important, thus his arguments over the nature of Jesus. In the eleventh chapter, however, he used πισ′τος in a wider sense. He was saying to his readers that they could survive persecution by sharing with their spiritual ancestors a thoroughgoing commitment to the God who sustained those ancestors and who had revealed the divine nature through the high priest, Jesus.

A clear understanding of the nature of suffering was necessary to withstand the persecution. The position taken by the writer on this topic is the opposite of that taken by both the editor of Deuteronomy and the editors of the materials describing the history of Israel. Suffering was not a sign of God's displeasure, but the means by which people of faith were tested. Jesus was so tested (4:15), and thus those facing persecution could see their fate in a similar light. It was through suffering that Jesus learned obedience and was made perfect. (5:8)

The writer praised his readers for their reaction to the pain they had already encountered. They "endured a hard struggle with sufferings," sometimes "being partners with those so treated." They "accepted the plundering of your possessions, knowing that you yourselves possessed something better and more lasting" (10:32–34).

Finally, a profound sense of community would sustain the people in their difficult encounter with persecution. Though the faith community could no longer identify itself as a closely knit ethnic group, the writer continued to see them as a people with strong attachment to one another. Evil could be overcome as long as they "exhort one another every day" (3:13).

The sense of community went backward in time as well as outward to contemporaries. Having listed the ancestors of their tradition who persevered through faith, the writer gave his readers a compelling reason why they, too, should stand firm: "Therefore, since we are surrounded by so great a cloud of witnesses,...let us run with perseverance the race that is set before us" (12:1).

The writer was confident his readers would survive their persecution, because they had faith in the great high priest, the pioneer in a salvation that had been brought about through suffering. They knew that suffering could be a sign that God had chosen them for testing and for training in obedience. He was confident of their survival because they were part of a continuing, supportive community.

The book of Hebrews attests, as much as any other book of the New Testament, a sense of continuity with Christianity's Jewish ancestry. Jesus was interpreted by use of an illustration taken from the Jewish nation: the role of high priest. The people were called to imitate the faithful response of their religious ancestors. It is surprising (perhaps "shocking" is not too strong a term) to see, embedded in this Jewish-friendly document, a statement supposedly invalidating the traditional relationship between Jew and Yahweh. In speaking of "a new covenant," the writer seemed to have made the first one obsolete. (8:13) This passage has been quoted by those who wish to prove that Christians have replaced Jews as the chosen people, and that Jews no longer have standing before God. The widely quoted statement by a contemporary Christian pastor that "God does not hear Jewish prayers" is an especially egregious, though hardly isolated, application of what this sentence seems to imply.

A look at the passage in its larger context, however, shows an entirely different meaning. The material just before this statement (vv. 8–12) is taken from Jeremiah 31:32–34. That remarkable prophet had seen the evolving covenant between Jew and God moving away from a compulsive application of rigid rules toward an internalized attitude of love. The old covenant which the writer of Hebrews insisted was obsolete had been set aside since the time of Jeremiah. The Jewish community, through its interpretation of the Torah, had long since reached the same conclusion about legalism. To put this verse in the service of anti-Jewish propagandists is an absolutely incorrect and highly destructive use of scripture.

Thus the book of Hebrews is a strong link in the chain of continuity that holds together faith's family album. It affirms the Jewishness of Jesus. It restates an understanding of suffering similar to that in Second Isaiah. It uses the ongoing community as a source of strength for those enduring persecution. Finally, it identifies the Christian understanding of covenant with that of the prophet, Jeremiah.

Revelation

The book of Revelation was another book written to help the Christian community cope with persecution. It used an approach very different, however, from that of the books just discussed. In contrast to other New Testament writers who tried to shift blame for the crucifixion to the Jews and thus to make peace with the Romans, this writer clearly pointed to Rome as the source of Christian suffering.

The author identified himself as "John" writing from the island of Patmos. (Revelation 1:1, 9) Patmos was a prison island to which the writer may have been sent as part of a general persecution of Christians by Rome. He seemed to have been writing during a time of general persecution, which would date it late in the reign of the Emperor Domitian (81–96 C.E.).

John's tactics in helping Christians deal with persecution were threefold. First, he wanted his readers to understand that Rome was the embodiment of evil. God would allow this evil to have its way for a short time. Rome would bring plagues of various sorts, would cause pain to the church, and would seem for a time to be fully in control. Second, he wanted Christians to know that God remained in control even during the time of terrors and that divine authority would be reestablished in a later triumphant moment. Third, he assured his readers their suffering would be of short duration. Christ was coming soon to establish justice for all who had stood fast.

In order to get his material past Roman censors, John was forced to put his ideas in code. The Christians of the late first century probably understood most of what was said. Christians twenty centuries later understand little of it. Its images seem confusing, oftentimes frightening, and a bit bizarre. Like the Hebrew book of Daniel, it is fertile ground for those who want to make their own application to current events. (The beasts of Revelation delighted the anti-Communist movement; its members were confident the Bible was speaking of the Russian bear!) Such applications should be made with great care, if at all. They are usually the musings of thoroughly self-centered individuals who conclude that Revelation was written two millennia ago to apply to *my* time and *my* place.

Because the attention of this writer was focused on Rome and its mischief, few other matters were directly addressed. He said little about Jesus, other than to identify him as the Lamb of God sacrificed for human sin. (Revelation 5) He dealt briefly with the problem of false teachings in one of the seven churches to which he addressed his words. (2:2, 15) A special role for those of Jewish descent seems to have been acknowledged. In describing those who have the seal of God on their foreheads, he first listed 144,000 of the twelve tribes of Israel. His next sentence, however, shows that the faith community had been opened to all humanity: "After this I looked, and there was a great multitude that no one could count, from every nation, from all tribes and peoples and languages" (7:9).

One must wonder about the success of the writer's effort to keep his ideas away from Roman investigators. The most incriminating part of his book was his anger at the Empire. The code here was also easiest to break. "So he carried me away in the spirit into a wilderness, and I saw a woman sitting on a scarlet beast that was full of blasphemous names, and it had seven heads and ten horns." Who is this woman? "Babylon the great, mother of whores and of earth's abominations. And I saw that the woman was drunk with the blood of the saints and the blood of the witnesses to Jesus." Yet a few verses later: "This calls for a mind that has wisdom: the seven heads are seven mountains on which the woman is seated" (17:3–9). No Roman reader would have missed the meaning of this passage, or the hatred of Rome that generated it. It was Rome, not Babylon, that was famous for its seven hills.

The dangers of such intense feelings were twofold. First, Christians might have been encouraged to take desperate and violent action against this "mother of whores." Second, and more likely, it strengthened the view of Roman officials that they must see Christians as enemies of the Empire—the view that Luke/Acts and other New Testament writings had been designed to dispel. These were not empty possibilities. Iranaeus, a leader of the church a hundred years later, referred to Revelation as a book that had brought harm to Christians. Perhaps it was for this reason that the book was one of the last to win general approval as a book of scripture.

Revelation was finally included in the canon because it is a tribute to human endurance and to divine faithfulness. It must be read like a work of abstract art, observing patterns and colors rather than seeking meaning in details. It can be compared with the *Leningrad Symphony* of Shostakovich, which describes in minor keys the long siege of that city in World War II and then ends on a single major chord of triumph. The writer of Revelation skillfully introduced himself and his themes, then carried the reader through the depths of horrible plagues. In the final three chapters the reign of God was shown to be reestablished. The old order had given way to a "New Jerusalem, coming down...as a bride adorned for her husband" (21:2). Jesus, "the bright morning star," issued an invitation, and all who were thirsty for the water of life responded. (22:16–17)

Revelation serves an additional purpose. In its unmitigated hostility to the reigning government, it serves as a warning to Christians against becoming too closely allied with political powers. In this sense, Revelation serves as a counterweight to the advice of Romans 13:1–7 about obedience to the authorities. It can also correct any misunderstanding about blind obedience to the hierarchical structures so admired in Ephesians 5 and 1 Peter. There are, indeed, times to be obedient to the authorities, but there are also times when some form of resistance is the demand of faith.

Even while coping with the overwhelming problem of persecution, the writer did not forget that he belonged to a continuing community. The new order that would arrive after the time of testing would be a refurbished Jerusalem. To describe its meaning the writer reached back to the prophet Isaiah. (Isaiah 25:7–8) The chain of continuity remained unbroken.

A Link that Completes the Circle

Faith's family album began with writers who described its characteristics as covenant with God, a search for justice, commitment to community, and obedience to a body of law. The faith community had, across nearly fifteen hundred years, survived slavery, established a new nation, been sustained through captivity and invasion. The community had encountered a new crisis when its ethnic barriers were destroyed by the life and teachings of Jesus of Nazareth. This seemed, for a time, to be such a major distraction that the original community commitments were in danger of permanent loss. The final writer to be examined in this exploration of scripture returns readers to the basic values to which their spiritual ancestors were committed.

James

The book of James is as controversial in its own way as the book of Revelation. Neither won its way easily into the Christian Bible. As late as the sixteenth century Martin Luther could publicly regret that James had been included in the canon.

No evidence can be cited to suggest that this was the last book of the New Testament to be written. It was certainly among the last, and probably was not composed until the beginning of the second century.

It is discussed last because it completes, as it were, a circle. James (whoever he might have been; no identification other than this commonly used name is offered) wrote to remind his readers that their religious roots were the same as those who remained in other sects of the Jewish faith. He hoped to accomplish this by bringing Christianity, by then established separately from Judaism, closer to the understanding of Jesus offered by the Synoptic Gospels.

A brief review is in order. After Jesus had lived out the meaning of the suffering/inclusive Messiah, Paul had welcomed Gentiles into the faith community by relaxing specific laws. Followers of Jesus were free from the rigid application of the ancient Law, he wrote— free to apply the Law with love and maturity. Followers of Paul carried his thoughts much further, perhaps arguing on one occasion that Christians were free from responsibilities to the laws of Judaism altogether. (All these later writers believed Christians should act lovingly, and most gave specific instructions about what this life of love entails. All, however, hesitated to allow their instructions to be the basis of any moral code.) The writer of Hebrews carried this logic so far as to state that all the major ancestors in faith had been included in the divine love because of their "faith," not because of any mark in human flesh.

James apparently knew by experience the destructive possibilities of separating faith entirely from any defined rules of behavior. He had observed people who insisted they believed all the proper dogma about Christ, yet who lived on such a low ethical plane that they became an embarrassment to the entire church.

James's argument was neither new nor radical. It was corrective. It called Christians to remember their roots. Their faith had emerged from the prophets who insisted that people of faith oppose oppression and give special attention to those whom society had pushed to the margins—a prophetic tradition to which Jesus had attached himself. James took on the task of reminding his readers of something Jesus had said in another way: Jesus' authentic family were those who *do* the will of God. James was confident that the legal code could reflect both love and maturity.

James was no enemy of Paul, or of Paul's emphasis on faith. On the contrary, James called people to a life of faith. Only after that challenge did he discuss ethical responsibility. Faith should be sought in prayer, he wrote. Those who try to live without faith are "double-minded" and thus unacceptable to God. (James 1:5–8)

Faith, however, does not lift the burden of personal or communal responsibility. People must take charge of their own lives. Neither blame for evil nor credit for good can be passed on to others. James first corrected those who attempted to shift responsibility to God. "No one, when tempted, should say, 'I am being tempted by God'" (v. 13).

Christians were shown to be responsible, also, for seeking social justice, just as the eighth-century (B.C.E.) prophets demanded. The writer had observed the deference given the wealthy in church meetings and the way the poor were often ignored. (2:1–7) Such biased practices must stop, he wrote. In a particularly telling passage James reacted to the comments about faith given in the book of Hebrews. The eleventh chapter of Hebrews implied that faith alone had made Abraham, Moses, and many others acceptable to God. To James this was ridiculous. It was what these people *did* with their faith that allowed them membership in the community's shared history! "For just as the body without the spirit is dead, so faith without works is also dead" (3:26). Later he repeated the same theme: "Anyone, then, who knows the right thing to do and fails to do it, commits sin" (James 4:17).

To James, the tongue was a primary source of evil. Thus the tongue should be controlled. The words one says that slander another may seem a small thing, but "How great a forest is set ablaze by a small fire" (3:5b).

234 The Bible: Faith's Family Album

Other subjects that received the writer's attention included ignoring the needs of the poor, the dangers of wealth—and the pride that often accompanies wealth, adultery, judgments, exploitative business practices, and swearing.

In short, James called the faith community back to a code of moral responsibility. Since he was confident he was a part of the drama that had begun in Abraham, he was deeply committed to the Jewish Law. He made a sweeping statement of support for this code: "For whoever keeps the whole law but fails in one point has become accountable for all of it" (2:10). The statement may seem out of place—even offensive—at this stage of Christian development, yet it is not at all dissimilar to a statement included in the Sermon on the Mount. (Matthew 5:19)

James was silent on other issues before the church at this time. He had nothing to say about Jesus' nature—the degree to which he had been either human or divine. He offered no theories of atonement. He simply called Christians back to moral accountability.

Thus James affirmed the chain of faith commitments that attach the latter part of the New Testament to the Synoptic Gospels, and the Synoptics to Amos—the shepherd of Tekoa who, with his railings against the economic injustices of his day, gave us the first complete book of the Bible .

The Bible is one book. It centers on a single story line. It tells the unbroken history of a faith community. It is our faith's family album.

The Faith Community

As the sacred canon closed, the faith community had evolved until it stood in a precarious position. The newly-emerged Christian branch of the faith family could not identify itself by any ethnic designation. Unlike the Jews, who knew themselves to be Jews by their biological nature, Christians were forced to define themselves by their behavior or their beliefs or both. Unless a clear identity was established, Christians were likely to be quickly reassimilated back into the secular society from which they had come.

Definition was difficult. A certain reading (or, perhaps, misreading) of Paul meant that moral behavior was not important to the Christian life. People, according to this belief, were in a saving relationship to God through faith alone. They were released from any obligation to a code of conduct.

Thus belief alone became the identifying mark of the Christian. *Correct* belief, then, took on enormous importance. Their Jewish ancestors could be somewhat relaxed about most theological issues. The presence in the Jewish writings of many views of God, of at least two major views of the Messiah, and of conflicts over ethical approaches was not seen as fatal. Jews defined their community on other grounds. In contrast, Christians felt a need to be more precise. Christians thus began their bitter internal disputes with a strong sense that ultimate values were at stake. The disputes were many. Primary among them were disagreements over the dual nature of Jesus, interpretations of Paul's comments about the Law, and the degree to which Christians should participate in the structures of society. These disputes would later rip the Christian side of the faith community asunder.

Christians and Jews had begun within the same family. As they debated, then fought, and then split, Christianity suffered severe losses. One of the major losses was, of course, the lack of clear identity. Without a shared ethnic background, and having rejected outward behavior as an identifying mark, the church was left with but one slender reed on which to lean when it wanted to distinguish its members from non-Christians: "Everyone who calls on the name of the Lord shall be saved" (Romans 10:13).

Other losses could have been avoided. One was the loss of community consciousness. In Judaism, the nation was the primary focus of divine activity. The nation was held responsible for the behavior of its people, and especially for the faithfulness of its king. Christianity came into being as individuals made a commitment to Christ as savior. Yet the book of Acts points out that the early Christians saw themselves as a continuation of the Jewish model. In that model persons carried responsibility toward one another—responsibility that was both material and spiritual. Gradually, however, that sense of responsibility lessened. The letters of Paul show the lengths to which he had to go to convince the early followers of Jesus to care for one another. Christianity, without close ties to its Jewish roots, became a collection of individuals, each seeking a saving relationship with God, feeling minimal responsibility for others of the same faith.

As the New Testament closed, the hostility between Jew and Christian contributed to a reading of Paul that pulled these two groups even further apart. Christianity was supposedly free from any specific code of conduct. To have adopted such a code would, in the eyes of those alive at the time, meant a surrender to Jewish influence. Later, without any moral anchor, it was entirely too easy for the Christians, who thought they had converted Constantine, to be converted by Constantine into the secular world which he so thoroughly symbolized.

The hostility between Jew and Gentile Christian also caused a strong surge of anger to be embedded in the New Testament writings. This anger, when read in later centuries, contributed to a tragic history of anti-Jewish activity. As the hostility grew between Jew and Gentile, Christian writers depicted Jews as followers of a rigid, legalistic religion that had been disowned by God. Much more seriously, the Jews were accused of being Christ-killers. Christians, who believe deeply in the forgiving nature of God, must seek that forgiveness themselves for the fact that the seeds of the twentieth-century Holocaust were planted in the way the Gospel stories recorded the crucifixion of Jesus—an unjust blaming of Jews that is especially apparent in the Gospel of John.

Nearly two millennia have gone by since the last of the New Testament was written. It is not too late to reclaim the Jewish roots of the Christian faith, and the security, strength, and identification those roots can provide. Reading the Bible as faith's family album is a major step in that process of reclamation.

11

Is the Faith Family Album Also the Word of God?

The Dilemma

In 1685 John Locke, reacting to a just-published book that cast doubt on the divine inspiration of parts of the Bible, wrote to a friend:

> If everything in holy writ is to be considered without distinction as equally inspired of God, then this surely provides philosophers with a great opportunity for casting doubt on our faith and sincerity. If, on the contrary, certain parts are to be considered as partly human writings, then where in the Scriptures will there be found the certainty of divine authority without which the Christian religion will fall to the ground?[1]

Locke defined the dilemma in which Christians have found themselves. Both Jew and Christian have identified themselves as a people of the Book. Yet these same persons of faith have had enormous difficulty specifying the nature of this Book, its relationship to God, and the authority it exercises over the community of faith.

---

[1] John Locke, *The Correspondence of John Locke*, ed. E. S. De Beer, 2 vols. (Oxford: Oxford University Press, 1976).

Claims of Authority

This lack of definition is a problem confronted in many settings. When a nation debates sending armies into some violent conflict, people of faith quote scripture on two sides of the issue. Those who feel violence is against the will of God call on Micah's admonition to beat swords into plowshares (Micah 4:3), while those who feel that circumstances call for armed resistance will look to Joel for moral permission to reverse the action, beating plowshares into swords. (Joel 3:10) In the middle of the nineteenth century Americans argued across the Mason-Dixon line about the moral basis of slavery, with proponents pointing to Titus' admonition that slaves should be submissive to their masters (Titus 2:9), while opponents argued the implications of Onesimus, once a slave, but returned as a brother to his former owner, Philemon. (Philemon, the entire letter)

On issue after issue the process repeats itself. Proponents of a particular position want to co-opt the enormous authority that has been given to scripture. "The Bible says..." is a powerful weapon in any struggle to convince the undecided. The problem with this approach is suggested in the often-used admonition: "The devil quotes scripture." (The devil being, of course, those people on the other side of whatever is the current debate!) Somewhere, in the thirteen hundred or so pages that make up Holy Writ, a clever individual will be able to find a writer who says, or implies, the opposite of what some opponent is confident "the Bible says."

Debates, of course, are never between devils and angels, but between fallible human beings. Imperfect humans search not for perfect answers but for the better options—sometimes for the least objectionable evil—amid the imperfect choices life places before us. If the Bible is approached as if it were the place where God has hidden "the right" answer to complicated situations we will be stymied on two fronts. First, "right" answers do not exist in this ambiguous life; and, second, the Bible contains such a strong human element that it could not possibly offer, even in hidden form, the precise answers for which humans hunger.

In what sense, then, can the Bible be an authority for our lives and our faith? In what way can this faith family album—this arena in which people of various persuasions debate the most important issues of human life—be embraced as the Word of God? Where, if at all, can we find divine inspiration in this collection of very human writings?

To put the question another way, the scriptures clearly are, for all those who read them without prior assumptions, a product of their age and society. How, then, can these time- and culture-bound words hold a truth that transcends time and place?

Inspiration: A Gentle Concept

The question is often couched in a simple form: Is scripture inspired? Yet, even to answer that in the affirmative settles little.

The word *inspiration,* is interesting in itself. Neither the secular nor the sacred users of the word can give it clear definition. The novelist Ernest Hemingway is said to have been inspired by the smell of salt water. But what does this mean? Did the ocean air grasp the novelist's hand and ensure that he wrote compelling material?

In truth, the word *inspiration* belongs to the religious world. The concept becomes an orphan in secular settings. It is bred from its two roots. In its center is the word *spirit,* preceded by *in.* To be inspired is to be, in some indefinable sense, invaded by a power beyond oneself. This religious heritage is even clearer in the Greek word used to define the role of God in scripture. (2 Timothy 3:16)[2] θεο'πνευστοσ (theópneustos) is composed of the word for God plus the word that means both *spirit* and *breath.* (Both Hebrew and Greek use single words to express what in English is meant by "wind," "breath," and "spirit.") Some older translations used "God-breathed" here.

The association of "breath" and "spirit" remind the reader of several important biblical passages. In Genesis, after God had made human forms from dust, divine breath was shared with them, bringing them to life. This did not mean perfection for humankind. On the contrary, Adam and Eve shared in God's freedom—a freedom they misused. It simply meant that human beings, even in their imperfection, became carriers of a divine spark. A similar event is recorded in Ezekiel. Dry bones were brought together and covered with muscle and skin. This material remained inanimate, however, until the breath of God came from the four winds to bring this flesh to life.

---

[2] This is the only time the scripture makes any claim for special status for itself. In this setting it refers to the scripture recognized at the time: the Hebraic (Old Testament) books, especially the Torah. It is the only time this word occurs in the New Testament.

The statement that God has breathed divinity into scripture is equally important. This is not, as is often assumed, a claim for perfection for every biblical word or phrase. "God-breathed" means that the otherwise inanimate pages of a book can become a living document, a unique carrier of divine grace.

The essential question is this: How does God inspire writers? An important clue in searching for an answer to this question comes from this fact: "inspiration" is a gentle word. Its root, as has already been stated, implies the inbreathing of a spirit. Persons who are inspired are enabled to express the best of their own powers. They are not given powers they did not possess before; they surely are not *over*powered. From the point of view of a writer, being inspired is quite different from—almost the opposite of—having a foreign will imposed on one's efforts. What comes from the pens of those who are inspired continues to be a product of their own will and skill.

Inspiration, in its gentleness, stands over against the concept of coercion. Sadly, when inspiration of scripture is discussed among religious folk, it is with the assumption of coercion. To say that God inspired the Bible implies, for many believers, that God *controlled* the outcome. The word means nothing of the sort. Divine inspiration of scripture means that God was *involved* in the writing, translation, and interpretation of these sacred pages. It does not, however, wipe out human involvement, or human limitations.

Force-Field Concept

Sociologists have given us the helpful concept of the "force-field theory." It helps explain how human decisions are reached. It also gives handles by which those decisions might be positively changed.

The "force-field theory" states that all major human decisions are made within a maelstrom of forces pushing in opposite directions. A helpful example is that of a young man of the late 1960s faced with a notice from his draft board that he must join the military forces and fight in Vietnam. The man is not a pacifist; he believes there are circumstances in which organized violence is the lesser of evils. But he has severe moral reservations about the particular war he has been called to fight. The secular law makes no provision for his moral stance. Should he go, then, and participate, or find some way to flee from his draft notice?

In making this choice, the man will be pushed toward participation by his patriotism, by his sense of commitment to friends who have already been drafted, and perhaps by a father who feels the family name would be tarnished if he had a "draft-dodger" as a son.

On the other hand, he will be encouraged to refuse to go by his own reading of the Sermon on the Mount, by philosophic discussions of nonviolence he has shared with teachers, and by a fiancée who does not want him killed for what she sees as an immoral goal. The force-field can be envisioned thus:

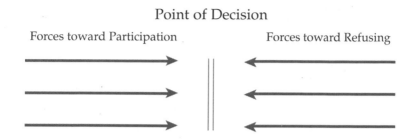

Point of Decision

Forces toward Participation   Forces toward Refusing

As the young man ponders his options, he knows that his decision can be expedited either by strengthening the forces on one side of the partition, or by decreasing the strength of those on the other side. Being a person of religious faith, he searches deep inside himself to determine his genuine priorities. The Sermon on the Mount takes on greater strength as an influence; the opinion of friends decreases in strength. He also prays for assistance from God. He knows at some deep level of his being—though he may not be able to articulate the matter in this way—that God may offer guidance but will not make the decision for him. Or, to put the same matter in a different form, *God is willing to allow the Holy Spirit to be one factor among many forces.*

The man struggling with this awesome decision can, if he wants his religion to be the major part of his decision, either pray that God will increase the volume of the sacred voice within him, or he may learn to turn down the volume of competing voices so he may concentrate directly upon the guidance of God.

Likewise, the Bible is *inspired* because God's voice is added to the cacophony of noises writers hear as they compose their thoughts. The degree of inspiration is measured in the skill of the writers in focusing on that one voice and allowing it to influence their work.

An Electronics Illustration

The world of electronics offers yet another illustration. Our home has special wiring that allows our stereo system to play through speakers in the living room and also in the back of the house. We also have a radio in the kitchen, which my wife will often tune to the same FM station that I have chosen to hear through the main speakers. Occasionally, however, on a stormy day, she may turn her radio to an AM station to hear a weather report. As I come from the back of the house on those days, I arrive at a point when I can barely hear the AM station battling against four speakers of the FM station. But if I stop and concentrate, I can make out the forecast. This, however, requires concentration, and some desire to block out competing sounds.

The Bible was written by a great variety of people over a very large span of time. These writers had varying abilities to (and motivation for) hearing the divine voice and blocking out competing allegiances.

Feminist Insights

The last decades have been enriched theologically by the writings of feminists who have attempted to make the churches more sensitive to the problems of viewing God exclusively as patriarchal and hierarchical. They have insisted, correctly, I believe, that our theology will be enriched as we envision a God who is relational and who respects the freedom of humanity. A God who "inspires" by coercing a writer, until the writer becomes not a participant but a medium, is paternalistic and autocratic. A God who enters into relationship with a writer, producing a document that has both divine and human characteristics, is a far different God, one who can be identified with traits both feminine and masculine. As this review of biblical writings has shown, the feminist scholars can make a strong case for their position from the nature of the varied biblical material.

This second, less gender-specific view of God answers two major concerns. In the first place, this view introduces us to the only kind of God who could be involved in the task of *inspiring* scripture. More traditional views turn God into a controlling autocrat, not an inspirer. The second concern is based partly on a personal desire to experience continuity in the nature of God. I have felt some rare moments of inspiration. They were pleasant, compelling, experiences; they never made me feel I was being forced in some direction or to some conclusion. The less autocratic view of God allows me to know that the God who touches me is the same God who touched my ancestors in faith. It assures me that this God does not deal with people of the current generation differently than those of the ancient past.

Degrees of Inspiration

One implication of this line of argument is that there can be degrees of inspiration. A person might respond in a limited way to the gentle prodding of the Spirit, but compromise the message in light of other voices. Or, on another occasion, that same person might respond to the nudging of the Spirit in a much more complete manner. The honest reader of scripture will acknowledge that there are passages, such as the genocide supposedly called for by God in the book of Judges, or the narrow nationalism of Obadiah, in which a writer has mistaken another sound for the voice of God. This need not be disturbing. When one accepts the Bible as faith's family album such passages can be accepted as a valued part of the whole, alerting us to the survival pressures felt by the community at that time. On the same basis, we can dismiss the idea that such texts must be viewed as carriers of divine guidance. On other occasions the reader might come across some moral command such as "give...eye for eye" (Exodus 21:24), and acknowledge that it was a much higher ethic (and in that sense somewhat inspired) than the common practice of the day—exacting vengeance tenfold. Yet these words are still not an ethic that can stand scrutiny today. Current readers have the benefit of many more centuries of increased understanding of a compassionate God.

Other texts show much clearer signs of divine influence. But in no case does the reader come in contact with pure divinity. A God who works through people in subtle and gentle ways would never seize a writer and force that writer to put ideas in some precise fashion. Therefore, even the most inspired passages of scripture contain some distortions caused by the limits of human frailty.

The gentleness of the word *inspiration* ensures that its effects will be uneven. The unevenness will be observed between different writers. At times it will be observed within one writer; a particular writer will have moments when he (or she) is able to concentrate more effectively on the guidance that comes from beyond. In another passage the same writer has been so obviously attuned to God that the insight offered is one which humanity still attempts to understand and incorporate.

In still other cases, the impact of the gentle prodding of the Spirit must be observed as it gradually makes its impact felt across hundreds of years. Just as a long series of moral insights had to accumulate before the Western world outlawed slavery, so a gradual accumulation of moral insights was required before there could be any decrease in the degree to which violence was accepted in the life of the faith community. Across time the reader moves from the blood-soaked effort to win the Holy Land, recorded in Joshua and Judges, to the awareness of moral responsibility for foreigners reflected in Ruth and Jonah, to insistence by both Second Isaiah and Jesus that suffering is sometimes to be accepted rather than imposed. This process is called "progressive revelation." The movement of progressive revelation is uneven (the book of Daniel is, in terms of violence, a throwback to the time of Joshua). On certain issues, however, it is obviously present.

The uneven nature of inspiration should be no surprise. While some might argue that God's inspiring Spirit touches all scripture alike, no one could deny the uneven impact of the writings that make up its varied literature. Even the widely used and highly respected Common Lectionary schedule of readings for worship devotes entire years to readings from Matthew, Mark, or Luke; it contains no suggested readings from the book of Obadiah, Jude, or other "less spiritual" books. The concept of uneven inspiration of scripture is universally accepted in practice. Sadly, it is almost universally denied in the public statements of even the most progressive of church people!

Identifying the Divine Spirit

Since God inspires in a gentle fashion that produces mixed results, the task is laid on the reader to answer this crucial question: How can I, within this complex family album, find indications of divine involvement? Or, to approach the matter from a slightly different angle, "How can I, the reader, identify the guiding Spirit within me that will assist me in hearing the voice of the Spirit within the text?"

Locating the inspiration in scripture need not become a totally subjective undertaking. It is possible to describe six ways in which the divine Spirit makes itself known in the pages of the Bible.

1. *The Divine is found in those passages that are personally inspiring.* This, on the surface, sounds like nothing but a truism: the Bible is accepted as inspired because it is inspiring to *me*. The truth here, however, emerges from a deeper reality. Something takes place in the personal encounter with scripture that can be quite moving. Generations of people whose faith has been quickened by reading

scripture cannot be ignored. The psalmist described the experience in a poetic image: "Deep calls to deep" (Psalm 42:7).

The insights of a particular individual, however, must be constantly shared with and corrected by the experience of the religious community, or the danger exists that a person will be "inspired" only by those passages that reinforce one's own biases. The theme of this volume is this: the Bible is more than an individual's faith resource. It is the history-bearing document of a *community* of persons, and must be understood in a community setting.

Despite the dangers of subjectivism and individualism, the fact that the Bible has been inspiring to many people in many ages is the first evidence that something beyond human nature is at work in its pages.

2. *Inspiration can be found in passages that are especially framed*. Inspiration can be a vivid experience. When certain writers were especially aware that they were communicating a clear message from God—that is, when the competing voices and noises of life had been pushed to the background and the divine voice was clear—the writers found ways to alert the reader to the importance of particular passages. For example, a reader of scripture quickly recognizes that anything which happened on the holy mountain must be taken with utmost seriousness. This would include the Ten Commandments, the Sermon on the Mount, and the transfiguration.

Another interesting example of framing came when Jesus returned to his childhood home and read scripture before a hometown audience. The stage was carefully set. (Today, when a person wants to run for high public office, the tradition is to return to one's hometown, and announce in the presence of family and friends, "I am running for the United States Senate!") At the beginning of his public ministry, according to Luke, Jesus returned to his hometown, accepted the honor of reading the text of the day, and then associated himself with one of the important traditions of his faith family. He would minister in the manner of the prophet. The writer has "framed" the passage as being of unique importance. This second evidence for divine inspiration is not something we bring to the Bible, but results from the writer's effort to identify ideas and events of special importance.

3. *Inspiration can be found in those passages that show concepts or ethical behavior different from that normally expected from human nature.*

Normal behavior, for any group that values its community, is to act in ways that offer maximum protection for that group. When, for example, Joel counseled his nation to beat their plowshares into swords he was saying what most people expect to hear when a nation is in danger. His words certainly reflect the actions of nations throughout recorded history. However, when the behavior of a people moves in an opposite direction, when prophets or others insist that the nation take risks in order to relate to others on a equal level (as did both Micah and Isaiah in insisting that swords be converted to plowshares), then one can assume that some outside influence has been at work.

The changing attitudes toward suffering offer an example of an unexpected insight. Through several centuries the belief within Judaism was that God rewarded them with prosperity and punished them with pain. It would seem logical that when the Babylonians defeated the Jews and took most of their people captive this attitude would have been reinforced. Instead, an exiled writer made a remarkably different interpretation of that event. Second Isaiah concluded that suffering can be a mark of divine calling, an invitation to participate in the redemption of humanity. The idea that faithfulness to God might bring additional, future suffering certainly ran counter to the perceived best interest of the nation!

Whenever I come to the Suffering Servant passages of Second Isaiah, and remember the way those passages, under the most horrid of circumstances, turned the concept of suffering on its head, I feel I must take off my shoes. This is sacred ground. Something is at work here that cannot be attributed to the normal processes of human logic or human self-preservation. The book of Job similarly rises far above expected human insights as it delves into the meaning of this same subject.

Another example of behavior that is different from what would be normally expected is the outcome of the argument between Peter and Paul over inclusion of non-Jews in the religious community. Since there is a tendency in such discussions for fear of the new to prevail—the narrower view almost always wins—it is amazing that Peter changed his mind and Paul's position triumphed. Modern churches continue to struggle to work out the implications of the astounding fact that in Christ there is neither Jew nor Gentile, slave nor free, male nor female.

When writers lift the ethical and spiritual level far above what would be expected from ordinary people, then we must assume that they have been visited by a power beyond themselves.

4. Similarly, *inspiration can be found in the work of writers who, working against a primitive and anthropomorphic concept of God, gave a view of God that is stunning in its depth.*

The most striking example of the redefinition of God comes in the third chapter of Exodus. Previous writers had dealt with a God who walked in the garden of Eden, argued with Adam and Eve, and was unable to find that couple when they hid in the bushes. Their concept of God was simply a reflection of themselves. In early Exodus, however, God is defined and named by the verb "to be." God is to be known as "Yahweh," the essence of Being itself. Likewise, the writer of the Eighth Psalm could understand God as the mystery associated with a creation whose vastness the writer could not comprehend. Amazingly, these understandings have stood the test of time over three millennia and continue to be intellectually respectable in the wake of the explosion of scientific knowledge that characterizes the current age.

Some insights into God seemed quite inadvertent and therefore offer further evidence of some power beyond human consciousness at work. For example, the two stories of creation, so different that the editor could not blend them but had to lay them side by side, give us the basis of some of the paradoxes which have been central to our understanding of the Divine. God is both immanent and transcendent; God is both merciful and demanding. Richard Friedman, a professed nonbeliever who has written extensively about the opening books of scripture, was nonetheless deeply impressed with the result of this blending:

> When the [editor] combined all the sources, he mixed two different pictures of God. By doing that, he formed a new balance between the personal and the transcendent qualities of the deity. It was a picture of God as both universal and intensely personal... The fusion was artistically dramatic and theologically profound...Ultimate things are at stake, but every human being is told, "The master of the universe is concerned with you."[3]

---

[3] Richard Elliott Friedman, *Who Wrote the Bible?* (New York: Harper and Row, 1987), p. 238.

Another example of inadvertent definition of God came from Paul, whose purpose was to make room in the faith community for persons of all ethnic backgrounds. In that process he gave a picture of a God who is extravagant, even reckless, in extending love and grace.

Virginia Mollenkott feels similarly about the fact that some writers from within a rigid, paternalistic society could, on occasion, describe God with feminine characteristics.

> For me, it is one of the signs of inspiration from beyond themselves that the biblical authors were sometimes able to reach beyond their socialization to depict God as a woman.[4]

5. *Inspiration can be found in certain stories that have been told and retold in the unique environment of the biblical people, being driven deeper with each telling until they probe the depths of human faith and the human psyche.*

An example of such a story is the Genesis account of Jacob's wrestling with an angel at Peniel. (32:22–32) The story has become, through its retellings, more than a tale about a person suffering internal conflict. It has been pushed to the more important level of myth (a story with divine overtones). In the story, Jacob was ready to cross a river in order to encounter his brother, Esau, whom he had not seen for years. Since Esau was the twin brother that he once cheated out of a birthright, Jacob was not sure what to expect from their meeting. In his deeply troubled state he found himself wrestling with a seemingly demonic being. (The story has roots in an ancient and pagan culture, a culture that believed that river demons guarded their bodies of water and prevented people from crossing them from dusk to dawn.) Throughout the night Jacob and the "demon" wrestled, and Jacob gradually began to realize that his antagonist was in a mysterious way a messenger of God. Though contending with God, Jacob was able to prevail. He held his antagonist until sunrise, when the river demon/angel needed to depart. Jacob asserted that he would not let go until he was given a blessing. The blessing was given, and Jacob was able to proceed across the river to a reconciling meeting with his brother. But in the encounter he had been injured, and would always walk with a limp.

---

[4] Virginia Mollenkott, *Godding: Human Responsibility and the Bible* (New York: Crossroad, 1987).

Jacob struggled with a demon/angel. He survived and matured, yet was wounded. The story suggests the way all people cope with the forces that would prevent forward movement. We wrestle with our demons and then recognize that even they can have divine content. We overcome them, then go away wounded but remarkably empowered. Such depth of human understanding could not be generated in any one writing; it was the product of constant telling and alteration by persons of faith, each honing it until it digs deep into the human soul.

Additional examples of stories with similar depth can be found among the other remarkable stories of Genesis and among Jesus' parables. Indeed, a keen eye can detect such profound insights in surprising places. William Faulkner recognized in the account of David and Absalom a story that explains much of the troubled race relations in the old South—half-brothers and half-sisters who destroy one another in their awkward efforts toward sex and power.[5]

Some biblical stories have been told and retold in the atmosphere of faith until they reach deep into the meaning of what it is to be human and what it means to exist in relation to God.

6. *On certain ethical issues, inspiration is identified not in any position taken by a single biblical writer, but by the direction in which ethical understandings evolve.*

Here we explore more fully the "progressive revelation" that was described earlier. Progressive revelation is seen in the area of sexual ethics and gender roles.

The earliest sexual ethic of the emerging faith community was an effort to produce the maximum number of births. Israel was a small nation surrounded by hostile neighbors. It needed male children to become soldiers to fight off the Canaanites and the Philistines. It needed female children who would mature to produce more soldiers. Two ethical standards came from this concern for procreation. One was that women were valued primarily as mothers of male children. The other viewed every sexual contact which had no chance of producing a child as an "abomination." With their understanding of the process of procreation, any waste of male semen was seen as a threat to the very existence of the nation. Thus[6] masturbation was an abomination, nocturnal emissions made a man unclean, homosexual activity between men was an abomination, as

---

[5] See his novel *Absalom, Absalom* (New York: Random House, 1966).
[6] See especially Leviticus 15ff.

was having sexual intercourse with one's wife during her time of infertility.

Another part of that sexual ethic was polygamy. Since one man can keep many women pregnant, a man was allowed as many wives as his finances would permit. For a man of unlimited wealth, such as David, this meant an unlimited number of wives and concubines. Jacob, father of the twelve sons from whom came the twelve tribes of Israel, produced these sons through two simultaneous wives and two concubines. The biblical writers gave no hint of judgment on such an arrangement.

As the community developed, the sexual ethic and the attitude toward the role of women underwent gradual transformation. Polygamy became less accepted (despite the fact that they still needed soldiers—an indication of something beyond the human sphere at work); women took on additional, important roles of leadership. In the New Testament women gave significant leadership (and even financial resources) to the disciples and the early church.

This transformation never brought women to full equality, nor did it fully affirm monogamous marriages. In one of the last scriptural books to be composed a writer told Timothy that if he aspired to the office of bishop he had best be married to only one wife! (1 Timothy 3:2) Thus, at no place in scripture does the reader find an ethic that allows woman and man to stand on equal ground or children to be born out of love rather than legal or social necessity.

Attempting to transfer the biblical sexual ethic to other times and cultures can be a delicate, even dangerous procedure. In the modern world overpopulation is a major threat to the human community. Strong, monogamous families are essential to the task of preserving culture. Birth control is necessary and homosexuality is no longer a threat. *We thus find our guidance in the direction in which the Spirit has nudged people for the centuries in which the Bible was written and the direction in which that same Spirit continues, gently, to encourage us today.* That direction is definitely toward gender equality and monogamous relations based on justice and love.

Subjectivism

The precise criteria for finding inspiration in scripture will differ from reader to reader, for inspiration is not only in the writing but also in the reading. All of what has been said about identifying the Spirit of God can be criticized as open to abuse. What one person identifies as inspiring, another may find thoroughly bland.

Judged against Standards of Jesus

Subjectivism, however, need not rule entirely. In addition to the six criteria given above, the Gospel accounts become another objective point of reference. If one believes that something definitive came into human life in the person of Jesus, then all the remainder of scripture must be judged by that high standard. If God taught, through Jesus, that people of faith are to overcome evil through redemptive suffering, then the calls to respond to evil by violence—calls attributed to God in the early history of Israel—must have come from some other voice. Also, the idea found in the Deuteronomic code that all suffering is just punishment visited on human sin, must be tossed on the scrap heap of outmoded concepts. By reaching out with compassion to persons outside his ethnic community, and by making a Samaritan the hero of a story defining "neighbor," Jesus rose above Nehemiah's harsh attitude toward foreigners. Using the life and teaching of Jesus as a touchstone keeps the search for divine inspiration from becoming entirely individualistic and subjective.

Embracing the Whole Volume

There is a yet another level in which subjectivity is decreased. While the level of inspiration varies within the passages of the book, *the volume as a whole is the vessel that holds the divine Spirit.*

The "problems" of the Bible need not be problems when they are viewed against the whole of scripture. Because the Bible is varied, because it is uneven in its moral vision, because it offers imperfect role models, every human being can find a home in its pages. It is hard, if not impossible, to imagine an act or thought, redemptive or destructive, that has not been foreshadowed in the biblical pages. The moral level of the Bible as a unit is not so high as to make any person feel excluded from the ongoing drama of the faith community. The belief systems developed by its various writers are often quite different from the orthodoxy of either that day or this. Sometimes beliefs expressed there appear weak or heretical. Yet this, also, need not be a barrier. Often, just as I am about to despair within what Annie Dillard calls "this anachronistic, semibarbaric mass of antique laws and fabulous tales from far away,"[7] I find a description of God that nourishes me or a moral challenge that lifts me. *The Bible, as a whole, becomes an instrument of grace.* No one is kept out. For those who are depressed, the door of Ecclesiastes is opened. For those struggling with the erotic, the door of the Song of Solomon is opened. For those seeking devotional helps, the Psalms offer entree. Those seeking to know the breadth and depth of the love of God find admittance through the parables of Jesus. Those wanting to know how to carry out the will of God toward the marginalized and how to structure societies for maximum justice will enter through the door held open by the eighth-century prophets.

Intentionality

Unfortunately, most Christians have been taught habits of Bible reading that complicate the process of experiencing it as a whole. Thus they miss the experience of receiving it as one's own book written about one's own faith family.

Philosophers have long known that the way we anticipate the world has an enormous effect on the way we actually experience it. "Intentionality" is the term put on this phenomenon. What we *intend* to hear and see largely determines what we actually *do* hear and see.

When one turns to the Bible *intending* to hear the direct voice of God in every word and phrase, much of the real message is blocked. It is as if an uninitiated individual were told, just before hearing a recording of a symphony, that the orchestra were only one organ-like instrument being played by a single individual. The result would be a certain flatness of hearing. Only as the listener is able to envision one hundred musicians making their contribution to the whole is the richness of the music experienced and the message of the composer—often given in melody and counter melody—fully encountered.

Only by coming to the Bible expecting to encounter the separate personalities of more than seventy writers, knowing that this remarkable diversity creates a whole greater than the sum of its parts, do we "hear" the Bible in all its richness.

Krister Stendahl, describing the diversity found in even one writer (Paul), also makes the argument that the total message of scrip-

---

[7]*Auteous* (Autumn 1989), p. 989.

ture, captured in the life of the community, is the medium through which the divine message is delivered.

> How, then, does the church, the Christian, the preacher, the individual Bible reader live with the richness of diversity? First we must overcome our defensive instincts. We need not defend God or the Bible. While we may find and rejoice in themes, lessons, and concepts that seem to hold the Bible together, we should not think that such an enterprise is actually what holds it together. The unity of the Scriptures is rooted in the experience of the church which found these various ways of speaking and thinking to be authentic witnesses to the one Lord.[8]

Tunnel Vision

Since the Bible as a whole is the primary conduit of the divine Spirit, tunnel vision (looking at one sentence or paragraph without reference to any context) can become a major barrier to effective interaction between the reader and the spiritual content of the Bible. In issues relating entirely to an individual, tunnel vision may, at times, be appropriate. Persons, for example, looking for assurance of full acceptance might read a chapter of Romans to the exclusion of all other parts of scripture. Nonetheless, tunnel vision is more often a danger. Those looking for guidance on how to conduct a particular part of the business of life need to examine each appropriate passage against the broad sweep of scripture. Else slave owners will continue to find ways to justify slavery, followers of some new Stalin or Hitler will quote a few brief passages to call people to obedience to oppressive governments, women will be kept from leadership in congregations, and violence between nations will be accepted as normal.

Removing the blinders that create tunnel vision will help, also, in keeping certain issues in perspective. One of the family arguments that has been observed from beginning to end of the biblical drama is that of prophetic religion over against priestly religion. Prophetic religion was seen in the words of the eighth-century prophets, bringing the judgment of God to bear on the injustices of the

---

[8] Krister Stendahl, *Paul Among Jews and Gentiles* (Philadelphia: Fortress Press, 1976).

economic order. It was seen, as well, in Jesus, as he reached out to the dispossessed of his day. James called the faith community back to prophetic religion in his comment that faith without works is dead. On the other hand, priestly religion insists that proper worship of the Divine is the essence of religion. The editors of the books of Chronicles, making David a temple leader rather than a military or political leader, attempted to give priority to priestly faith. The many Psalms with their liturgical beauty, and the book of Hebrews' description of Jesus as the high priest, are all efforts to strengthen this aspect of faith.

The truth, of course, is that prophetic and priestly religion need one another. The argument between these two should never be either/or; it is always a both/and. The concern must be over how to apply both styles of religion under constantly shifting circumstances. Any strong, continuing social group needs both goal-oriented tasks (for the church, its prophetic ministry) *and* maintenance tasks (for the church, its ritual and fellowship). In the life of the faith community, prophetic religion was especially important in the eighth century when the nation, through its kings and laws, was able to apply concerns of justice. During the exile, however, when the people were powerless to determine the quality of their communal life, it was only the precious rituals that allowed the people to remain united with one another and with their tradition. Because of the tendency to read only favorite portions of the Bible and the failure to put those passages against the total message of the Bible, the church continues to be split between those who want to pour almost all their energy into social action (the prophets) and others who want to put energy exclusively into ritual and dogma (the priests). It would be a tragedy for the church if either of these extremes were to banish the other.

Ethical Guidance: Defining the Self

What does the Bible say about the issues that still are debated within the faith family? On ethical and theological issues, it says many things on many subjects. The words of scripture will not, by themselves, make decisions for modern readers. The ancient writers will lay out the boundaries of the historic debates, debates that have raged over the most important issues in human living. Also, because the Bible is a volume of grace, it will invite each reader into that debate.

Instead of dealing in simple answers, the Bible traffics in matters of identification and community context. "Who am I?" is the first basic question confronted in scripture. The individual is a product of dust, into which has been breathed a divine Spirit. The believer is part of a unique community that has struggled for more than three thousand years with the issues of responsible living.

The Bible tells me who I am. It also tells me to whom I belong. I belong to a community of similarly motivated seekers, people who have undertaken responsibility for me and to whom I have reciprocal responsibility. The choices I make concerning my life are made in the context of a "great cloud of witnesses" whose influence I dare not attempt to escape.

Scripture informs me that a few basic assumptions of the faith community are no longer open to argument. These assumptions include the fact that the world is created and ruled by a Divine Being who is worthy of our worship; that the only meaningful measure of life is the degree to which we respond to this Divine Being. Included among these assumptions is the fact that we are not simply isolated individuals bumping against and often bruising each other as we pursue divergent goals; rather, we are tied together in an intricate web of caring and responsibility that reaches to the ends of the world. The faith community has always assumed that we should give special attention to those who are being crushed at the bottom of the social pyramid, and that we should attempt to usher all persons into secure communities of peace and justice.

Ultimately, the scriptures insist, we belong to God—God who called the faith community into being—God who made heaven and earth—God who is from everlasting to everlasting—God who has no patience with the idols we build to ward off our insecurities.

In the face of difficult moral concerns, the Bible forces on us this one question: *"How can we, a part of the faith community that lives in response to God, confront current ethical issues in a way that preserves continuity with the past and creates integrity toward the present and future?"*

The effort to treat the Bible as inerrant and to find the word of God buried in every human word and phrase is, tragically, a search for perfection that cannot be achieved by anything within the boundaries of human life. Such an effort attempts to transform the Bible from a message about the Divine into the substance of the Divine. In short, it creates an idol. Idols are dangerous to the degree they stand close to the sacred. Because the Bible is a channel of divine grace, it is potentially a very dangerous idol. On one thing there is little debate among the scriptural writers: nothing is infallible that human minds have touched and helped construct. The only infallible is the Sovereign Being whom the faith community is called to serve. To chase after full security is to run away from faith and, ultimately, to run away from life. This should come as no surprise. Jesus told his friends: "Those who try to make their life secure will lose it" (Luke 17:32).

Accepting the Bible as a faith family album allows the scriptures to be central to faith without becoming an idol. Such acceptance allows biblical insights to guide without controlling. It allows scripture to point toward, without competing with, the God in whom we live and move and have our being.

Postscript: Listening within the Noise

The child just across the aisle, beyond several broad planks in the historic meetinghouse, was restless. Well he might be. Quaker meetings—an hour of shared silence—can be difficult for the uninitiated adult, but agony for an energetic child. He whispered to his mother, turned pages in his coloring book, and finally shared the silence by going to sleep. Farther across the room was a woman suffering from allergies. She coughed. She honked. Immediately in front of us was a woman with back problems. She made no sound, but her pain-filled movements were distracting.

Despite the very human noises, a holy stillness descended across the meeting for worship. The Society of Friends takes seriously the psalmist's invitation: "Be still, and know that I am God" (Psalm 46:10). Nothing, for a Quaker worshiper, is so sacred as silence. Nothing, according to this tradition, draws individuals into a worshiping community so effectively as the shared hush that settles over a place where ancestors in faith have worshiped and witnessed.

Human distractions cannot ultimately deny the pervading Spirit of the Holy One. Quite the opposite: human realities authenticate the presence of the Spirit.

The Bible is a collection of varied writings, punctuated by human distractions that cannot, finally, deny its sacred reality.

This volume began with my frustration with the human "noises" that can bewilder any serious reader of the Bible. Indeed, the human element is quite real. The moral level of some parts of scripture sinks distressingly low. The pre-scientific assumptions of the writers are obvious and embarrassing. The buoyant optimism of many of the psalms runs aground on the shoals of pessimism in the book of Ecclesiastes. It is easy to develop sympathy for those who have attempted to read the Bible for guidance but instead have surrendered in the face of its seemingly intractable problems.

After a long period of intense involvement in the scriptures, however, I find myself writing now in appreciation of a sacredness that no amount of human noise can deny. Despite all the problems—the variety of views given by different writers, and the highs and lows of moral development—a mysterious holiness pervades the whole.

I write in hopes of helping others find the sacredness that moves silently in and around the Bible's earthy environment.

History of Biblical Writings

DATE	BOOKS WRITTEN *CONCERNING* THIS TIME	DECISIVE EVENTS	BOOKS WRITTEN (EDITED) *DURING* THIS TIME
Before recorded time, until 1,700 B.C.E.	Genesis	Creation of the world. Development of living things, including human life Beginning of Jewish nation. Sarah and Abraham	
1,600		Joseph and the entry into Egypt. Jewish people fall into slavery	Perhaps the earliest fragments of historic materials were written during this time: examples are the Song of Deborah (Judges 5), and the earliest edition of the Ten Commandments. Oral traditions also developed, but no complete books were written during this time
1,500			
1,400		Years of slavery	
1,300			
	Exodus	Moses and the release from slavery. Wandering in the desert	
1,200	Joshua and Judges	Entry into the promised land Continued warfare between Israel and Canaanites	
1,100	Leviticus and Numbers		

259

260 *The Bible: Faith's Family Album*

DATE	BOOKS WRITTEN *CONCERNING* THIS TIME	DECISIVE EVENTS	BOOKS WRITTEN (EDITED) *DURING* THIS TIME
1,000 950	1 and 2 Samuel, 1 and 2 Chronicles and 1 and 2 Kings	Hebrew kingdom organized under Saul. David overthrows Saul and leads the nation to its greatest triumphs and its greatest wealth.	
		King Solomon builds the temple. Solomon dies.The kingdom is divided (922)	Perhaps early Psalms
900 850 800	Ruth	Many different kings (and one queen) rule Israel and Judah from 922 until 721	Fragments of historic documents
750 700	Amos, Micah, Hosea, 1 Isaiah (1—39)	Assyrians invade Israel, and take the people captive. This is the end of the Kingdom of Israel (721). Assyrians also invade Judah. Judah begins to pay tribute to Assyria (701)	Amos, Micah, Hosea, 1 Isaiah (1—39)
650 600 550	Jonah Daniel, Jeremiah, Nahum, Ezekiel, Lamentations, 2 Isaiah (40—56), Esther	The reforms of Josiah (640) Assyrians defeated by a new power, Babylonia. Babylonians invade Judah twice (598 and 587), taking captives each time. Captivity begins	Deuteronomy Jeremiah, Ezekiel, 2 Isaiah (40—56), Genesis—Numbers (edited), Nahum, Joshua and Judges, Lamentations, 1 and 2 Samuel, 1 and 2 Kings, 3 Isaiah.
500 450 400	Ezra, Nehemiah, Obadiah, Zechariah, Zephaniah, Haggai, Malachi, Joel, 3 Isaiah, Habakkuk	Exiles return (538). Rebuilding begins. Jews remain under Persian control (538–331)	Ezra, Nehemiah, Zechariah, Zephaniah, Obadiah,Haggai, Malachi, Ruth, Jonah, Additional Psalms, Ecclesiastes, Song of Solomon
350 300		Alexander the Great conquers Holy Land and surrounding region. Alexander dies, and empire divided (323)	Joel, Proverbs 1 and 2 Chronicles

DATE	BOOKS WRITTEN *CONCERNING* THIS TIME	DECISIVE EVENTS	BOOKS WRITTEN (EDITED) *DURING* THIS TIME
250			Job Psalms completed
200		Antiochus IV attempts to impose Greek culture on Jews. The temple is violated.	Daniel
150		Judas Maccabaeus rebels (167) Temple worship is restored (164)	
100		The Jews enjoy brief period of autonomy	
50		Rome spreads its power over Mediterranean world. Herod appointed king of Judea (37–4 B.C.E.)	
0	Matthew, Mark, Luke, John	Jesus born in Nazareth (6 B.C.E.)	
50 C.E.	Acts of the Apostles	Jesus is crucified (27 C.E.) Paul becomes a follower (38). Jerusalem Jews rebel against Rome (66). Temple is destroyed. Jews are scattered through Greek and Roman world.	
100			1 Thessalonians, 1 and 2 Corinthians, Romans, Galatians, Philippians, Philemon. Mark, Matthew, Luke-Acts.
		Domitian becomes emperor, persecution intensifies	Revelation, 1 and 2 Peter, John, 2 Thessalonians, Pastoral Epistles, Epistles of John.
150		The church continues to grow. Persecution moderates. Hostility between followers of Jesus and traditional Jewish community intensifies	1 and 2 Peter, Jude, James
200			
250			
300		Constantine is converted. Future of Christian movement, even if in altered form, is assured	

Study Guide

The Bible is the story of a community attempting to formulate and broaden its faith. The Bible is thus best studied in community settings.

Some individuals will read *The Bible: Faith's Family Album* alone. Those people will, it is hoped, find the suggestions for study offered here helpful. Nonetheless, the preferred mode of study is in a group. Sharing allows ideas to be exchanged and tested. Tasks, such as assignments for intensive study of particular scriptures, can be distributed.

Some who read this book will find its ideas significantly different from their previous understanding of the Bible. A group setting can be supportive as new ideas struggle against the old. On the other hand, when a new way of understanding the Bible answers a long-standing question, the joy can be shared.

Two types of groups are anticipated. One will move rather quickly through the chapters of this book, using about one week to cover each of the twelve chapters. Parts of the Bible can be probed to illustrate points made in the book, but no in-depth study of scripture can take place in this format. This brevity is quite acceptable. There are times to grasp the contours of the forest without attention to individual trees.

Other groups may want to take a year or more to make their way through this volume. The greater time will allow the primary text—the Bible itself—to be examined in depth. This study guide will offer suggestions for enrichment material that will help make the extended study worth the larger investment of time.

Members of study groups are encouraged to supplement this volume with their own biblical investigation. Here are some aids in doing this:

- Simply reading several good translations of the same text will illuminate the meaning of the original languages. Some translations recommended include *The New Revised Standard Version*

(New York: Oxford University Press, 1989); *The New Jerusalem Bible* (New York: Doubleday, 1985); and *The New International Version* (Grand Rapids: Zondervan, 1978). In addition, *An Inclusive Language New Testament* by the Priests for Equality (Brentwood, Md., 1994) gives insights into the problems of a fair and just translation.

- For those who wish to dig deeper, *The New Interpreter's Bible* (Nashville: Abingdon Press) is a massive but user-friendly group of books. Another helpful series is known as *Interpretation* (Louisville: Westminster/John Knox Press); it is written in clear and helpful language. *The Women's Bible Commentary* (Louisville: Westminster/John Knox, 1992) shows how meager are our interpretations when restricted to any one (for example, white male) point of view. Alongside these Bible commentaries, most groups will want to have a good Bible dictionary—any one of several put out by major religious publishing houses.

Introduction:

Encountering the Whole Bible

The group may want to make two lists on chalkboard or newsprint. The first list will be of "Ways the scriptures have been helpful in my spiritual growth." The second list will be of "Difficulties I have encountered in reading the scriptures." The purpose of the study is to strengthen items on the first list, and to eliminate or lessen the impact of items on the second list. Preserve these lists, then check from time to time to see what advances are being made in these areas.

Jack Good proposes that the Bible as a whole is the bearer of divine truth. To use a metaphor suggested in the Introduction, we must be willing to hear all the instruments in order to receive the full impact of a symphony. Are members of the group willing to encounter the entire scripture, even if it means listening to instruments and hearing chords that may be less than pleasing to the ear?

Members of the group may share family mementos—collections of letters or photographs. What is the purpose of collecting family lore?

Seeing the Bible as the effort of a community to preserve its values implies a new approach to the scriptures. Discuss the implications of this shift of focus from a book about God to a volume about a community seeking to understand itself in relationship to its Creator.

Look carefully at the "freeing assumptions" given in the Introduction. Are these assumptions likely to remove barriers to Bible study?

Enrichment resources for those moving at a more deliberate pace:

In introducing the idea of the Bible as family album, the writer states that genealogies are developed by historians, but family albums are put together by poets. What is meant by this? What are the implications?

Discuss the difference between traditional and nontraditional societies. What are the dangers of each? Is the Bible sometimes used for nonreligious purposes, primarily to prevent *any* change in the life of society?

The group may want to spend time discussing the impact of Darwin's ideas on people of the late nineteenth century. List the ways his concepts would have proved threatening. Were there ways Darwin could have been received as the carrier of good news?

The group should discuss the phrase "biblical criticism." In what ways has biblical criticism been helpful to persons seeking spiritual guidance in scripture? In what ways is it threatening?

Good suggests that the Bible is not to be treated as a how-to guide, a self-help book, or a book of recipes. Can anyone think of exceptions to these general rules?

Looking Ahead:

The eighth-century prophets' are the first biblical books to be discussed. Three of these are short enough to be read in the time between study sessions; 1 Isaiah (chapters 1—39) may be divided. Encourage members of the group to choose one of these to examine over the coming week.

Chapter One:
The Community Defines Itself: Justice

The *Parable* that opens each chapter of biblical explanation is intended to nudge the reader out of the mindset of "The Bible is about God" and into a mindset of "The Bible is about a community." Discuss the four ways that the island community related to the surrounding sea. Do these capture the ways the Jewish community related to Jehovah?

Review the social realities of Israel and Judah in the eighth century B.C.E. To what degree do we face similar conditions today?

Each person needs to understand the meaning of *the theory of retribution*. Is this concept still encountered in religious circles?

Receive the reports from those assigned to read each of the four eighth-century prophets. Pay careful attention to the insights gained by these class members.

Review the identifying marks of the faith community offered by these earliest biblical books. To what degree are these identifying marks still visible in churches and synagogues today?

Enrichment resources for those moving at a more deliberate pace:

The group may enjoy a role-playing exercise in which an individual is assigned to be one of the four eighth-century prophets. (Those who have made reports on each prophet would be prime candidates to be so cast.) The four could have a conversation among themselves about their reactions to conditions of the modern day. The remainder of the "audience" could put questions to these "experts." Do not be afraid to let a sense of humor pervade this drama.

Micah, whose village would have been on the front lines in the event of hostile attack, counseled his people to "beat their swords into plowshares" and trust in God for national defense. Compare this to Isaiah's vision of a militarily strong messiah. Should either—or both—of these prophetic words be taken seriously today?

The prophet is defined as one who speaks the wisdom of God to the present time. Who, then, have been the prophets of your lifetime?

Looking Ahead:

The book of Deuteronomy is the subject of the next chapter. As assignments for further study, the Ten Commandments (chapter 5) and the Great Commandment (Shema—chapter 6) should receive special attention. The remainder of the chapters might be divided at random.

Chapter Two:
The Community Defines Itself: Law

The group should discuss the role of law in human life. Can communities exist without law? When is law an annoyance? (April 15 could be mentioned!) Note the particular role that law plays in Jewish tradition.

Hear reports from those who have read portions of Deuteronomy. What, in particular, impressed these readers about the assigned material?

Describe the variety of legal requirements contained in the book of Deuteronomy. Do you feel the same degree of loyalty to all types of law?

Jack Good distinguishes the laws that relate primarily to priestly religion from those that relate primarily to prophetic religion. Make sure that all members of the class have a clear understanding of the difference between these two.

Enrichment resources for those moving at a more deliberate pace:

The book of Deuteronomy strongly connects God's gift of freedom and God's gift of the law. Talk about this. Is freedom found in obedience or disobedience?

In modern Western societies the religious law and the secular law have been separated. Or have they? What role does each play, and to what degree do they overlap?

Jack Good notes that religious law is pliant. Do members of the group see evidence of evolutionary change in religious law today?

Some laws in Deuteronomy call for actions that we today would condemn as genocide. Others are a special burden to women. How should we relate to these laws?

Looking Ahead:

The next chapter will cover a large amount of scripture. Members of even a large class will find it difficult to read and report on all the material. The following are suggested assignments: the first two chapters of Genesis; the escape from slavery described in the first twelve chapters of Exodus; the Code of Holiness (Leviticus 17—26). Other class members could compare the story of Jewish entry into the Holy Land given in Joshua (see chapter 8) with that of Judges (see chapter 2). Other members of the group can read and review passages that they find especially interesting.

Chapter Three:
The Community Traces Its History

Has anyone in the group helped write a family history? If so, have the person(s) describe the process by which that history was written. Did members of different branches of the family ever clash over contrasting interpretations of facts? If so, how were these conflicts reconciled?

Receive the reports of those who have read the first two chapters of Genesis. Review the material in chapter 3 that points to two creation stories. Note the implications for an understanding of God.

A report from those examining the early part of Exodus will provide an excellent opportunity to reinforce one of the major themes of this volume: the primary purpose of the biblical writers is to tell about the community. When a reader comes to the first chapters of Exodus asking, "What does this tell us about God?" the answer is brutal and unappealing. The group should shift the focus and ask, "What is this passage saying about the religious community?" The same shift of focus is important in dealing with the material in the Code of Holiness.

Those assigned to read Joshua and Judges will note the differences in reporting the same historic events. What is each editor saying about the community of faith?

Jack Good states that the historic material of scripture was written less to convey facts than to "justify the ways of God toward humankind." Is there, then, no validity in the historic information?

Many episodes of violence are recorded in both Joshua and Judges. Are the explanations (not excuses) given in chapter 3 satisfying?

Enrichment resources for those moving at a more deliberate pace:

The word *myth* is introduced as a way of understanding parts of the book of Genesis. What does this word mean to the members of the group? A dictionary may help open a discussion of the various ways this word may be used.

Members of the group may enjoy staging a debate over one of the issues before the faith community. Half the group, using only biblical material covered in this chapter, could argue for: *God is a demanding Deity whom we must approach in awe.* The other half, also using the same biblical works, could argue for: *God is a gracious Deity who embraces all people in divine love.*

Here is another debate the group may have. Does the Bible, by showing the conditions in which women lived in ancient Israel, reinforce women in subservient roles; or does it add strength to women by showing how individuals were able to rise above the roles assigned their gender?

Looking Ahead:

Understanding the trauma that awaited the nation at its next stage is essential to the continuing story. One or more members should be encouraged to study the Babylonian exile. Other class members will look into the works of Jeremiah and Ezekiel. At least one member should investigate the suffering servant passages of 2 Isaiah.

Chapter Four:
The Community Survives Crisis

Receive the reports of those examining the conditions of the exile. What is the role of a people's sacred writings in helping the group survive under such circumstances?

Describe the smug attitude of the nation during Jeremiah's early years. Have we as a church or nation—or as individuals—ever refused to listen to prophetic words of warning?

Habakkuk challenged the theory of retribution with his insistence that "judgment comes forth perverted." Note the importance of this insight for all people in pain.

Examine Ezekiel's vision of dry bones and their renewal. Is this vision optimistic? pessimistic? realistic? To what degree is it all three?

Receive a report from members of the class who have studied the Suffering Servant passages. Try to imagine how these words would have been received by the people of the exile. Review the contributions of 2 Isaiah. Does the writer of 3 Isaiah carry on these same themes?

Read a brief portion of the description of David given in 1 and 2 Chronicles. Compare this with the portrait of David given in the historic books described in chapter 3.

Review the family arguments before the faith community at this point. Give special attention to the evolving understandings of suffering.

Enrichment resources for those moving at a more deliberate pace:

The group may want to spend a few minutes discussing the prophets Nahum and Obadiah. Can a biblical book have no role other than to describe the anxieties and angers of our religious ancestors?

The work of Ezekiel offers an opportunity to review the difference between a priest (which Ezekiel was early in life) and a prophet (which he became). In what ways was each role helpful to his people?

Examine carefully the other Suffering Servant passages listed in the footnotes. Try to imagine a dramatic setting for each. Do any of these poems imply that the *nation* may be asked to suffer for all humankind?

After encountering 2 Isaiah, Joel will impress some as a throwback to a narrow, violence-saturated view of the Divine. Is this surprising? Do such pendulum swings take place in the history of other human groups?

Have members of the group report on the contributions of Haggai, Zechariah, and Malachi.

Two radically different views of a coming messiah are now before the faith community. Compare and contrast these.

Looking Ahead:

The short books of Ruth and Jonah make good assignments. Someone with time to invest might be willing to examine varying interpretations of the book of Job. Other members of the group may want to read and report on their favorite psalms. Exploring the book of Daniel can be an adventure. A person who is not embarrassed by matters erotic might be willing to report on the Song of Solomon.

Chapter Five:
The Community Produces Artists and Philosophers

Receive the reports of those who gave special attention to the books of Ruth and Jonah. Show how these two story writers addressed, in quite different ways, the same subject.

Does the idea of humor in scripture seem strange? Refer back to the story of Balaam's talking mule (Leviticus).

Discuss the reasons why the Song of Soloman and Esther, neither containing any reference to the Divine, are included in the Bible.

A significant portion of this class session may be devoted to a discussion of the book of Job. Note the way the dramatist has described Job as blameless. Discuss the meaning of the phrase "Job's comforters." Share evidence that we continue to find ways to blame the victim when illness or other disasters strike. Jack Good insists that the book of Job calls us "to be faithful when faith has no guaranteed rewards." Are members of the class willing to "serve God for naught"?

The book of Ecclesiastes offers the thoughts of a deeply depressed philosopher. Someone in the group may be willing to describe the experience of being severely depressed. How would it feel, in the depth of spiritual darkness, to read scripture written by someone who was battling a similar despair?

The book of Daniel is as much about patriotism as about religion. Discuss the differences in the relationship between God and country in biblical times and in modern times. To what degree do patriotism and religion strengthen each other? Does mixing the two constitute a danger?

Encourage the total class to experience the book of Psalms. Look through a modern hymnal and identify texts based on Psalms. If the hymnal includes a Psalter, note its importance to modern worship. How have the Psalms been able to speak to the spiritual needs of people across more than two thousand years?

Enrichment resources for those moving at a more deliberate pace:

The book of Proverbs is a collection of wise sayings. To what degree are these more than truisms? Make sure that all members of the group understand the meaning of Wisdom as used by the writer of Proverbs. Discuss the view of women given in the thirty-first chapter. Is this a compliment to women, or a potentially destructive reinforcement of society's expectations that women should be "super-moms"? Discuss the differences in child-rearing practices in biblical times and modern times.

Identify the particular messages the writer of Daniel wanted to offer those struggling against Greek dominance. To what degree are these messages valid for the modern day? Is it possible to hear the assurance of divine care without the trappings of violence and revenge?

Looking Ahead:

Since the next chapter is a transition, this is a good time to review the lists set up at the beginning of the study. Has the class thus far helped its members strengthen their previous positive experiences of scripture? Has this study helped overcome barriers to biblical understanding? Class members should meditate on these questions through the following week.

Chapter Six:
The Community in Transition:
Between Hebrew and Greek

Evaluation and review are appropriate. Are the goals of the class being achieved? If not, what changes in procedure will help? Does every member of the class feel that his/her questions and contributions are heard and respected?

This chapter describes the impact of different original languages on our understanding of scripture. Any bilingual individuals in the group might share their insights about the ways languages both express and shape human thought.

Review the assumptions concerning the continuity of the Hebraic and Christian scriptures. In particular, discuss the implications of the fact that both Jesus and Paul began and ended their lives as faithful Jews.

What does the author mean by his statement that Paul was the Jonah of the New Testament?

Discuss the implications of Jesus' teaching of a kingdom, especially as this impacts the rampant individualism of many modern churches.

Members of the class might share any incidents of anti-Semitism they have witnessed. Talk about the roots of this attitude.

Enrichment resources for those moving at a more deliberate pace:

Jack Good is critical of the practice of reading Christian themes into Hebraic writings. In contrast, he attempts to recognize "the Jewish nature of the Christian writings." Are members of the class willing to consider this quite different approach to the relationship of the two parts of scripture? Note the dangers for Christianity of failing to recognize our Jewish heritage.

Looking Ahead:

The subject for the next session will be the life of Jesus and his impact on the ongoing faith community. The Gospels themselves will wait for a later chapter. But it is not inappropriate for members of the group to refresh their memories by reading through one or more of the four Gospels. Any who are willing to read more extensively might look at any of the excellent studies of the historic Jesus now on the market. Marcus Borg, Luke Timothy Johnson, and John

Dominic Crossan have written well—if controversially—on the subject. Highly recommended is a small volume, structured in question and answer form, by Crossan and Richard Watts: *Who Is Jesus*, published by HarperPaperbacks in 1996.

Chapter Seven:
The Community Encounters a Unique Figure

Describe the impact social circumstances of the first century had on the unity of Jewish life. Note how the expectation of the end of the world altered Jesus' ministry and affected the ways that ministry was received.

Trace the development of hostility toward Jesus. Given the circumstances of the time, could Jesus have been faithful to his mission without causing controversy and danger to himself? Note especially the three options he faced late in his career.

The significant features of Jesus' life are noted in this chapter. Members of the class may want to add to or subtract from this list.

Note the ways that Jesus' interpretation of the nature of God both reinforced and differed from that of his religious ancestors. Is the term "radical" appropriate in describing the parable of the prodigal son?

Jesus lived out the meaning of prophetic religion. Does this mean he ignored the priestly side of faith? Explain.

"Jesus intended to preserve the faith community in essentially its original form, but with its boundaries made permeable." Discuss the implications of this statement for the current relationship between Jews and Gentiles.

Which of the interpretations of suffering given him by his ancestors did Jesus most intimately embrace? Did he reject other interpretations?

List incidents from Jesus' life in which his attitude toward women may have angered the leaders of a patriarchal society.

Review the two visions of a saving individual (messiah) given in Hebraic Scriptures. Discuss how Jesus' temptations in the wilderness related to these two views.

One of the final paragraphs of chapter 7 is a summary of the contributions made by Jesus to his religious tradition. Note these carefully.

Enrichment resources for those moving at a more deliberate pace:

On chalkboard or newsprint, list the major events in the development of the Jewish nation. In a second column, list the major events of Jesus' life and death. Note any similarities.

Introduce the phrase "the kingdom of God." How did Jesus' use of the word "kingdom" differ from the common understanding of that term?

Review the distinction between prophetic and priestly religion, especially as it is lived out in the life of the modern church.

The Gospels show how Jesus simultaneously built upon and expanded his religious tradition. Discuss how this occurred in his teachings about the meaning of suffering and in his attitude toward women.

Looking Ahead:

To prepare for the next session, class members should gather information about conditions in first-century Jewish and Greek societies. A member of the group may be willing to read a biographical account of Paul, perhaps in a Bible dictionary. Assign the letters of Paul to class members who are willing to read ahead; longer letters, such as Romans, should be divided among several people. The seven letters usually attributed to Paul are: 1 Thessalonians, Romans, 1 and 2 Corinthians, Galatians, Philippians, and Philemon.

Chapter Eight:
Paul Broadens the Community

Hear reports of those who have studied social conditions of the first century. List the problems faced by the evangelists of that time.

According to chapter 8, Paul's purpose was more practical than theological. Does this contradict previous understandings?

Review the various ways in which the word *law* can be used. Receive, also, the report on the life of Paul. Examine the evidence given that Paul was not "converted" from Judaism, but was called to a particular mission within his faith. How did Paul's introduction to Jesus affect his understanding of Jesus?

Receive a report from the class member who read 1 Thessalonians in preparation for this class. Give special attention to Paul's comments about Jews who killed Jesus. Note the comments in chapter 8 explaining this.

Paul wanted his Gentile converts to come into the faith community with no stigma of second-class citizenship. Why would this argue for receiving them on the basis of divine grace rather than through a full application of the law? On what basis had Abraham been originally chosen?

Jack Good argues against the idea that Judaism is a religion of laws while Christianity is a religion of grace. To what degree are law *and* grace found in both faiths?

Paul instructed his readers to be subject to the governing authorities. Would he have said the same had he lived long in Jerusalem?

Discuss Paul's advice to women. Female class members, though biblically instructed to be silent, should join vigorously in the discussion!

Describe the way other letters of Paul, especially those to the churches in Corinth, Galatia, and Philippi, expanded the arguments he had made in Romans and 1 Thessalonians.

If time permits, read the entire letter of Philemon. What do the letter's references to slavery tell about Paul's social conscience?

Enrichment resources for those moving at a more deliberate pace:

The group may want to stage a debate, with one individual taking the role of Peter and another of Paul. Peter will argue that the full body of religious law should apply to all new converts; Paul will argue that the law of circumcision is unnecessary. Questions and comments can come from "the audience."

Review the evidence that Paul did not intend to release Gentile followers of Jesus from the basic body of Jewish law. What does Krister Stendahl mean when he says that Paul was not addressing "the introspective conscience of the West"?

Discuss the way the unique problems in Corinth altered the tenor of the evangelist's advice.

The letter to Philemon is but one of many biblical references to slavery. How would members of the group explain to a non-Christian neighbor that many biblical writers seem to accept the reality of human slavery?

Looking Ahead:

After Paul sent his letters, four persons composed biographies of Jesus. One of them added a history of the continuation of Jesus' ministry in distant places. Assignments can include the birth stories in Matthew and Luke, the Sermon on the Mount (Matthew 5—7), Luke's account of the launching of Jesus' ministry (chapter 4), John's prologue (chapter 1), the crucifixion and resurrection stories in Mark, the account of Pentecost (Acts 2), and the summons to Paul on the Damascus road (Acts 9).

Chapter Nine:
The Community Records the Stories of Jesus

Receive reports from those assigned to special readings for this week. From these, and from the material in this volume, list the unique characteristics of each of the four Gospel writers.

Jack Good suggests that both Mark and Matthew may have been written, in part, to correct misunderstandings left by the letters of Paul. What particular misunderstandings were involved?

In what ways did John reinforce the position of Paul?

Briefly trace the process by which Jesus is spiritualized; trace this from Mark through John.

From the record of the three Synoptic Gospels, defend the idea that Jesus saw himself as a continuation of the prophetic tradition.

Trace and explain the development of conflict with "the Jews" in the four Gospel stories.

Describe how the Pentecost story contributes to the internationalization of the faith. Explain, also, the importance of the transition of leadership from Peter to Paul.

Review the evidence that Paul, at the end of his three missionary journeys, continued to see himself as a Jew in good standing.

Make a list of the significant differences between the portrait of Jesus found in the Synoptic Gospels, and that found in the Gospel of John.

Enrichment resources for those moving at a more deliberate pace:

What are the implications of the absence of any birth stories in the earliest of the Gospels? Describe the emotions that, according to Mark, energized Jesus' activity.

What is the evidence that Matthew was writing to a Jewish audience? Trace Matthew's account of Jesus' turn toward the non-Jewish world.

Describe Jesus' attitude toward the Law in the book of Matthew. Compare his teaching with what Paul had said about the Law. Do class members sense the vigor of the argument being carried on in the early church?

Describe the evidence that Luke was writing to a Gentile audience. What is the significance of the fact that Luke traces Jesus' genealogy to Adam, while Matthew traces it only to Abraham?

Compare the concept of God, given by Jesus in the book of Luke, with concepts of God found in Hebraic Scripture. Defend (or oppose) the statement made in chapter 9: "Ethical living plays an insignificant role in the Gospel of John."

An entire session might be set aside to discuss the differences between the concepts of a Jewish Messiah and a Greek Christ. Personal statements of faith would be appropriate in this discussion.

Looking Ahead:

A variety of late New Testament writings are examined in chapter 10. Encourage some members of the group to read Ephesians; at least one should be prepared to report on James. The first five plus the last two chapters of Revelation will give a reader a taste of that cryptic book. Other members of the group can choose assignments according to their interests.

Chapter Ten
The Community Copes with Persecution

Enumerate the faith family arguments that pushed followers of Jesus away from their Jewish background. A second set of conflicts tore at the Christian community; list these, also.

Briefly note the central messages of 2 Peter and Jude. Note, also, how the writer of 1, 2, and 3 John sometimes reinforces, and sometimes disagrees with, the themes of the Gospel of John. Be specific about the ways the writer of Ephesians and Colossians attempted to dampen the hostility between Jews and Gentiles.

The writers of 2 Peter and Hebrews attempted to help people cope with persecution. With what faith statements did they accomplish this?

Discuss the ways the book of Hebrews strengthened the link between the emerging Christian church and its Jewish heritage.

Imagine yourself as a first-century Christian under persecution. How would the book of Revelation have comforted and strengthened you?

Note the ways the book of James completes the circle. Compare the writer's understanding of the faith community with that of the eighth-century prophets. Review the summary given at the end of chapter 10. Has the continuity of scripture been effectively established?

Enrichment resources for those moving at a more deliberate pace:

Describe how both Christian theology and church structure were influenced by the unique circumstances of the early second century. In what ways were the pastoral letters responding to the particular needs of that moment?

Describe the ways the writer of Hebrews contributed to an understanding of the meaning of suffering.

Do any members of the group recall hearing the book of Revelation used to predict current events? Is this a proper use of scripture?

Explain why belief systems were more important for the emerging Christian church than for the Jewish community.

Chapter Eleven:
Is Faith's Family Album Also the Word of God?

If this is the final session for the group, allow some time for questions and summary statements at either the beginning or end of the time. The lists made in the first session should be reviewed.

Class members should be encouraged to share their own beliefs about the authority of the Bible. To what degree has the Bible been a source of support—and to what degree has it been a source of confusion?

Additional sharing can take place around the concept of inspiration. Let members of the group describe moments in which they felt inspired. Did they remain in control of their own lives? Did limitations vanish?

List on newsprint the six identifying marks of divine revelation in scripture. Members of the group may want to add to (or subtract from) the list.

Discuss this question with the group: Are we willing to be guided and inspired by the Bible, knowing that human frailty has touched its original words, its translation, and its reading?

Jesus warned his followers that "Those who try to make their life secure will lose it." Relate this truth to the role of the Bible in human life.

The postscript states that "human realities authenticate the presence of the Spirit." Do members of the group agree, in relation to the Bible? Does this insight also apply to the total life of the religious community?

Enrichment resources for those moving at a more deliberate pace:

Encourage some member of the group to describe a personal dilemma. On newsprint, use the force-field concept to visualize the forces on each side of the issue. Which forces can be lessened? Which can be strengthened? Show from this how God chooses to be one force among many in our ethical decisions.

List and discuss the ways we can lessen the dangers of reading our own biases into the scripture.

Good states that "The words of scripture will not, by themselves, make decisions for modern readers." How, then, can the Bible help us confront the ethical dilemmas of modern life?